Explaining Variation in Juvenile Punishment

This research monograph provides a comparative analysis of juvenile court outcomes, exploring the influence of contextual factors on juvenile punishment across systems and communities. In doing so, it investigates whether, how, and to what extent macro-social context influences variation in juvenile punishment. The contextual hypotheses under investigation evaluate three prominent macro-social theoretical approaches: the conflict-oriented perspective of community threat, the consensus-oriented perspective of social disorganization, and the organizational perspective of the political economy of the juvenile court.

Using multilevel modeling techniques, the study investigates these macro-social influences on juvenile justice outcomes across nearly 500 counties in seven states—Alabama, Connecticut, Missouri, Oregon, South Carolina, Texas, and Utah. Findings suggest that the contextual indicators under investigation did not explain variation in juvenile court punishment across communities and systems, and the study proposes several implications for future research and policy.

This monograph is essential reading for scholars of juvenile justice system impact and reform as well as practitioners engaged in youth policy and juvenile justice work. It is unique in taking a comparative perspective that acknowledges that there is no *one* juvenile justice system in the United States, but many such systems.

Steven N. Zane, Ph.D., J.D., is an assistant professor in the College of Criminology and Criminal Justice at Florida State University. He received his Ph.D. from Northeastern University and his J.D. from Boston College Law School. His research focuses on juvenile justice, racial disparities, and evidence-based social policy, and has appeared in *Criminology & Public Policy*, *JAMA Network Open*, *Journal of Criminal Justice*, *Journal of Quantitative Criminology*, *Justice Quarterly*, and *Youth Violence and Juvenile Justice*.

Routledge Studies in Juvenile Justice and Delinquency

Juvenile justice matters are of critical concern in both the United States and around the world. Books in the *Routledge Studies in Juvenile Justice and Delinquency* series explore mechanisms, consequences, insights, and innovations in the field of juvenile justice and its responses to delinquency. Each monograph will examine new areas of empirical and theoretical inquiry, provide an agenda-setting discussion of important concepts and controversies surrounding juvenile justice and delinquency, and seek to encompass a transnational or global approach to the issues addressed. The series will be a resource for the international community of undergraduates, post-graduates, researchers, practitioners, and policymakers concerned with juveniles and families caught up in or at risk of engagement in delinquency and justice system involvement.

Series editor David L. Myers

Contextual Characteristics in Juvenile Sentencing
Examining the Impact of Concentrated Disadvantage on Youth Court Outcomes
Rimonda Maroun

Due Process Protections for Youth
Defense Counsel Policies and Disparity in the Juvenile Justice System
Emily K. Pelletier

Norms of Violence
Violent Socialization Processes and the Spillover Effect for Youth Crime
Aimée X. Delaney

Explaining Variation in Juvenile Punishment
The Role of Communities and Systems
Steven N. Zane

Explaining Variation in Juvenile Punishment

The Role of Communities and Systems

Steven N. Zane

Routledge
Taylor & Francis Group
NEW YORK AND LONDON

First published 2022
by Routledge
605 Third Avenue, New York, NY 10158

and by Routledge
2 Park Square, Milton Park, Abingdon, Oxon OX14 4RN

Routledge is an imprint of the Taylor & Francis Group, an informa business

Library of Congress Cataloging-in-Publication Data
Names: Zane, Steven N., author.
Title: Explaining variation in juvenile punishment: the role of communities and systems / Steven N. Zane.
Description: New York, NY: Routledge, 2021. |
Series: Routledge studies in juvenile justice and delinquency |
Includes bibliographical references and index.
Identifiers: LCCN 2021002581 (print) | LCCN 2021002582 (ebook) |
ISBN 9780367471866 (hardback) | ISBN 9781003034469 (ebook)
Doi: 10.4324/9781003034469
Subjects: LCSH: Juvenile delinquency. | Juvenile corrections. |
Juvenile justice, Administration of. | Social problems.
Classification: LCC HV9069 .Z36 2021 (print) | LCC HV9069 (ebook) |
DDC 364.6083/0973–dc23
LC record available at https://lccn.loc.gov/2021002581
LC ebook record available at https://lccn.loc.gov/2021002582

ISBN: 9780367471866 (hbk)
ISBN: 9781032038155 (pbk)
ISBN: 9781003034469 (ebk)

Typeset in Bembo
by Newgen Publishing UK

Contents

Tables

Introduction

The Context of Juvenile Punishment

Any inquiry into juvenile punishment is complicated by the fact that the juvenile court is historically premised on the notion that it does not punish at all. Instead, juvenile court decision-making is guided by an individualized consideration of each juvenile offender with an eye to the best interests of the child. Juvenile sanctions may thus be viewed, on the one hand, as punitive, and on the other hand, as the appropriate intervention for a particular child's rehabilitation. While this tension between treatment and punishment has always existed within the juvenile court, many observers claim that it has become exacerbated in the "punitive" era of the late twentieth century (see Feld, 2017). Of course, the notion of "punitiveness" is also complicated. While incarceration rates are most often utilized in measuring the level of punitiveness in the criminal justice system more broadly, this only represents one dimension of punishment. As Matthews (2005) has argued, "punitiveness remains a 'thin' and undertheorized concept" (p. 178). Whitman (2003), for example, develops a conceptual framework for penal harshness that distinguishes between harshness in *criminalization*—what kinds of behavior are treated as criminal?—and harshness in *punishment*—what is the response to this criminal behavior? Moreover, the author distinguishes harshness in the law of punishment (e.g. sentence length), harshness in the application of punishment (e.g. prison conditions), and harshness in the formalism and inflexibility of punishment (e.g. mandatory minimum sentences). In the context of criminal justice more broadly, Matthews (2005) observes that "the division of sanctions into 'punitive' and 'non-punitive' is itself too simplistic and does little to account for the diversity and variability of penal developments" (see also Frost, 2008).[1]

In juvenile justice, then, we are faced with the dilemma of what constitutes the "punitive" outcomes to serve as our object of study. There are also different stages of juvenile justice processing that might be more or less punitive. Each stage of processing involves different decision-making units with different goals and priorities. While much research focuses on custodial outcomes as the best measure of punitiveness, this leaves out much of what happens in the juvenile justice system. Indeed, most cases that are referred to the juvenile justice system are not even adjudicated delinquent, let alone sentenced to custodial placement (Hockenberry & Puzzanchera, 2020). Diversion provides a good illustration. As Mears (2017, p. 131) writes, diversion "constitute[s] a mainstay of juvenile justice systems, yet its implementation and impacts remain largely unknown." Is diversion to informal processing, such as informal probation supervision, a punitive outcome? For any individual case it appears less punitive than formal probation and certainly less punitive than residential placement, but could diversion also result in net-widening that reflects a *more* punitive system in some other sense?

Much has been written on this tension in juvenile justice, along with the historical evolution of juvenile punishment from the inception of the juvenile court in 1899 to the "punitive turn" in the late twentieth century (see, e.g., Bernard & Kurlychek, 2010; Feld, 2017). Much of this prior work focuses on *the* juvenile justice system as its subject. While this aggregation is understandable as a method for examining general trends in juvenile justice sanctions, a central motivating theme of the present study is that there is no *one* juvenile justice system. As Tanenhaus (2012, p. 420) observes, "the juvenile court is an elusive institution. The diversity of juvenile court practices within and among states has made it nearly impossible to study *the* juvenile court." Instead, there are 51 separate juvenile justice systems, as well as many juvenile courts within each state. The heterogeneity in juvenile sanctions across systems thus complicates any aggregate analysis, such as looking at national rates of juvenile justice punishment over time.[2] It is possible that juvenile courts vary in orientation—treatment versus punishment—such that it is difficult to generalize about *the* juvenile justice system. When it comes to punishment practices, then, there is "remarkable variation among America's juvenile justice systems" that is arguably more important than any overall assessment of punitiveness in the juvenile justice system (Kutateladze, 2009, p. 213).[3]

While we understandably seek generalizable answers about *the* juvenile justice system, this approach can miss out on important nuances. As noted above, one is that every state has its own juvenile justice system. Another is that even within states, different courts may vary according to community characteristics as well as organizational differences between courts. To that end, the central question of the book is whether juvenile justice systems operate differently according to *community context*.

The Present Study

The present study provides a comparative analysis of juvenile court outcomes across multiple states, exploring the influence of contextual factors on juvenile punishment practices across hundreds of courts. Data were obtained from the National Juvenile Court Data Archive for 475 counties across seven states—Alabama, Connecticut, Missouri, Oregon, South Carolina, Texas, and Utah—for years 2010 (*N* = 246,729 referrals) and 2000 (*N* = 301,641 referrals). These datasets are used to investigate whether, how, and to what extent community and system characteristics explain variation in juvenile justice processing.

The study improves upon prior literature in several ways. First, rather than focusing on any one theoretical perspective, the study is guided by a systems perspective that takes account of myriad theoretical perspectives (Mears, 2017). To that end, the study borrows from community threat theory, social disorganization theory, and organizational theory, testing 20 contextual effects on juvenile justice processing. Relatedly, the study examines all major outcomes of juvenile justice from intake to final disposition. Second, the study takes a comparative approach to the juvenile justice system by examining contextual effects across several different states. This approach treats contextual effects as multidimensional, ranging from court-level differences (i.e. community-level differences) to system-level differences—the latter of which may be especially underappreciated.

Book Overview

The book is structured as follows. Chapter 1 describes the history of the juvenile court from its inception in 1899 in Cook County. As part of this history, the original mission of the juvenile court and its evolution over the course of the twentieth century are described. Chapter 2 explains the different stages of processing within the juvenile justice system, with special attention to how these stages may differ across states, or even across courts within a single state. Chapter 3 examines major theoretical perspectives that might explain whether and how context influences juvenile punishment practices across different stages of processing. The chapter is organized around three main perspectives: community threat, social disorganization, and the political economy of the court. The chapter emphasizes that a range of theoretical perspectives might be needed to understand why juvenile justice outcomes vary across communities and systems. Chapter 4 then summarizes prior empirical research that investigates contextual hypotheses for juvenile justice, with special focus on the theoretical perspectives discussed in Chapter 3. Crucial to such research is a multilevel approach, as single-level studies of contextual relationships are likely to produce biased estimates.

Chapter 5 then describes the methodology of the present study, including research hypotheses, a detailed overview of the data, the operationalization of key variables, and the analytical approach employed to test the research questions of interest. The study employs three-level hierarchical regression modeling, with juvenile referrals nested within counties nested within states. Chapter 6 reports on the results of the main analyses for the full, multijurisdictional sample for the year 2010. Twenty contextual hypotheses, corresponding to community threats, social disorganization, and political economy, are evaluated for each of five major juvenile justice outcomes. Chapter 7 similarly reports on the results of the analyses for the full, multijurisdictional sample for the year 2000. This provides an independent assessment of the contextual hypotheses evaluated in the main analyses in Chapter 6. Chapter 8 then reports on the results of supplemental analyses that examine variation in juvenile court outcomes *within* states. Each analysis is repeated for state-specific samples using two-level hierarchical regression modeling (with Connecticut excluded due to small sample size at the county level). Chapters 6–8 are quite technical and each chapter includes a summary of findings that provides an overall takeaway for readers who wish to skip these technical details. Chapter 9 provides an overall summary and discussion of the findings presented in Chapters 6–8. The chapter also discusses study limitations and how future research can build upon the present study in investigating contextual influences on juvenile court processing using a comparative approach. The chapter also explores several possible interpretations for the main findings. In concluding, Chapter 10 discusses the implications for future theory, research, and policy.

Notes

1 Matthews (2005) argues further:

> There is a preoccupation with limited oppositions and polarities that fail to do justice to the diversity, contradictions, reversions and tensions in current crime control policy. In this twin-track, bifurcated and zero-sum world of punitive versus non-punitive, inclusion versus exclusion, populism versus elitism, 'new' versus 'old' penologies, 'civilizing' versus 'decivilizing processes', we are in danger of becoming lost in a series of false dichotomies.
>
> (p. 195)

2 As Zimring and Hawkins (1991, p. 136) describe in the context of U.S. prison statistics: "Of special importance in the study of imprisonment policies is the fact that there are fifty-one different political units with very different rates of imprisonment and priorities in the administration of penal laws." As the authors put it, analysis of state and regional data is more informative than "aggregating those values into a single national figure" (p. 217).

3 Kutateladze (2009) points out that this is especially important for cross-national comparisons, where US variation in punishment is ignored and "the darkest sides of America's criminal justice system" are used for comparisons to other countries (p. 1).

References

Bernard, T. J., & Kurlychek, M. C. (2010). *The cycle of juvenile justice* (2nd ed.). New York, NY: Oxford University Press.

Feld, B. C. (2017). *The evolution of the juvenile court: Race, politics, and the criminalizing of juvenile justice*. New York, NY: New York University Press.

Frost, N. (2008). The mismeasure of punishment: Alternative measures of punitiveness and their (substantial) consequences. *Punishment & Society*, *10*(3), 277–300.

Hockenberry, S., & Puzzanchera, C. (2020). *Juvenile court statistics 2018*. Pittsburgh, PA: National Center for Juvenile Justice.

Kutateladze, B. (2009). *Is America really so punitive? Exploring a continuum of U.S. state criminal justice policies*. El Paso, TX: LFB Scholarly Publishing.

Matthews, R. (2005). The myth of punitiveness. *Theoretical Criminology*, *9*(2), 175–201.

Mears, D. P. (2017). *Out-of-control criminal justice: The systems improvement solution for more safety, justice, accountability, and efficiency*. Cambridge, UK: Cambridge University Press.

Tanenhaus, D. S. (2012). The elusive juvenile court: Its origins, practices, and re-inventions. In B. C. Feld & D. M. Bishop (Eds.), *The Oxford handbook of juvenile crime and juvenile justice* (pp. 421–441). New York, NY: Oxford University Press.

Whitman, J. Q. (2003). *Harsh justice: Criminal punishment and the divide between American and Europe*. New York, NY: Oxford University Press.

Zimring, F. E., & Hawkins, G. (1991). *The scale of imprisonment*. Chicago, IL: The University of Chicago Press.

Chapter 1

The Mission and History of Juvenile Justice

Origins of Juvenile Justice

The US juvenile justice system officially began with the passage of the Illinois Juvenile Court Act of 1899, which granted original jurisdiction over cases involving any juvenile matters to a separate, non-criminal court which "may, for convenience, be called the 'Juvenile Court'" (Illinois Juvenile Court Act of 1899, §3). Prior to its passage, the idea of a separate system for children who committed crimes had been considered for some time, and other juvenile courts soon appeared across the country, notably in New York (1901), Wisconsin (1901), Ohio (1902), Maryland (1902), and Colorado (1903).[1] By 1925, 48 states—all but Maine and Wyoming—had created separate juvenile courts.

Under the common law doctrine of infancy, children were considered incapable of committing crimes. Youth who were younger than seven years old were deemed *doli incapax*: they automatically did not have the capacity to commit crimes, an "irrebuttable presumption" that they were unable to form the requisite criminal intent. On the other hand, youth aged 14 and above were deemed to have adult capacity and were treated as adults by the criminal legal system—meaning they were tried and sentenced. For youth aged between seven and 14 years, however, there was a rebuttable presumption of *doli incapax*: while these children were presumed to lack capacity, this presumption could be rebutted in specific cases by evidence of criminal intent. This allowed children as young as seven years old to be tried and sentenced as adults, including execution, if they were deemed to possess criminal intent; it also provided for no legal response to a 13-year-old offender who was deemed to lack criminal intent.

The philosophy of the juvenile court sat in stark contrast to this common law approach. The institutional origins of the American juvenile court are often traced to the Houses of Refuge in New York, Boston, and Philadelphia in the 1820s, which represented the most notable state response to the problem of juvenile delinquency at the time. Placement in these institutions was not considered criminal punishment but rather "reformation" of the delinquent (or vagrant) child, including "imbuing their minds with principles of morality and religion" and "separating them from the corrupting influence of improper associates" (*Ex parte Crouse*, 1839, p. 11). Most children in the Houses of Refuge were actually not delinquent, but merely vagrant—street children. The Houses of Refuge included daily regimens of education and work, with strict discipline being enforced. Children were committed until age 21 for boys and age 18 for girls, and typically released from the Houses into apprenticeships—farm work for boys and maid service for girls (Bernard & Kurlychek, 2010).

The Houses of Refuge represented an unprecedented intervention into the lives of children by the government. As Scott and Steinberg (2008) note, "It is no great exaggeration to describe parental rights until the late nineteenth century as akin to property rights; children 'belonged' to their parents in concrete ways that would be foreign to us today" (pp. 61–62). To justify the state's interference with children, the Pennsylvania Supreme Court applied the English common law doctrine of *parens patriae*—literally, "parent of the fatherland." In *Ex parte Crouse* (1839), Mary Ann Crouse was committed to the Philadelphia House of Refuge on grounds of incorrigibility. Her father filed a write of *habeus corpus* to challenge the detention, arguing that it was unconstitutional to detain Mary without a trial by jury. The Pennsylvania Supreme Court unanimously upheld the detention, reasoning that the House of Refuge was a *reformatory* and did not constitute criminal punishment: "The House of Refuge is not a prison, but a school. Where reformation, and not punishment, is the end, it may indeed be used as a prison for juvenile convicts who would else be committed to a common jail" (p. 11).

The Court pointed to *parens patriae*, a legal concept that harkened back to English Chancery Courts that exercised jurisdiction over matters of guardianship, as well as administration of trusts and estates for orphaned children. This served as legal precedent that the government could act *in loco parentis* where children were in a vulnerable state of dependency without their natural parents. Yet here, the Court was suggesting that it could intervene in situations where parents were perceived as failing to raise their children properly. This was indeed a radical departure from notions of children as property of their parents. The right of parents to raise their children was now viewed as a "natural, but not an unalienable one" (p. 11). In some cases, the government must intervene:

> To this end may not the natural parents, when unequal to the task of education, or unworthy of it, be superseded by the *parens patriae*, or common guardian of the community? It is to be remembered that

> the public has a paramount interest in the virtue and knowledge of its members, and that of strict right, the business of education belongs to it. That parents are ordinarily entrusted with it is because it can seldom be put into better hands; but where they are incompetent and corrupt, what is there to prevent the public from withdrawing their faculties, held, as they obviously are, at its sufferance?
>
> (p. 11)

While this *parens patriae* power was not unlimited (see *People ex rel. O'Connell v. Turner*, 1870), this precedent would ultimately serve as the legal justification for an independent juvenile court, where the "common guardian of the community" has the right to displace natural parents when necessary (see, e.g., *Commonwealth v. Fisher*, 1905; *Lindsay v. Lindsay*, 1913).

The First Juvenile Court

While other states had adopted various innovations for dealing with juvenile delinquency, such as trying juveniles separately in Massachusetts (in 1874) and New York (in 1892), the first juvenile court was established by statute in Chicago (Cook County) in 1899. This new institution, a hybrid of a criminal court and a social welfare agency, was marked by several notable features. The Court had original jurisdiction over cases involving "dependent and neglected" children as well as "delinquent children" (Illinois Juvenile Court Act of 1899, §7, 9). Delinquent child was defined as "any child under the age of 16 years who violates any law of this State or any city or village ordinance," while dependent and neglected child was defined broadly—possibly to include any poor children living in the city of Chicago.

While not unaware that delinquency was different from dependency, early reformers may have sought to elide them for purposes of justifying the interventionist approach of juvenile court: "Because the image of 'child' and 'criminal' are discordant, the intersection of childhood and criminality poses a difficult dilemma. The Progressive era reformers resolved the dilemma by redefining the offense as something less than a crime" (Scott & Steinberg, 2008, p. 96). By the 1890s, the majority of criminal prosecutions against boys under age 16 were dismissed by grand juries unwilling to submit these children to criminal punishment. While the House of Refuge had been designed to prevent this kind of jury nullification, it was now clear that a separate system was needed for juvenile offenders to be perceived as "dependents" rather than "criminals" (Feld, 2017). As Bernard and Kurlychek (2010) observe, "officials in Chicago faced the same dilemma as did officials in New York City seventy-five years earlier: either punish harshly or do nothing. Both options seemed to increase crime among juveniles" (p. 75).

The primary motivation for the juvenile court was thus diversionary: an alternative to the criminal justice system for juvenile offenders (Zimring, 2000a). Still, an important secondary rationale, more ambitious and more controversial even at the time, was interventionist: the need to rehabilitate the juvenile offender (Tanenhaus, 2004). Julian Mack was an early proponent of this interventionist approach, which he laid out in his classic article, "The Juvenile Court." There, Mack (1909) argued that the juvenile court had ancient foundations in the Chancery Courts of England and their power of *parens patriae*: "Why is it not just and proper to treat these juvenile offenders, as we deal with the neglected children, as a wise and merciful father handles his own child whose errors are not discovered by the authorities?" (p. 107). At the time, rehabilitation was the dominant ideology in criminal justice as well, as illustrated by the "distinctly American idea of the 'penitentiary'" (Whitman, 2003, p. 173; see also Meranze, 1996). But in addition to adhering to the more universal rehabilitative ideal, the early juvenile court was also premised on the notion of *non-punitive* interventions—any kind of punishment being viewed as ineffective and possibly harmful. According to its foundational philosophy, "[w]hat the juvenile court does ... is not 'real' punishment" (Zimring, 2000b, p. 276).

Guided by the Progressive vision the government could fix broken children, turning them into productive, law-abiding citizens—most states had followed suit and established independent juvenile courts by 1925 (Tanenhaus, 2004). These new courts shared several important similarities: they included a separate staff from the criminal court, mostly probation officers; court sessions were typically held in a more informal setting, such as around a table instead of a traditional courtroom; and they included a complaint system by which many cases could be disposed informally, without judicial involvement. Unlike criminal court judges, the juvenile court judge performed a therapeutic function. They should "have legal training, acquaintance with social problems, and understanding of child psychology" (Children's Bureau, 1923, p. 2). The judge represented a kind of hybrid of law and social work. As such, judges were granted broad latitude and discretion and not encumbered by procedural regulations that would undermine their role: "Just as a lawyer would not accompany a patient to a physician's examination, juvenile court judges viewed lawyers as an unnecessary intrusion" (Feld, 2017 p. 34).

The juvenile court, characterized by a social work and social welfare approach, also employed different terminology from the criminal court that illustrates the non-punitive, treatment-oriented philosophy. Youth were not arrested, but "referred" to the court. Charges were not filed against them, nor were they indicted: instead, there was a "petition of delinquency"—"a formal request for the court to look into the case of this particular child" (Bernard & Kurlychek, 2010, p. 79). If petitioned, the case was named *In re*

John Doe instead of *State v. John Doe* to emphasize the non-adversarial nature of the proceeding: the State was not prosecuting the child, but examining its situation and assessing its needs. The juvenile court hearing was not a "trial" but an "adjudication": a simple, non-adversarial determination of the facts by the judge. If "adjudicated delinquent"—rather than "convicted"—the juvenile offender was not sentenced to a punishment but rather was given a non-punitive "disposition." Most often, this disposition was not institutionalization, as had been the practice in the days of the Houses of Refuge, but supervision in the community by a probation officer.

Probation was a central component to these early juvenile courts and what made them unique. Probation officers were in charge of the *interventionist* mission of the court: rather than incarcerate juvenile offenders, they could remain in the community under the supervision of a probation officer who would look after them and execute the dispositional plan attendant to their individualized needs. Probation had already emerged in the nineteenth century as a tool for accomplishing greater social control over wayward youth. In Boston, probation first emerged informally during the Civil War, when delinquent boys were often released by police to the Children's Aid Society for placement in suitable foster homes. In the final decade of the nineteenth century, Massachusetts began to require probation officers for all juvenile cases—prior to establishing any separate juvenile court (Tanenhaus, 2004). Probation officers could then essentially operate as social workers for the court, but with coercive powers that ordinary social workers did not possess (Bernard & Kurlychek, 2010).

Child Saving: The Interventionist Vision of Juvenile Justice

The interventionist approach of the juvenile court was inspired by the Progressive movement sweeping through America in the final decade of the nineteenth century. Progressivism was largely a response to a rapidly changing society, with urbanization and industrialism causing massive "structural changes and dislocations" (Feld, 2017, p. 22). Leonard (2016) points out that these Progressives were elites and not victims of their turbulent times—but they found the conditions of urban cities to be deplorable and believed they could change them. They perceived themselves as "disinterested agents of reform" who, armed with scientific expertise, could solve the problems of society—such as crime and poverty. In the terminology of the day, they preached a social gospel: "The progressives' urge to reform American sprang from an evangelical compulsion to set the world to rights, and they unabashedly described their purposes as a Christian mission to build a Kingdom of Heaven on earth" (Leonard, 2016, p. 12). The

Child-Saving movement was deeply influenced by other Progressive social reforms for children occurring at the same time, such as advocating for publicly funded education, compulsory school attendance, and restrictions on child labor (Scott & Steinberg, 2008). This movement was made up largely of "Gilded Age patrons," society women who were part of a "transatlantic social movement in the 1880s and 1890s to solve the problems of crime and poverty" (Tanenhaus, 2004, p. 5). As Leonard (2016) documents, these were overwhelmingly descendants of "old New England families of seventeenth century Massachusetts Bay" (p. 11). These elites believed they could remake society.

Central to this belief was an environmental determinism that displaced traditional notions of individual responsibility and free will. Instead, crime and poverty were re-described as social problems that could be cured through scientific investigation and treatment. As such, juvenile delinquents were not responsible for their crimes—rather, they were victims of their social environments. Intervention was thus needed to steer their lives away from pauperism and delinquency. As Tanenhaus (2004) observes, an early defense of the juvenile court in the *Chicago Tribune* in 1899 argued, "Society makes criminals; environment and education make criminals, but they are not born so" (p. 26). The early juvenile court proceeded on the assumption that juvenile delinquency could be treated like a medical disease—that delinquent youth could "be helped if a scientist could discover the causes of delinquency, much like Louis Pasteur had successfully isolated the germs that destroyed plant, animal, and human life" (Tanenhaus, 2004, p. 112). Thus, the medical model of crime replaced the adversarial model of the criminal justice system.

This more deterministic and positivist outlook challenged traditional legal principles: "progressive reformers questioned classical legal conceptions of free will, the due process of law, and the benefits of limited state intervention into social relations" (Tanenhaus, 2004, p. 25). In place of what they called "laissez-faire"—the classical liberal model where "a well-ordered society channelled self-interested market behavior into socially beneficial outcomes"—these reformers sought to improve society through the administrative state and its application of science to identifying and solving social problems (Leonard, 2016, p. 21). The goal of science-driven social control replaced "quaint and retrograde" notions such as individual liberty (Leonard, 2016, p. 24).[2] As Tanenhaus (2012, p. 423) observes, "the needs of children mattered more than due process."

Some revisionist accounts of the juvenile court highlight that it was easier to justify state intervention in what was perceived as a vicious cycle of pauperism and unfit parents—often immigrants—who would fail to raise their children to be productive members of society. In this way, the early juvenile court also reflected the "quintessential tension in progressive thinking, which simultaneously regarded the poor as victims deserving uplift and as threats requiring restraint" (Leonard, 2016, p. 119). Rothman (1971) argues that the "attempt to eliminate delinquency ended up as a practical method for getting rid of delinquents" mostly made up of "foreign-born and lower classes" (pp. 255, 257). While some conflict theorists have insisted that the juvenile court was created to control the conduct of lower-class youth and stave off potential revolutionary movement of the lower classes (see, e.g., Platt, 1969) it is dubious that this was the primary motivation of the early reformers. One critic of the revisionist perspective points out that "the greatest obstacle to interpreting juvenile court acts as instruments of class oppression is the evidence that *parents* liberally availed themselves of the courts' broad jurisdiction and easy access by turning in their own children" (Schultz, 1973, p. 472). As Singer (1996) argues, "the idea that juvenile justice was created exclusively on the grounds of class ignores other internal interests that are more often related to the concerns of those in existing child-care bureaucracies" (p. 16). In the final analysis, the motivation for early juvenile courts represented a blend of Progressive idealism about social reform driven by positivistic science, the Child-Savers' desire to prevent harm to "dependent" children, and a need to exert social control over "potential paupers," many of whom were immigrants (Bernard & Kurlychek, 2010).

The Failure of the Interventionist Vision

From its inception there had been opponents of the juvenile court who worried that the unbridled discretion and individualized approach would lead to abuse of power by the court, including imposing middle class values on working class Chicagoans (Tanenhaus, 2004).[3]

By the 1920s, many legal scholars had begun to criticize the juvenile court as being "socialized courts" that "disregarded the rule of law in the pursuit of 'individualized' justice" (p. 60). As Tappan (1946) wrote in his influential critique of the juvenile court,

> These various methods of applying court treatment without a full and fair judicial trial of the issue of guilt of a particular offense, despite their seductive rationale, appear to the writer to be peculiarly hazardous and unnecessary. … In general denial of the validity of the current procedures, the writer maintains that they resemble too closely in some respects the philosophy of the Star Chamber. For their greatest fault is in failing to give to the defendant some of the most basic protections of due process which inhere in our modern legal system.
>
> (p. 309)

Evidence also began to emerge in the 1920s and 1930s that the juvenile court's intervention in the lives of young delinquents was not meeting its aspirations. One of the earliest evaluations of the juvenile court was performed by Sheldon and Eleanor Glueck, who found high recidivism rates for boys from the Boston juvenile court who were traced and followed up (Glueck & Glueck, 1934, 1940). These findings were particularly alarming since Massachusetts was considered to be "taking the lead" in providing reformatories that were educational and not juvenile prisons (Mack, 1909). If the Boston juvenile court did not reform juvenile offenders, it seemed to follow that the juvenile court must be an abject failure. As one of the Gluecks' colleagues, Dr. Richard C. Cabot, observed:

> I now believe that even the very *best* juvenile courts,—such as Fred Cabot's,—are largely useless due to our ignorance of the fact that delinquent children are hardened habitual thieves and are not going to be changed on any hypothesis that assumes that they are very like the rest of us when we were small, that their bad environment is largely responsible for their actions, or that they simply have too much energy.
>
> (as cited in Evison, 1995, p. 361, emphasis in original)[4]

Given that the main justification for lack of due process in juvenile courts was their treatment-oriented mission, the lack of evidence of rehabilitation undermined the original Progressive enthusiasm for the juvenile court.[5]

The Due Process Revolution

The disillusionment with the juvenile justice system led to some state-level reforms, such as providing the right to an attorney for juvenile offenders in California and New York in the 1950s and early 1960s (Bernard & Kurlychek, 2010). But it was the Supreme Court's due process revolution of the 1960s where a series of juvenile justice cases forever changed the nature of the juvenile court (Manfredi, 1998). These cases emerged as part of the Warren Court's due process jurisprudence, extending the constitutional rights of criminal defendants in such famous cases as *Mapp v. Ohio* (1961) and *Miranda v. Arizona* (1966).[6]

The first juvenile justice case to appear before the Supreme Court of the United States was *Kent v. United States* (1966). The D.C. juvenile court had waived jurisdiction over a 16-year-old juvenile referral, Morris Kent, who was charged with robbery, rape, and breaking and entering. The judge did not hold a waiver hearing or provide a written opinion before transferring Kent to criminal court for prosecution, but simply stated, "after full investigation, I hereby waive" (p. 546). Kent was subsequently found guilty in criminal court and sentenced to 30–90 years imprisonment, which he appealed on grounds that his transfer to criminal court had been unconstitutional. The United States Supreme Court agreed, and held that the waiver was invalid. In its reasoning, the Court observed,

> [T]here is no place in our system of law for reaching a result of such tremendous consequences without ceremony—without hearing, without effective assistance of counsel, without a statement of reasons. It is inconceivable that a court of justice dealing with adults, with respect to a similar issue, would proceed in this manner.
>
> (p. 554)

Here, we can see that the juvenile court is being treated as a kind of criminal court, and no longer as a social welfare agency that is owed unbridled discretion due to its interventionist goals.

While the *Kent* holding itself was limited to the transfer decision, the Court also went out of its way to express skepticism about the juvenile court and its ability to act as *parens patriae*:

> There is much evidence that some juvenile courts, including that of the District of Columbia, lack the personnel, facilities and techniques to perform adequately as representatives of the State in a *parens patriae* capacity, at least with respect to children charged with law violation. There is evidence, in fact, that there may be grounds for concern that the child receives the worst of both worlds: that he gets neither the protection accorded to adults nor the solicitous care and regenerative treatment postulated for children.
>
> (pp. 555–556)

This was quite a shift from earlier cases that had optimistically adopted the *parens patriae* rationale of the juvenile court. Put more strongly: "*parens patriae* was dead, and rising to take its place … [a] new juvenile court was being born" (Bernard & Kurlychek, 2010, p. 101).[7]

One year later, the Court decided *In re Gault* (1967), the most important case in the history of the juvenile justice system. Fifteen-year-old Gerald Gault had been adjudicated delinquent and committed to the Arizona State Industrial School until age 21 for making a lewd phone call to a neighbor. His parents filed a writ of habeas corpus, arguing that the proceedings were unconstitutional for violating several due process rights. Moreover, they argued, this lack of due process had resulted in a severe disposition—potentially six years under commitment—for a crime for which the adult maximum punishment was only 60 days in jail.

In its decision, the Court first reviewed the history of the juvenile court. In so doing, the Court expressed concern with the power and discretion of juvenile courts to interfere in the lives of children without even minimal due process—as well as some degree of cynicism about the original mission of the juvenile court: "The absence of substantive standards has not necessarily meant that children receive careful, compassionate, individualized treatment. ... Departures from established principles of due process have frequently resulted not in enlightened procedure, but in arbitrariness" (pp. 18–19). The Court rejected the argument that minimal due process protections would interfere with juvenile court's mission. Instead, the Court insisted that due process rights are essential components of individual liberty and that "the features of the juvenile system which its proponents have asserted are of unique benefit will not be impaired by constitutional domestication" (p. 22). The Court then overturned Gault's adjudication of delinquency and disposition, holding that the lack of due process was unconstitutional. Going forward, the Court held that several due process rights were required in juvenile courts: notice of the charges, the right to an attorney, and the privilege against self-incrimination. In sum, the Court held that the juvenile court may technically be considered a "civil court" under state laws—but for practical (and constitutional) purposes, it was a criminal court. This followed from the fact that juvenile offenders who were adjudicated delinquent were *punished*: "commitment is a deprivation of liberty. It is incarceration against one's will, whether it is called 'criminal' or 'civil'" (p. 50).

As noted above the concerns raised in *Gault* were not new. Following the establishment of the juvenile court in Chicago, for example, many judges did not assert original jurisdiction over juvenile criminal cases due to "concerns about the constitutionality of the state's juvenile law, including the possibility that the Illinois Supreme Court might determine that the law's procedural informalities did not provide adequate due process protections to children and their families" (Tanenhaus, 2004, p. 43). These concerns had been present for the first half-century of the juvenile court's existence, creating a perennial tension between the Progressive mission of the juvenile court and the problem of dealing with juvenile criminals. *Gault* finally resolved that tension in favor of due process rights and criminal court procedures: "*Gault* marked the beginning of the end of the traditional juvenile court" (Scott & Steinberg, 2008, p. 8).[8]

The Criminalization of Juvenile Justice

Following *Gault*, several other Supreme Court opinions solidified what Barry Feld (1993) calls the "criminalization" of juvenile justice. First, in *In re Winship* (1970), the Court held that juvenile courts must determine delinquency according to the criminal burden of proof—"beyond a reasonable doubt"—rather than the lower standard of "preponderance of evidence" that many states employed. In doing so, the Court again disagreed with the argument that juvenile courts should use lower standards because they were "civil" rather than "criminal." This difference in labels obscured the fact that an adjudication of delinquency was the juvenile court equivalent of a criminal conviction. Once again, the Court reasoned that the juvenile court was, in fact, a criminal court for juvenile offenders—not the Chancery Court that Mack (1909) had described sixty years earlier.

Next, in *Breed v. Jones* (1975), the Court held that double jeopardy attached to adjudicatory hearings in juvenile court, again noting that these hearings were the functional equivalent of criminal trials. The 17-year-old defendant, Gary Jones, was adjudicated delinquent for robbery, then transferred to criminal court via judicial waiver. Jones argued that he had already been prosecuted for the same crime in juvenile court, such that waiver to criminal court violated the Fifth Amendment's Double Jeopardy clause. While the lower appellate court held that Jones had not been placed "in jeopardy" because the adjudicatory hearing was not a criminal trial, the Supreme Court disagreed, holding that jeopardy *does* attach to an adjudicatory hearing: "in terms of potential consequences, there is little to distinguish an adjudicatory hearing ... from a traditional criminal prosecution" (p. 530). Once again, the Court separated the ideal from the reality of the juvenile court.

With these decisions, the juvenile court became even more formal and adversarial—moving further away from its original *parens patriae* orientation. The Court stopped short of full criminalization of the juvenile court, however. In *McKeiver v. Pennsylvania* (1971), the Supreme Court held that jury trials were *not* constitutionally required for juvenile courts. The Court did acknowledge that juvenile courts were more like criminal courts than originally envisioned: "We must recognize ... that the fond and idealistic hopes of the juvenile court proponents and early reformers of three generations ago have not been realized" (pp. 543–544). Still, the Court insisted, jury trials did not represent a fundamental due process right because the fact-finding mission of the court could be accomplished by the judge. Moreover, the Court was not ready to sound the death knell for the juvenile court as an interventionist institution. The Court maintained that "the juvenile court proceeding has not yet been held to be a 'criminal prosecution,' within the meaning and reach of the Sixth Amendment" (p. 541). While the due process revolution had criminalized the juvenile court, the Court nonetheless concluded: "If the formalities of the criminal adjudicative process are to be superimposed upon the juvenile court system, there is little need for its separate existence" (p. 551).

While the conferral of (most) due process rights was viewed by many as a welcome improvement over the pre-*Gault* juvenile court, some have observed a dark side to this otherwise beneficial development. Specifically, giving juveniles due process rights makes the court more formal, as "[p]rocedural informality is the concomitant of substantive discretion" (Feld, 2003, p. 256). In Weberian terms, formal rationality replaces substantive rationality, and the juvenile court becomes "criminalized"—essentially, a criminal court for juvenile offenders. This stood in stark contrast to the Progressive vision of the juvenile court, which involved reformation of the youth as its chief mission. Juvenile delinquents thus came to be perceived as criminal defendants instead of wayward children in need of supervision (Bernard & Kurlychek, 2010). One consequence of this was to dismantle the traditional fusion of delinquency with dependency. Non-delinquent youth, such as status offenders, would now be treated less punitively—with a major push toward deinstitutionalization (Zimring, 2000a).[9] Correspondingly, more serious juvenile offenders would be treated more punitively—as serious criminals (Feld, 1993).

A More Punitive Juvenile Court

Soon after the due process revolution in juvenile justice, another major transformation occurred. Early opponents of the juvenile court believed that the new institution "coddled criminals" and was too "soft" on crime, and these arguments continued to challenge the court through the twentieth century (Tanenhaus, 2000, p. 27). Rising juvenile crime in the 1980s and 1990s gave new force to these old arguments (Zimring & Rushin, 2013). As Scott and Steinberg (2008) argue,

> By the late 1980s, two key premises of the rehabilitative model had been largely discredited. The first was that young offenders were blameless but misguided children who were simply in need of redirection with the guidance of the court. . . . The second premise, related to the first, was that the sole purpose of state intervention in delinquency cases was to promote the welfare of delinquent youths through rehabilitative interventions.
>
> (p. 7)

Bernard and Kurlychek (2010) argue that juvenile delinquents thus came to be perceived as "hardened criminals" and were met with an even more punitive response. Most notably, this involved a shift in juvenile court dispositions toward more residential placement, reduced confidentiality of juvenile court proceedings, higher rhetorical emphasis on the accountability of juvenile offenders, and more juveniles being transferred to criminal court.

First, beginning in the late 1970s, a majority of states enacted legislation to make their juvenile justice systems more punitive and formalistic (Feld, 2017). Many states changed their laws to require more punishment for juvenile offenders, such as 16 states that required minimum periods of residential placement for more serious offenses, as well as blended sentencing statutes in 14 states that granted juvenile courts the power to impose *criminal* punishments. Second, many states relaxed restrictions on the confidentiality of juvenile court proceedings and records, allowing release of some juvenile court information to other justice agencies, social services, schools, and victims (Jacobs, 2014). Third, many states modified the "purpose" clauses in their juvenile justice statutes—emphasizing public safety and offender accountability in addition to, or in some cases in place of, the best needs of the child. This is also reflected in probation supervision shifting from a "therapeutic" orientation to a more "law-enforcement" orientation (Hafoka et al., 2017).

Fourth, juvenile courts transferred increasing numbers of juvenile offenders to the criminal justice system during this time. Judicial waiver to criminal court had always been part of the juvenile justice system—but was typically reserved for the most serious juvenile offenders who posed a danger to other juveniles and did not belong in juvenile facilities. During the 1980s and 1990s, however, the juvenile justice system experienced an increase in the number (and proportion) of juvenile offenders that were transferred to the criminal justice system. The primary mechanism for this were non-judicial forms of waiver of jurisdiction: prosecutorial waiver, where the prosecutor decided whether to charge a juvenile offender in juvenile or criminal court, and legislative waiver, where cases with certain characteristics were statutorily excluded from juvenile court jurisdiction. These newer forms of waiver reflected a shift in power that has transformed waiver from a decision guided by consideration of the best interests of youth—the mission of the original juvenile court—to one guided by public safety considerations of state governments (Zimring, 2010).

The expansion of transfer perhaps best reflects the shift to a more retributive philosophy of juvenile punishment, with more juveniles being viewed as mature enough to be held accountable as adults. Others have observed that the expansion of transfer was largely "an attempt to expand prosecutorial power in juvenile justice" and wrestle decision-making away from juvenile court judges who were traditionally allocated more discretionary power than criminal court judges (Zimring, 2010, p. 4). Non-judicial forms of transfer thus emphasize characteristics of the offense rather than offender, and reflect "the retributive values of the criminal law" in contrast to the more treatment-oriented mission of the juvenile court (Feld, 2000, pp. 84–85). Importantly, prosecutorial and legislative waiver today account for the majority of juveniles in criminal court (see Griffin, Addie, Adams, & Firestine, 2011).

The Developmental Turn: Juvenile Justice in the Twenty-First Century

The first two decades of the twenty-first century have marked another change in juvenile justice, what Feld (2017) refers to as the "kids are different" era. Most states have reversed course from the "get tough" era, and ushered in reforms aimed at making the juvenile court more lenient (Bernard & Kurlychek, 2010). This includes several notable changes, such as deinstitutionalizing status offending, reducing preadjudication detention, increasing the use of diversion from formal processing, and limiting the use of adult sanctions for juvenile offenders in criminal court through practices such as reverse waiver and blended sentencing (Feld, 2017). Grounded in developmental science, the vision of children as "hardened criminals" has been tempered by evidence that even adolescents are fundamentally different from adults in terms of their culpability (Scott & Steinberg, 2008; but see Maroney, 2014).

This shift in perception of juvenile offenders is best illustrated by Supreme Court jurisprudence that has recognized the constitutional significance of age, holding that juvenile offenders cannot be punished as harshly as adults. The landmark decision is *Roper v. Simmons* (2005), which held that the death penalty was unconstitutional—violating the Eighth Amendment's prohibition against "cruel and unusual punishment"—for offenders under 18 years old.[10] Two decades earlier, in *Thompson v. Oklahoma* (1988), the Court had ruled that capital punishment was "cruel and unusual" for juveniles under 16 due to their reduced culpability as well as a national consensus that had formed against such a punishment.[11] One year later, however, in *Stanford v. Kentucky* (1989), the Court held that capital punishment of juvenile offenders aged 16 and 17 was *not* "cruel and unusual."[12] The Court declined to extend *Thompson*'s "under sixteen" prohibition on capital punishment to "under eighteen." The swing vote was Justice O'Connor, who had concurred in *Thompson* but joined the majority in *Stanford* based on the national consensus test:

> The day may come when there is such general legislative rejection of the execution of 16- or 17-year-old capital murderers that a clear national consensus can be said to have developed. … I do not believe that day has yet arrived.
>
> (pp. 381–382)

That day *would* arrive 16 years later in *Roper v. Simmons* (2005).

In *Roper*, the majority opinion observed three general differences between juveniles and adults that together demonstrated that juvenile offenders "cannot with reliability be classified among the worst offenders," such that capital punishment is "cruel and unusual" in violation of the Eighth Amendment (p. 569). First, youth are less culpable due to lower maturity and greater impulsivity, including a diminished ability to consider long-term consequences. Second, they are more vulnerable to outside negative influences and have diminished control over their behavior. Third, their character is less well formed than adults, meaning they are more malleable and have a higher capacity for rehabilitation. This reasoning broadly tracks that of juvenile justice reformers who argue based on developmental science that adolescents are more impulsive and immature, more short-sighted and risk-taking, and highly influenced by peer groups (Scott & Steinberg, 2008). Second, the Court also applied the national consensus test to determine whether a punishment was "cruel and unusual" in light of "evolving standards of decency" in society. The majority reasoned that a national consensus against the use of capital punishment for juvenile offenders had emerged. Since the *Stanford* decision, the Court observed, five states with the death penalty had abolished it for juvenile offenders. As a result, the "majority of States have rejected the imposition of the death penalty on juvenile offenders under 18, and we now hold this is required by the Eighth Amendment" (p. 568).[13]

Since *Roper*, the Supreme Court has reaffirmed the diminished culpability of juvenile offenders, and extended constitutional protection in the context of two additional punishment issues. In *Graham v. Florida* (2010), the Court held that juvenile offenders could not be sentenced to life without parole (LWOP) for non-homicide offenses. In addition to reiterating that juvenile offenders are less culpable than adults (citing *Roper*),[14] the Court argued that a national consensus had emerged against LWOP sentences for juvenile non-homicide offenders convicted in criminal court. Two years later, in *Miller v. Alabama* (2012), the Court held that mandatory sentences of LWOP for juvenile homicide offenders were likewise unconstitutional. *Miller* established that juveniles should not be automatically sentenced to LWOP—the most serious punishment for juveniles post-*Roper*—under a mandatory sentencing scheme. Since juveniles are generally less culpable than adults, the Court reasoned, mandatory LWOP was "cruel and unusual punishment" because it violated the proportionality principle to impose the harshest possible sentence without any individualized assessment of the juvenile's culpability. Here, we can see the Court channeling the notion of individualized justice that defined the philosophy of the original juvenile court.

Conclusion

This latest era of juvenile justice may reflect a newfound perception that most juvenile offenders are "naïve risk takers," as Bernard and Kurlychek (2010, p. 216) have put it. In their scheme, the "cycle of juvenile justice" involves different perceptions of juvenile offenders over time, which, in turn, produce different social responses to crime committed by juveniles. As we saw, many juvenile offenders were originally simply treated as ordinary criminals. In the common law, certain children were simply too young for capacity, while others were deemed mature enough to be treated as adults. In the early nineteenth century, juvenile offenders came to be viewed as "potential paupers." The concern was that so long as these children remained on the streets, they would inevitably grow into adult vagrants and criminals. The response was to create juvenile institutions that would mold these at-risk youth into law-abiding, productive members of society.

By the end of the nineteenth century, with the philosophical momentum of the Child-Saving movement and Progressive social reform more generally, juvenile delinquents came to be perceived as dependent and neglected children. It was not enough for the State to institutionalize children and teach them hard work and discipline—instead, the State must act as *parens patriae* in place of natural parents who are unable or unwilling to provide proper care and discipline. The Progressive vision of juvenile delinquency gave rise to the original juvenile court: an interventionist, non-criminal system in which juvenile offenders could be individually treated and ultimately reformed.

The "due process" revolution then marked a shift to thinking of delinquents as "criminal defendants" instead of dependent children. Juvenile defendants deserved due process rights because they *were* at risk of being punished. As the juvenile court became more due process oriented, it underwent what Weber called a rationalization process: the juvenile justice system became more formal, resembling the criminal justice system. In effect, the juvenile court was now a criminal court for younger offenders. Here we see that the original mission of the juvenile court—individualized consideration of each juvenile offender—is in striking tension with formal rationality, which emphasizes uniform decision-making in accordance with rules and regulations to produce predictable results. This is the model of criminal justice in the late twentieth century, moving away from indeterminate sentencing schemes and toward more determinate sentencing whereby criminal punishments are based on the "principle of the offense" rather than contingencies of each particular case (Feld, 1993). This was only exacerbated by social changes in the late twentieth century that contributed to a general "get tough" movement, with juvenile punishment reaching its peak severity in the mid-1990s (Feld, 2017).

In the first decade of the twenty-first century, however, a new vision of juvenile offenders, informed by developmental science, began to take over. Elements of the original treatment-oriented vision of the juvenile court have re-emerged, but now exist in tension with considerations of due process as well as public safety and retributive justice. Today, the juvenile court continues to exhibit an organizational tension in its overall mission: punishment, accountability, and public safety, on the one hand, and individualized treatment of the juvenile offender, on the other hand.[15] This sets the context for the present research.

Notes

1 Similarly, there was an international movement toward establishing juvenile courts. This included the 1908 Juvenile Delinquents Act in Canada, the Children Act of 1908 in England, a revised Penal Children's Act in the Netherlands in 1921, the German Youth Court Law of 1923, and New Zealand's Child Welfare Act of 1925.

2 In 1913, Dean of Harvard Law School Roscoe Pound argued that the Bill of Rights "were not needed in their own day, [and] they are not desired in our own," while President Woodrow Wilson referred to inalienable rights as "nonsense" (quoted in Leonard, 2016, p. 25).

3 The juvenile court was also criticized for interfering in the natural parent-child relationship and invading the privacy of the home. Part of the concern was that juvenile courts actually created dependency and relieved parents of their natural obligations. In 1925, President Calvin Coolidge stated, "Too many people are neglecting the real well-being of their children, shifting the responsibility for their actions, and turning over supervision of their discipline and conduct to the juvenile courts" (quoted in Tanenhaus, 2004, p. 81).

4 Cabot's (1934) review of this book caused a minor controversy. In a personal letter to Cabot, *Survey* editor Paul Kellogg wrote: "Quite a hornet's nest has been stirred up by your article on the Glueck book .... It is quite natural that the probation people are stirred up and apprehensive. A good many of them do not feel too secure in the record of work done by the juvenile courts and there is the further fact which they are disinclined to bring out into the open that they fear discussion such as this of the juvenile court may lead to abolishing some of them" (as quoted in Evison, 1995, p. 360).

5 The idealism of the original interventionist vision is apparent in the focus on "individualized" treatment of juvenile offenders. As Sowell (1996) argues, "Arguments for 'individualizing' the punishment to the criminal, rather than generalizing punishment from the crime, presuppose a result rather than specifying a process. Whether or not such a result is desirable, the question must first be faced whether courts can in fact do it" (p. 282).

6 In *Mapp*, the Court established the exclusionary rule, holding that evidence obtained during an illegal search would be inadmissible as evidence in court. In *Miranda*, the Court held that suspects must be provided with a series of warnings

prior to custodial interrogation for any statements to be admissible as evidence in court.

7 In fact, the doctrine of *parens patriae* has continued to shape juvenile court jurisprudence. For example, in *Schall v. Martin* (1984), the Supreme Court held that preventative detention of a juvenile offender prior to being petitioned was not unconstitutional because the State can act as a natural parent under *parens patriae*: "Children … are assumed to be subject to the control of their parents, and if parental control falters, the State must play its part as *parens patriae*" (p. 265).

8 In his prescient dissent in *In re Gault*, Justice Stewart observed that the majority holding effectively ended the traditional juvenile court, arguing that it "serves to convert a juvenile proceeding into a criminal prosecution" (p. 79).

9 The Juvenile Justice and Delinquency Prevention Act (JJDPA) of 1974 targeted several reforms, including removing status offenders from detention, separating juveniles from adults in correctional facilities, and removing juveniles from adult jails. Zimring (2000a) argues that these reforms reveal a "diversionary" rather than an "interventionist" purpose—noting that the focus was on preventing harm to juvenile offenders and no longer treating status offenders as delinquents, the latter of which being "one of the great failings of the interventionist theory of the juvenile court" (p. 2490).

10 Simmons, age 17, was convicted of first degree murder and sentenced to death. Along with two younger accomplices, Simmons had broken into a woman's home, kidnapped her, tied her up, wrapped her face in duct tape, and then thrown her off a bridge. When asked about his motivation, Simmons replied that he had planned the event because he "wanted to murder someone" (*Roper*, p. 556).

11 Thompson, age 15, was convicted of first degree murder and sentenced to death for killing his former brother-in-law, whom he and several older peers shot, cut his throat, and then chained his body to concrete and threw him into a river.

12 Stanford, age 17, was convicted of first degree murder and sentenced to death for raping and killing a female gas station attendant during a robbery.

13 Both the O'Connor and Scalia dissents argued that the national consensus test was clearly not driving the majority opinion in *Roper*. Justice O'Connor observed that the majority "refrains from asserting that its holding is compelled by a genuine national consensus" (p. 588). More forcefully, Justice Scalia argued: "Words have no meaning if the views of less than 50% of death penalty States can constitute a national consensus" (p. 609). Instead, as Justice O'Connor put it, the majority had determined as "its independent moral judgment" that the death penalty for juvenile offenders was disproportionate—and thus cruel and unusual— as a matter of principle (p. 588).

14 The majority opinion also observed that juvenile offenders "should not be deprived of the opportunity to achieve maturity of judgment and self-recognition of human worth and potential" (p. 79). According to this argument, even if a juvenile offender commits a serious non-homicide crime, the juvenile should be afforded an opportunity to "grow up" before being incapacitated for the rest of their life. This may suggest a return to the "second chance" philosophy underlying the original juvenile court.

15 Zimring (2000a) argues that while due process requirements may interfere with the interventionist mission of the juvenile court, they do not interfere with its diversionary mission:

> For an informal and interventionist court, standards of proof and defense lawyers are a major drawback to identifying children in need and providing them with help. Due process is therefore a major handicap to achieving such an informal juvenile court. But if saving kids from the gratuitous harm inflicted by the criminal process is the aim, there is no inherent conflict between due process and the court's main beneficial functions.
>
> (p. 2487)

References

Bernard, T. J., & Kurlychek, M. C. (2010). *The cycle of juvenile justice* (2nd ed.). New York, NY: Oxford University Press.
Breed v. Jones, 421 U.S. 519 (1975).
Cabot, R. C. (1934). 1000 delinquent boys: First findings of the Harvard law school's survey of crime. *Survey, 70*(2), 38–40.
Children's Bureau (1923). *Juvenile court standards*. Washington, D.C.: United States Department of Labor.
Commonwealth v. Fisher, 213 Pa. 48 (1905).
Ex parte Crouse, 4 Wharton 9 (1839).
Evison, I. S. (1995). *Pragmatism and idealism in the professions: The case of Richard Clarke Cabot, 1869–1939* [Unpublished doctoral dissertation]. The University of Chicago.
Feld, B. C. (1993). Criminalizing the American juvenile court. *Crime & Justice, 17*, 197–280.
Feld, B. C. (2000). Legislative exclusion of offenses from juvenile court jurisdiction: A history and critique. In J. Fagan and F. E. Zimring (Eds.), *The changing borders of juvenile justice* (pp. 83–144). Chicago, IL: The University of Chicago Press.
Feld, B. C. (2003). The politics of race and juvenile justice: The "due process revolution" and the conservative reaction. *Justice Quarterly, 20*(4), 765–800.
Feld, B. C. (2017). *The evolution of the juvenile court: Race, politics, and the criminalizing of juvenile justice*. New York, NY: New York University Press.
Glueck, S., & Glueck, E. T. (1934). *One thousand juvenile delinquents*. Cambridge, MA: Harvard University Press.
Glueck, S., & Glueck, E. T. (1940). *Juvenile delinquents grown up*. New York, NY: The Commonwealth Fund.
Graham v. Florida, 560 U.S. 48 (2010).
Griffin, P., Addie, S., Adams, B., & Firestine, K. (2011). *Trying juveniles as adults: an analysis of state transfer laws and reporting*. Washington, D.C.: Office of Juvenile Justice and Delinquency Prevention.
Hafoka, M., Woo, Y., Hsieh, M. L., van Wormer, J., Stohr, M. K., & Hemmens, C. (2017). What legally prescribed functions tell us: Role differences between adult and juvenile probation officers. *Federal Probation, 81*(3), 32–47.
In re Gault, 387 U.S. 1 (1967).

In re Winship, 397 U.S. 358 (1970).
Jacobs, J. B. (2014). Juvenile criminal record confidentiality. In F. E. Zimring and D. S. Tanenhaus (Eds.), *Choosing the future for American juvenile justice* (pp. 149–168). Chicago, IL: The University of Chicago Press.
Kent v. United States, 383 U.S. 541 (1966).
Leonard, T. C. (2016). *Illiberal reformers: Race, eugenics, and American economics in the Progressive era*. Princeton, NJ: Princeton University Press.
Lindsay v. Lindsay, 257 Ill. 328 (1913).
Mack, J. W. (1909). The juvenile court. *Harvard Law Review, 23*(2), 104–122.
Manfredi, C. P. (1998). *The Supreme Court and juvenile justice*. Lawrence, KS: University Press of Kansas.
Mapp v. Ohio, 367 U.S. 643 (1961).
Maroney, T. A. (2014). The once and future juvenile brain. In F. E. Zimring and D. S. Tanenhaus (Eds.), *Choosing the future for American juvenile justice* (pp. 189–215). Chicago, IL: The University of Chicago Press.
McKeiver v. Pennsylvania, 403 U.S. 528 (1971).
Meranze, M. (1996). *Laboratories of virtue: Punishment, revolution, and authority in Philadelphia, 1760–1835*. Chapel Hill, NC: The University of North Carolina Press.
Miller v. Alabama, 567 U.S. 460 (2012).
Miranda v. Arizona, 384 U.S. 436 (1966).
People ex rel. O'Connell v. Turner, 55 Ill. 289 (1870).
Platt, A. M. (1969). *The child savers: The invention of delinquency*. Chicago, IL: The University of Chicago Press.
Roper v. Simmons, 543 U.S. 551 (2005).
Rothman, D. J. (1971). *The discovery of the asylum: Social disorder and disorder in the new republic*. Boston, MA: Little, Brown & Co.
Schall v. Martin, 467 U.S. 253 (1984).
Schultz, J. L. (1973). The cycle of juvenile court history. *Crime & Delinquency, 19*(4), 457–476.
Scott, E. S., & Steinberg, L. (2008). *Rethinking juvenile justice*. Cambridge, MA: Harvard University Press.
Singer, S. I. (1996). *Recriminalizing delinquency: Violent juvenile crime and juvenile justice reform*. Cambridge, UK: Cambridge University Press.
Sowell, T. (1996). *Knowledge and decisions*. New York, NY: Basic Books.
Stanford v. Kentucky, 492 U.S. 361 (1989).
Tappan, P. W. (1946). Treatment without trial. *Social Forces, 24*(3), 306–311.
Tanenhaus, D. S. (2000). The evolution of transfer out of the juvenile court. In J. Fagan & F. E. Zimring (Eds.), *The changing borders of juvenile justice* (pp. 13–43). Chicago, IL: The University of Chicago Press.
Tanenhaus, D. S. (2004). *Juvenile justice in the making*. New York, NY: Oxford University Press.
Tanenhaus, D. S. (2012). The elusive juvenile court: Its origins, practices, and re-inventions. In B. C. Feld & D. M. Bishop (Eds.), *The Oxford handbook of juvenile crime and juvenile justice* (pp. 421–441). New York, NY: Oxford University Press.
Thompson v. Oklahoma, 487 U.S. 815 (1988).

Whitman, J. Q. (2003). *Harsh justice: Criminal punishment and the divide between American and Europe*. New York, NY: Oxford University Press.

Zimring, F. E. (2000a). The common thread: Diversion in juvenile justice. *California Law Review*, *88*(6), 2477–2496.

Zimring, F. E. (2000b). Penal proportionality for the young offender: Notes on immaturity, capacity, and diminished responsibility. In T. Grisso & R. G. Schwartz (Eds.), *Youth on trial: A developmental perspective on juvenile justice* (pp. 271–289). Chicago, IL: The University of Chicago Press.

Zimring, F. E. (2010). The power politics of juvenile court transfer: a mildly revisionist history of the 1990s. *Louisiana Law Review*, *71*(1), 1–15.

Zimring, F. E., & Rushin, S. (2013). Did changes in juvenile sanctions reduce juvenile crime rates? A natural experiment. *Ohio State Journal of Criminal Law*, *11*(1), 57–69.

Chapter 2

The Contemporary Structure of Juvenile Justice

Juvenile Referrals

In the most recent year for which data is available (2018), juvenile courts nationwide handled approximately 744,500 delinquency cases.[1] This number has declined from a peak of nearly 1.9 million cases processed in 1998, decreasing most steeply in the past ten years (from 1.6 million in 2008). Since 2005 alone, there has been a 55 percent reduction in delinquency cases. The majority of referrals to juvenile courts, approximately 82 percent in 2018, are based on arrests by law enforcement rather than by parents, school officials, or probation officers. For personal, property, and drug offenses, police make approximately 90 percent of referrals. This is lower for public order offenses, in large part due to probation violations where the probation officer may refer the youth without police involvement. (Here, only 58 percent of referrals involve police.) The number of juvenile arrests in 2019 was the lowest in decades (Hockenberry & Puzzanchera, 2020).

The number of delinquency referrals varies considerably across juvenile justice systems, however. In 2018, for example, the average rate of juvenile arrests for robbery was 52 (per 100,000), ranging from 2 in Wyoming to 190 in Illinois. For aggravated assault, the average rate was 84, ranging from 19 in Maine, Kansas, and Kentucky to 305 in Nevada. For simple larceny, the average rate was 413, ranging from 56 in West Virginia to 891 in Louisiana. For weapons offenses, the average rate was 50, ranging from 2 in Kansas to 209 in Illinois. For drug offenses, the average rate was 269, ranging from 24 in Massachusetts to 1,082 in Wyoming (Puzzanchera, 2020). Each state juvenile justice system thus has its own unique juvenile crime problem—although there are discernible trends over time, such as juvenile crime increasing steadily from 1962 to 1996, then decreasing slightly for the next decade and decreasing more dramatically from 2006 to 2018 (Hockenberry & Puzzanchera, 2020).

Preadjudication Detention

Upon referral, the first major decision is whether to place the juvenile in a short-term secure detention facility or to release them to their parents or guardian, pending petition of adjudication. An intake department official (i.e. probation officer) will first recommend that a juvenile be detained, and the juvenile court judge must decide whether detention is warranted, and, if so, issue the detention order. This decision is made based on considerations of community safety, the juvenile's safety, and ensuring appearance at future court hearings, as well as for evaluation of the juvenile (Barton, 2012). For example, in a recent ethnographic study a juvenile court judge recounted one such decision: "I am thinking if I let this kid go back into the community, this kid's coming back in a body bag" (Clair & Winter, 2016, p. 343). Detention can occur before a formal petition of delinquency is filed, but most often it occurs after petition but before adjudication. Typically, a detention hearing for "probable cause" must occur within 24 hours of the initial referral. For adults, bail can only be denied based on strong evidence that the defendant is a "flight risk" or a "danger to community" (*US v. Salerno*, 1987). For juveniles, however, preventative detention is more common and subject to a lower standard. Specifically, preventative detention has been held to be constitutional in the juvenile context since preadjudication detention does not constitute punishment and there remains a strong *parens patriae* interest in promoting the welfare of children (*Schall v. Martin*, 1984).

Nationally, 26.2 percent of delinquency cases were detained prior to adjudication in 2018 (Hockenberry & Puzzanchera, 2020). While the total number of detained cases nationwide has declined from almost 400,000 in 2006 to less than 200,000 in 2018, the proportion of referrals that are detained has hovered around one quarter—although this can vary considerably from state to state.[2]

Intake and Petition of Delinquency

Youth can be referred to juvenile court processing by a variety of means, including law enforcement, school referral, and parent or guardian referral. The first point of contact with the juvenile court itself is the intake department, which screens referred cases and decides whether the case should be handled formally (i.e. petition of delinquency), informally (i.e. diversion), or dismissed. Historically, delinquency cases could be referred directly to the juvenile court judge by police or parents, but this created an enormous burden on the juvenile court due to the quantity of referrals requiring an adjudicatory hearing before a judge. In the early twentieth century Judge Mack came up with the *complaint* system, where the probation department would screen cases before they appeared before the judge, investigating complaints and possibly handling them without judicial involvement (Tanenhaus, 2004). This remains the model today, as most referred youth are handled informally. The intake decision typically involves three factors: first, whether the juvenile court has original jurisdiction; second, whether there is probable cause; and third, whether formal processing is in the best interests of the child and the community. The major options at intake, then, are to refer the case to formal processing (i.e. petition of delinquency), divert the case to some informal disposition, or dismiss the case (often for lacking probable cause). The second outcome, diversion, requires the juvenile offender to admit the delinquent act in exchange for some informal sanction or intervention program.

Traditionally, as we saw in Chapter 1, intake processing was almost exclusively the province of intake officers, usually the probation department. Today, the intake agent can vary across jurisdictions and may involve the prosecutor, judge, or even special agency outside the court. The decision whether to formally or informally proceed with a case is one of the most important, and most open to discretion. Mears (2012) explains the five major arrangements for intake processing (from strongest to weakest role for traditional intake agents): (1) intake officers wield high discretionary power and file petitions that prosecutors review; (2) intake officers must seek prosecutor approval in order to dismiss or divert a referred case; (3) prosecutors must review all intake officer recommendations, for formal as well as informal processing; (4) serious charges bypass the intake officer and are sent directly to the prosecutor; and (5) the prosecutor reviews all cases and makes petition decisions.

Importantly, probation officers and prosecutors can have quite different priorities in deciding what is "best" for the child and community. On the one hand, probation officers tend to have more of a social welfare orientation. This means they will consider many non-legal factors such as likelihood of success in diversion programs, problems at school or home, and the overall attitude of youth and parents (e.g. cooperation). Prosecutors, on the other hand, are more guided by due process and legal considerations. They are better trained to assess strength of the evidence, but may focus more on the nature of the offense and the prior record than non-legal factors. In 15 states, the intake decision is determined principally by the probation officer, while in ten states it is principally the prosecutor. In 11 states, it is some combination (i.e. categories 2–4 above). And in another 15 states, the decision largely follows statutory guidelines developed by the legislature; in practice, this means the prosecutor has the power (see Zimring, 2010). States also vary in whether there are time limits on informal sanctions (i.e., diversion), with pre-petition time limits in 34 states, post-petition time limits in 29 states, and no time limits in 10 states (22 states have both pre- and post-petition limits). These differences may also be related to contextual characteristics within states such as urban versus rural courts (see Fairchild, Gupta-Kugan, & Andersen, 2019).

If the intake department decides that a case should be handled formally, a petition of delinquency is filed by the prosecutor and the case is placed on the juvenile court calendar for an adjudicatory hearing. This is the juvenile court equivalent of charges being filed. In 2018, 56.7 percent of referrals were formally petitioned, 25.8 percent were diverted to informal processing, and 17.5 percent were dismissed (Hockenberry & Puzzanchera, 2020).[3]

Waiver to Criminal Court

The intake department may also recommend that a juvenile case be removed from the juvenile court's jurisdiction and transferred to criminal court. This process is called "waiver" because the juvenile court waives its original jurisdiction over the case, allowing the juvenile to be prosecuted in criminal court. While transfer to adult court usually occurs before the adjudication stage of processing, it is considered the "capital punishment of juvenile justice" since it places juvenile offenders in the formal, adult criminal court—and thus opens the door to more severe punishments than are available in juvenile court (Zimring, 1981, p. 193). As noted in the last chapter, judicial waiver represents the original form of transfer and is most consistent with the court's original mission. For this traditional form of transfer, the prosecutor files a petition of waiver, requesting that the juvenile court judge waives original jurisdiction. At the transfer hearing, which is subject to the due process requirements laid out in *Kent v. United States* (1966), the juvenile court judge decides whether the juvenile case merits criminal prosecution based on the evidence presented by the prosecutor.[4] Nationally, approximately .5 percent of petitioned delinquency cases were waived by juvenile court judges from 2005 to 2018. The age distribution is quite varied, however. Among juveniles age 16 and older, approximately 1.5 percent of petitioned cases were waived to criminal court in 2018. Among juveniles under age 16, approximately .2 percent of petitioned cases were waived. This has to do with the age of eligibility for discretionary judicial waiver. For felony offenses, the most common age of eligibility is 14, shared by 19 states. Sixteen states set the age of eligibility higher (age 16 for ten states and age 15 for six states), while five states set lower age limits (ranging from 10 to 13) and six states have no age of eligibility specified by statute (Hockenberry & Puzzanchera, 2020).

Other mechanisms of waiver have also emerged in recent years. First, concurrent jurisdiction, also called prosecutorial waiver, takes the decision out of the hands of the juvenile court judge and places it with the prosecutor, who has statutory authority to file charges in juvenile or criminal court. No waiver hearing is required because there is concurrent jurisdiction, and there is no constitutional right to juvenile court processing. Second, statutory exclusion, also called legislative waiver, sends juvenile cases to criminal court based on certain case characteristics (typically age and offense type) as determined by the state legislature (Feld, 2000). As noted in Chapter 1, prosecutorial and legislative waiver statutes reflect a transformation of the practice of transfer from a decision guided by consideration of the best interests of youth and the juvenile justice system to one guided by the interests of the executive and legislative branches of state governments (Zimring, 2010).

While 46 states allow judicial waiver, compared to 37 states that have some kind of legislative waiver and only 14 states that have prosecutorial waiver, non-judicial waivers today account for the majority of juveniles in criminal court (see Griffin, Addie, Adams, & Firestine, 2011). This also includes states with lower ages of original jurisdiction for their juvenile court. While not technically waiver, courts with lower age of jurisdiction automatically send juveniles (i.e. 16- and 17-year-olds) to criminal court. In 2018, seven states used age 16 as their upper age of juvenile court jurisdiction—sending all 17-year olds to criminal court—while two states, New York and North Carolina, used age 15 as their upper age of jurisdiction—sending all 16-year-old offenders to criminal court. Additionally, 28 states allow for "reverse waiver," where criminal court judges can send some juveniles in criminal court to juvenile court instead. This provides some judicial oversight for juvenile offenders that are automatically transferred to criminal court. Many states have also developed blended sentencing as an alternative to transfer: 15 states allow juvenile courts to impose criminal sanctions and 23 states allow criminal courts to impose juvenile sanctions (Hockenberry & Puzzanchera, 2020).

Adjudication of Delinquency

Once a petition of delinquency is filed by the prosecutor, the case is placed on the juvenile court docket for an adjudicatory hearing. At the arraignment hearing following the petition, the judge will advise the juvenile defendant of his or her rights, read the full petition aloud, and allow the juvenile to admit or deny the petitioned charges. Most juveniles will admit the charges, equivalent to pleading guilty, such that something like 90–95 percent of delinquent cases result from admissions rather than formal adjudicatory hearings (Bernard & Kurlychek, 2010). As in criminal court, this typically involves negotiations with the prosecutor (i.e. plea bargains) to determine the best disposition for the juvenile offender.

If the juvenile denies the petitioned offense(s), then there will be a full adjudicatory hearing which functions as the juvenile court equivalent of a criminal trial. Here, the prosecutor presents evidence that the juvenile committed the petitioned criminal or status offense. This is the most formal, adversarial part of the juvenile justice process since the hearing is considered a criminal prosecution in most states, and rules of criminal evidence apply. Basic due process rights are also guaranteed at this stage. (Unlike criminal court, many juvenile defendants waive their right to counsel, one example of juvenile court proceedings remaining less adversarial than criminal prosecutions.) As in criminal court, the fact-finder decides whether the juvenile defendant is responsible for the petitioned offense, and if so, whether to declare the juvenile a "delinquent," a "status offender," or some other legal designation (e.g. "serious juvenile offender"). In ten states, juveniles can elect to have a jury trial, but typically the judge is the fact-finder. (This remains one of the major contrasts with criminal court.) The outcome of the adjudicatory hearing is either an adjudication of delinquency (equivalent to a guilty verdict), dismissal (equivalent to not guilty), or some informal outcome (i.e. diversion). Diversion at this stage usually involves a suspended or continued sentence (sometimes called an "adjudication withheld"), meaning that the juvenile must agree to some informal sanction in order for the case to be dismissed (but the juvenile avoids being officially adjudicated delinquent). This might involve volunteer work, paying restitution, or attending a treatment program such as drug counseling. If conditions of the informal court order are violated, however, the juvenile is adjudicated delinquent and receives a formal disposition without an additional adjudicatory hearing.

Nationally, 52.1 percent of petitioned delinquency cases were adjudicated delinquent in 2018 (Hockenberry & Puzzanchera, 2020). This means that nationally (in 2018), 30 percent of all *referred* cases were adjudicated delinquent while 70 percent of referrals did not result in a formal adjudication of delinquency (either not petitioned or petitioned but not adjudicated delinquent). Additionally, the proportion of petitioned cases that are adjudicated delinquent has been steadily declining over time, from 61 percent in 2005 to 52 percent in 2018. In 2005, however, a similar proportion of referrals were adjudicated delinquent (i.e. 33 percent). This reflects that more cases are being handled informally *after* being formally petitioned, what is called judicial diversion.

Judicial Disposition

For cases that are adjudicated delinquent, the juvenile court judge also determines the sanction to be applied to the delinquent juvenile. This occurs at a dispositional hearing, separate from the adjudicatory hearing, where the judge no longer focuses exclusively on the legal aspects of the case (e.g. offense severity, prior record, age, and strength of evidence), but considers what dispositional outcome would be in the best interests of the child and community. For this, the judge typically relies heavily on the predisposition report provided by the probation officer. This report includes a full assessment of the juvenile and their background and social environment based on the probation officer's investigation. (Since most juvenile delinquents admit the petition, the dispositional hearing is often the only time the judge becomes acquainted with the case.)

The primary dispositional options are residential placement (i.e. commitment) and community supervision (i.e. probation), although some juveniles are also released at this point (i.e., judicial discharge), possibly with a judicial warning or suspended sentence. Residential placement may involve commitment to a long-term secure facility or residential treatment center (the juvenile court equivalent of prison), placement in a group home or other short-term residential facility (e.g. a shelter), or special programs such as boot camps and wilderness camps. Community supervision may involve intensive probation supervision, regular probation, referral to treatment in a community setting, or other community sanctions such as community service. Nationally, 26 percent of cases that were adjudicated delinquent in 2018 resulted in residential placement while 63.2 percent received community supervision and 8.6 percent received some other disposition such as paying restitution (Hockenberry & Puzzanchera, 2020). Rates of placement versus probation have remained steady since 2005, with just under 30 percent of cases committed and just over 60 percent placed on community supervision. Nationally, then, only 7.7 percent of initial *referrals* to juvenile court resulted in residential placement (in 2018).

As was true at the inception of the juvenile court, community supervision remains the most common disposition for juvenile offenders. The probation officer is the backbone of the juvenile court and juvenile corrections system, performing initial screening of all cases at the intake stage, assessments and predisposition reports at the adjudicatory and dispositional stages, as well as performing community supervision for juveniles on probation. While originally part of the juvenile court and judicial branch, probation is now part of the executive branch of government (i.e. law enforcement) in 15 states, while it is a shared office between judicial and executive branches in another 15 states and only exclusively part of the judicial system in 20 states. Probation duties can include dozens of tasks, including, most notably: intake screening; predisposition investigation and report, including risks and needs assessments; coordinating direct services to youth and families (i.e. rehabilitation); supervision such as compliance checks and other forms of surveillance (e.g. electronic monitoring); coordinating programs; and enforcing conditions of probation and revocation upon violation.

Specific probation duties can vary widely across juvenile justice systems, however. For example, in the states included in the present study (Alabama, Connecticut, Missouri, Oregon, South Carolina, Texas, and Utah), prescribed statutory duties overlap less than expected. Of these, the only duty that is prescribed across all seven states is investigating cases. Generally assisting or advising the court is a prescribed duty in four states (but not in Connecticut or Utah), as is providing supervision (but not in Oregon or Utah). The law enforcer role is prescribed in three states—Connecticut, Missouri, and Oregon—while assisting in rehabilitation is prescribed in two states—Connecticut and Texas. Additionally, only two states prescribe diverting cases at intake and case management (Alabama and South Carolina) or prescribe performing risks/needs assessment (Connecticut and Missouri). While the traditional roles of investigating cases and advising the court appear universal, other probation tasks thus vary from state to state (Hafoka et al., 2017).

For youth who are placed in residential facilities, the most common options are long-term secure facilities (36.2 percent in 2018) and residential treatment centers (34.5 percent). Additionally, 11.6 percent of placements involved short-term detention facilities (also used for preadjudication detention) and 11.3 percent of placements involved group homes. Less common placements include shelters (1.1 percent), diagnostic centers (1.5 percent), boot camps (.5 percent), and wilderness camps (3.1 percent). Approximately 40 percent of these facilities are state-run while another 40 percent are privately operated (especially residential treatment centers), the rest being locally operated (e.g. detention centers). Close to 90 percent of residential facilities are secure (i.e. locks). The typical length of stay is between one month and one year (approximately 70 percent), with only 11.2 percent of commitments being longer than one year and approximately 20 percent being less than one month. Facilities commonly house between 21 and 200 youth, with only 12.3 percent of juveniles being placed in facilities with more than 200 residents (and approximately 17 percent placed in facilities with fewer than 20 residents). In terms of educational services for confined youth, about 87 percent of facilities provide high school education, while about 78 percent provide middle school, 77 percent provide special education, and 67 percent provide GED preparation services. In terms of onsite treatment services, about 85 percent of facilities provide mental health treatment and 69 percent provide substance abuse treatment, while only approximately 36 percent provide treatment for sex offenders and only 22 percent for serious violent offenders (Hockenberry & Sladky, 2018).

Placement rates also vary across states. While the national average in 2017 was 85 youth committed per 100,000, this ranged from states with low commitment rates such as Connecticut (13), Hawaii (19), and Vermont (22), to states with high commitment rates such as Oregon (185), West Virginia

(207), and Wyoming (233) (Hockenberry, 2020). The structure of juvenile corrections also varies considerably across states. First, corrections agencies vary. In 18 states, an independent juvenile agency handles juvenile corrections, while in 10 states the adult corrections agency also processes juveniles (although they are housed separately). Additionally, juvenile corrections are administered by a separate child welfare agency in 11 states and by a human services agency in 12 states. Second, states differ with respect to whether solitary confinement is allowed in juvenile facilities. In 31 states, solitary confinement is prohibited, while 15 states allow it in limited cases and five states allow it more broadly. Third, states differ in terms of who determines release from secure confinement. In 22 states, the corrections agency determines release, while this decision is made by the juvenile court in 10 states and shared between court and corrections agency in another 11 states. Additionally, the release decision is made by an independent parole board in 8 states (JJGPPS, 2020).

State Variation in Juvenile Justice Processing

In addition to the state-level variation noted for specific stages of processing above, several other notable differences between states involve the overall organization and mission of the state's juvenile justice system. Most notably, this includes the age-related jurisdiction of the court, the treatment of status offenders, the organization of the juvenile justice system (including judicial selection), and the statutory purpose of the juvenile justice system.

First, age limits the jurisdiction of the juvenile court at both ends: some offenders are too young to be referred to the court, while others are too old. The first is the lower jurisdiction of the court, also referred to as the "age of responsibility." As noted in Chapter 1, the common law set this limit at age 7, and created a presumption of infancy (i.e. no capacity) for children aged 7–13, becoming full-fledged adults for purposes of criminal prosecution at age 14. Today, 33 states have no lower limit of jurisdiction for their juvenile courts and may rely on this common law approach, treating age 7 as the lower jurisdiction of the court. Eleven states instead make 10 the lower age of jurisdiction, and the lower age ranges from age 6 to age 8 among the remaining seven states. In an international context, this represents a lower-than-average age of jurisdiction, which is typically 12–14 in other Western, developed countries (Tonry & Chambers, 2012).[5] In the states included in the present study, only one state specified a lower age of jurisdiction (as of 2010): age 10 in Texas.

For the upper age of jurisdiction, states are more uniform, with 42 states holding that juvenile court jurisdiction extends to age 17 (and adulthood begins at age 18). This is also the international consensus (Tonry & Chambers,

2012).[6] In seven states, however, juvenile court jurisdiction only extends to age 16, and in two states, it only extends to age 15. As mentioned in the section on waiver above, this means that in nine states, 16- and 17-year-old juvenile offenders are prosecuted in criminal court. In recent years, though, there has been a move toward "age 17" as the upper jurisdiction. In 2010, the upper age of jurisdiction was age 16 in ten states and age 15 in three states. Among the states in the present study, Connecticut has moved from age 15 (in 2010) to age 17 (in 2018), while Missouri, South Carolina, and Texas have retained age 16 as their upper jurisdiction. Alabama, Oregon, and Utah have set age 17 as their upper jurisdiction since before 2000 (JJGPS, 2020). Additionally, most states have extended jurisdiction for their juvenile justice systems, allowing for juvenile dispositions to extend beyond the upper age of original jurisdiction. In 36 states, jurisdiction is extended to age 20, while in 6 states it extends to ages 21–24. All states in the present study extended jurisdiction to age 20 (as of 2010), except for Oregon which extends jurisdiction to age 24 (JJGPS, 2020).

Second, the treatment of status offenders varies across states. This is reflected in different terminology that ranges from a "dependent" label to an "offender" label. Moving from "dependent" to "offender," they are labeled as "in need of care" in 6 states, "in need of services" in 12 states, "in need of supervision" in 12 states, "unruly" in 6 states, "status offender" in 13 states, and no separate label in three states. Among the states in the present study, status offenders are labeled "in need of services" in Connecticut, "in need of supervision" in Alabama, "status offender" in Missouri, South Carolina, and Texas, and no separate label in Utah. (In Oregon, status offenders are classified as "wards.") Jurisdiction for status offenses is the same as for delinquency in 29 states, but 14 states have a lower age of jurisdiction for status offenders—including Texas—while eight states have a higher age of jurisdiction for status offenders—including Missouri and Texas (JJGPS, 2020).

Third, the organization of the juvenile court varies across state systems. First, in terms of the overall integration of juvenile justice and child welfare, most states have a decentralized juvenile justice system (25 states), while seven states have a single, centralized juvenile justice system, eight states have an umbrella agency with separate divisions for juvenile justice and other child and family services, and 11 states have separate state-level agencies for juvenile justice, on the one hand, and child services, on the other hand. Second, systems vary in whether juvenile court services are provided locally or by the state. Detention services are typically locally operated (33 states), probation services are typically state operated (31 states), and reentry services are almost always state operated (46 states; JJGPS, 2020).

Fourth, most juvenile justice systems have a statutory "purpose" clause, prefatory language that explains the purpose of the juvenile justice system, and these statutes also vary across states. While each statutory purpose is uniquely worded, they can be grouped into four categories. First, the traditional "parens patriae" orientation is the guiding language of eight juvenile justice systems, including Missouri. Second, "due process" is the language of seven juvenile justice systems, including Texas. Third, and most popular, 29 states have language of "balanced and restorative justice," including Alabama, Connecticut, Oregon, South Carolina, and Utah. This represents a hybrid between the *parens patriae* orientation of the original juvenile court and the due process orientation of modern juvenile courts. Fourth, five states have a "developmental" focus in their statutory purpose (JJGPS, 2020). None of the states included in the present study have adopted this language.

Notes

1 These break down as follows: 235,000 violent (person) offenses (31.6 percent), 225,900 non-violent property offenses (30.3 percent), 101,000 drug law violations (13.6 percent), and 185,100 public order offenses (24.9 percent). Status offense cases are not included.

2 Several notable reform efforts have targeted preadjudication detention and attempted to reduce its use (see Barton, 2012). Most notably, this includes the Juvenile Detention Alternatives Initiative (JDAI), which uses objective risk assessment for detention screening and seeks to increase community-based alternatives to detention (e.g. home detention, electronic monitoring). Established by the Anne E. Casey Foundation in the 1980s with a pilot project in Broward County, FL, JDAI had expanded to 300 sites in 39 states by 2014. Interestingly, though, the proportion of referrals that are detained has still hovered around 25 percent of referrals since 2006.

3 Reforms aimed at deinstitutionalizing status offenders have resulted in a lower number of status offenses that are formally handled, although this varies by the type of status offense. Overall, petitioned status offenses declined from 192,600 cases in 2005 to 97,800 cases in 2018—a 49 percent reduction. This is not substantially different from the overall reduction in petitioned delinquency cases (52 percent), but certain categories of status offense were petitioned even less often. Most notably, the number of petitioned liquor law violations declined from 38,520 in 2005 to 8,802 in 2018 (77 percent), the number of petitioned curfew violations declined from 15,408 to 3,912 (75 percent), and the number of petitioned ungovernable youth declined from 25,038 to 8,802 (65 percent). On the other hand, the number of petitioned truancy cases only declined 15 percent, from 71,262 to 60,636 (Hockenberry & Puzzanchera, 2020). As such, there has been a shift in the kinds of status offenders that are handled formally.

4 *Kent* proposed eight criteria for judicial waiver, having to do with the seriousness of the offense, the youth's prior record, adult accomplices, the strength of the evidence, the youth's maturity, and considerations of public safety and rehabilitation.

5 The age of responsibility is as follows, from lowest to highest: age 8 in Scotland; age 10 in England/Wales, Ireland, Australia, New Zealand, and Switzerland; age 12 in Canada, the Netherlands, Portugal, and Turkey; age 13 in France,

Greece, and Poland; age 14 in Austria, Germany, Italy, Japan, and Spain; age 15 in Denmark, Finland, Norway, Sweden; and age 18 in Belgium. For Belgium and the Scandinavian countries, the high age of criminal responsibility reflects that there is no separate juvenile justice system (Tonry & Chambers, 2012).

6 The only exceptions to this are the Scandinavian countries, where criminal court jurisdiction begins at age 15, along with Scotland (age 16) and New Zealand (age 17).

References

Barton, W. H. (2012). Detention. In B. C. Feld & D. M. Bishop (Eds.), *The Oxford handbook of juvenile crime and juvenile justice* (pp. 636–663). New York, NY: Oxford University Press.

Bernard, T. J., & Kurlychek, M. C. (2010). *The cycle of juvenile justice* (2nd ed.). New York, NY: Oxford University Press.

Clair, M., and Winter, A. S. (2016). How judges think about racial disparities: Situational decision-making in the criminal justice system. *Criminology, 54*(2), 332–359.

Fairchild, A., Gupta-Kagan, J., & Andersen, T. S. (2019). Operationalizing intake: Variations in juvenile court intake procedures and their implications. *Children and Youth Services Review, 102*, 91–101.

Feld, B. C. (2000). Legislative exclusion of offenses from juvenile court jurisdiction: A history and critique. In J. Fagan and F. E. Zimring (Eds.), *The changing borders of juvenile justice* (pp. 83–144). Chicago, IL: The University of Chicago Press.

Griffin, P., Addie, S., Adams, B., & Firestine, K. (2011). *Trying juveniles as adults: an analysis of state transfer laws and reporting*. Washington, D.C.: Office of Juvenile Justice and Delinquency Prevention.

Hafoka, M., Woo, Y., Hsieh, M. L., van Wormer, J., Stohr, M. K., & Hemmens, C. (2017). What legally prescribed functions tell us: Role differences between adult and juvenile probation officers. *Federal Probation, 81*(3), 32–47.

Hockenberry, S. (2020). *Juveniles in residential placement, 2017*. Justice Juvenile Statistics National Report Series Bulletin. Washington, D.C.: Office of Juvenile Justice and Delinquency Prevention.

Hockenberry, S., & Sladky, A. (2018). *Juvenile residential facility census, 2016: Selected findings*. Justice Juvenile Statistics National Report Series Bulletin. Washington, D.C.: Office of Juvenile Justice and Delinquency Prevention.

Hockenberry, S., & Puzzanchera, C. (2020). *Juvenile court statistics, 2018*. Pittsburgh, PA: National Center for Juvenile Justice.

Juvenile Justice Geography, Policy, Practice & Statistics. (2020). Online. Available: www.jjgps.org/. Developed by the National Center for Juvenile Justice (NCJJ), with funding from the John D. and Catherine T. MacArthur Foundation.

Kent v. United States, 383 U.S. 541 (1966).

Mears, D. P. (2012). The front end of the juvenile court: Intake and informal versus formal processing. In B. C. Feld & D. M. Bishop (Eds.), *The Oxford handbook of juvenile crime and juvenile justice* (pp. 573–605). New York, NY: Oxford University Press.

Puzzanchera, C. (2020). *Juvenile arrests, 2018.* Justice Juvenile Statistics National Report Series Bulletin. Washington, D.C.: Office of Juvenile Justice and Delinquency Prevention.
Schall v. Martin, 467 U.S. 253 (1984).
Tanenhaus, D. S. (2004). *Juvenile justice in the making.* New York, NY: Oxford University Press.
Tonry, M., & Chambers, C. (2012). Juvenile justice cross-nationally considered. In B. C. Feld & D. M. Bishop (Eds.), *The Oxford handbook of juvenile crime and juvenile justice* (pp. 871–897). New York, NY: Oxford University Press.
US v. Salerno, 481 U.S. 739 (1987).
Zimring, F. E. (1981). Notes toward a jurisprudence of waiver. In J. C. Hall, D. M. Hamparian, J. Pettibone, & J. L. White (Eds.), *Major issues in juvenile justice information and training: Readings in public policy* (pp. 193–205). Columbus, OH: Academy for Contemporary Problems.
Zimring, F. E. (2010). The power politics of juvenile court transfer: a mildly revisionist history of the 1990s. *Louisiana Law Review, 71*(1): 1–15.

Chapter 3

Why Might Context Matter?

Theoretical Perspectives on Juvenile Justice

The present research is guided by the following broad question: Do juvenile justice outcomes vary across community and system contexts, and if so, *why* do they vary? Any attempts to answer this complex and important question first must develop a theoretical model of how the juvenile justice system operates, that is, a theory of the juvenile justice system. If we think of the juvenile justice system in terms of systems theory, as Mears (2017) rightly urges us to do, then "we cannot reasonably expect a single theory to explain all things" (p. 113).

Several definitions of the notion of "system" have been offered. One major difference in how systems are defined involves whether the notion of "goals" is incorporated into the definition. On the one hand, a *teleological* understanding of systems includes goals, for example, "the interaction of different units toward a common goal." On the other hand, a *functional* description of a system does not include goals, for example, "[a] whole which functions as a whole by virtue of the interdependence of its parts" (Mears, 2017, pp. 56–57). In thinking about systems in nature, there is some debate as to whether there is a biochemical basis for teleological language, or whether this necessarily involves unhelpful anthropometrism (see Dennett, 2013). Nevertheless, in the context of social systems such as juvenile justice, a goal-oriented understanding appears appropriate—although we may discover that social systems do not in fact function toward coherent goals (see Feeley, 1973). For our purposes, then, we can think of a system as "an interconnected set of elements that is coherently organized in a way that achieves something" (Mears, 2017, p. 56). As such, the juvenile justice system can be conceived as a complex social phenomenon with shared goals but different organizational inputs. For such a phenomenon, variation in outcomes across context is to be expected—but may also undermine the more uniform goals of the system. Efforts to understand this complexity thus begin with "simultaneously focusing on systems operations and impacts and using a diverse range of theories and empirical research … to understand the whole and its parts and how both can be improved" (Mears, 2017, p. 123).

Juvenile justice theory has not developed independently of criminal justice theory, and the latter will be employed to guide the present inquiry. Nevertheless, it is important to note at the outset a major difference between juvenile justice and criminal justice that complicates the analysis. As discussed in Chapter 1, the juvenile court is constrained by its traditional mission as *parens patriae*, serving the best interests of the child in addition to considerations of community safety and justice. The goal of the juvenile justice system is thus at least two-fold: justice and welfare. While the criminal justice system is constrained mainly by the goals of social control and punishment, the juvenile justice system has, from its inception, aimed primarily at *reforming* wayward youth. Since the juvenile court is premised on the individualized consideration of delinquent youth with the goal of reform, there is more room for discretion and thus more room for variation in outcomes compared to the criminal justice system (where legal considerations are more dominant). While clearly inappropriate in the criminal justice system, where notions of formal equality and due process reign supreme, we should thus not expect legal factors alone to determine outcomes in the juvenile justice system. To some extent, contextual factors will likely play a role. Less formal decision-making criteria coupled with higher discretion may even produce greater variation in outcomes across juvenile courts, in addition to greater variation within them, based on social context. With these preliminary observations in mind, we can turn to the main subject of the present chapter—theoretical frameworks for understanding the juvenile justice system.

Theoretical Frameworks for Juvenile Justice

If we are interested in answering basic questions about how juvenile justice outcomes are produced in the processing of referrals, we begin with three major questions. First, *what* variables are related to juvenile justice outcomes? This includes an examination of case-level legal variables such as type of offense, prior record, and age, case-level extralegal variables such as gender and race or ethnicity, and contextual variables such as poverty or urbanism in the surrounding community. Second, *how* are these variables related to juvenile justice outcomes? Most notably, is there a positive or negative relationship? Also, what is the magnitude of the relationship and is it linear or non-linear? Third, *why* are these variables related to juvenile justice outcomes? This third question involves the causal mechanisms by which different factors (i.e. independent variables) produce different outcomes (i.e. dependent variables). Answers to these questions will form the basis of a theory of the juvenile justice system.

Another way to characterize theories is by level of explanation (Snipes & Maguire, 2007). Often criminal justice theories are described at either the micro- or macro-level, with most theories having independent and dependent variables at the same level of analysis. Contextual theories, however, use independent variables from a higher level of explanation than the dependent variable of interest. In the case of the juvenile justice system, this involves predicting juvenile court outcomes—micro-level dependent variables—based on higher level community characteristics—macro-level independent variables. Worden (2007) outlines three conceptual domains where contextual characteristics might influence the court process: first, "court characteristics" such as local legal culture and organizational features of the particular court; second, "characteristics of community elites" such as characteristics of those in power in the court and the community more generally; and third, "community characteristics" such as socioeconomic or demographic characteristics of the community. Similarly, Mears (1998) enumerates several determinants of sentencing, including (1) goals of sentencing; (2) case-specific factors; (3) characteristics of court practitioners; (4) organizational context; and (5) cultural, political, and social context. These last two categories capture what Worden (2007) describes as court characteristics, community elite characteristics, and community characteristics. As such, we can think of the two dominant contextual perspectives from which such theories can be developed as *sociopolitical* and *organizational.*

Sociopolitical Perspectives

Perhaps the most basic distinction in theoretical perspectives on the criminal and juvenile justice systems involves two broad sociopolitical perspectives: consensus and conflict (see Snipes & Maguire, 2007). According to a consensus approach, theories will tend to assume that the juvenile justice system operates for the benefit of the entire community and is based on "broadly shared societal values in the punishment of criminal norm violations" for youthful offenders (Hagan, 1989, p. 116). Here, the system fulfills the most basic functions of government: protecting the public from predatory crime and promoting the rule of law by punishing those who violate it. For juvenile justice, we can add, a consensus approach would see the reformation of juvenile offenders as reflecting shared values and goals: namely, the desire to rehabilitate delinquent children so they do not grow up into hardened, adult criminals. This consensus perspective is strongly influenced by Émile Durkheim's view that some level of crime is functional for society: it brings the common public together around the acts they collectively view as deviant (see Durkheim, 1964). This consensus approach is sometimes also referred to as legalism or rationalism, invoking Weber's conception of a rational legal system (see Weber, 1954). Rationalism-legalism is the most basic and intuitive perspective of justice system processing: indeed, it is how the justice system is *supposed* to work. In the present context, this model supposes that the juvenile justice system is aimed toward certain goals—rehabilitation of juvenile offenders, public safety, offender accountability, and justice for victims—and that the system is rational to the extent that it efficiently achieves those goals in a uniform way (see Duffee & Allan, 2007).

On the consensus view, the variables that we would expect to be related to juvenile justice outcomes would be variables related to the goals of the system to promote public safety, punish offenders for wrongdoing, and in the case of juvenile justice, rehabilitate young, malleable offenders. The most predictive variables would thus be case-level *legal* variables (Hagan, 1989). Most notably, this would include severity of the alleged offense (related to culpability and dangerousness), age of the offender (related to culpability, dangerousness, and malleability), and prior record (related to dangerousness and malleability). For our purposes, what is most relevant is whether we should expect substantial variation in juvenile justice outcomes across different *contexts*. On the one hand, we might imagine that if the system is oriented toward the same consensus goals, we should not see variation in outcomes across different courts. On the other hand, some contextual factors may influence the rational goals of the juvenile court—namely, how to respond to the problem of juvenile delinquency in the surrounding community. Thus, the most relevant contextual factors would involve *social disorganization*, which might rationally require a formal social control response.

Alternatively, conflict theories posit that the criminal and juvenile justice systems are operating for the benefit of powerful elites and at the expense of the powerless. This perspective is strongly influenced by the Marxist view that society is characterized by class struggle between the haves and have-nots (Snipes & Maguire, 2007). Here, the system seeks to maintain the status quo and exert social control over certain traditionally disadvantaged groups. That is, the criminal and juvenile justice systems are seen as exerting a social control function not to fulfill the basic functions of the government—as in the consensus perspective—but to oppress certain populations with whom those in power are in perennial conflict. In more recent versions of conflict theory, "elites" has been replaced by "mainstream society" so that the conflict can be visualized as between "mainstream society" and the underclass (Hagan, 1989; Sampson & Laub, 1993).[1]

On the conflict view, the case-level extralegal variables that should *not* influence juvenile court outcomes according to a consensus perspective—race and ethnicity, gender, and socioeconomic status—would be expected to play a more important explanatory role. Similarly, different aspects of social context may condition juvenile court outcomes. Contextual conflict theories—such as racial threat, ethnic threat, and economic threat—posit that racial minorities and the underclass poor are subjected to greater social control by the juvenile court because they are perceived as a threat to those in power or to mainstream society (see, e.g., Sampson & Laub, 1993). Here, it could be posited that community conflict will produce harsher juvenile court responses.

While the consensus-conflict distinction provides a helpful starting point for thinking about how the juvenile justice system operates and why sanctions might vary across contexts, others have lamented that the distinction is of limited utility in explaining the complexity of criminal justice system processes and outcomes (Hagan, 1989). As Myers and Talarico (1987) emphasize:

> [C]riminologists must acknowledge the consensual *and* coercive characteristics of criminal punishment and recognize the complexity in any use of penal sanctions. It strikes us, then, as theoretically unsound to test the utility of either a conflict or consensus perspective because any such attempt is tantamount to setting up straw men for inevitable rejection. (p. 14)

On more fundamental grounds, Bernard and Engel (2001) object to framing theory in terms of sociopolitical perspectives at all: "Such a broad classification obscures difference among theories and research while adding little to increase clarity. … classifying theories according to their underlying theoretical assumptions is not useful" (p. 3). Instead, the authors propose that criminal justice research be guided first by the dependent variable of interest, and then by the independent variables thought to predict variation in the outcome of interest. This alternative framework does not assume that any theory could explain all juvenile justice outcomes—or variation therein—equally well. This important insight motivates independent investigation into different outcomes, each of which may be influenced by different factors. Nevertheless, it is important for the present inquiry to be theoretically grounded, even if we must keep in mind that there may be no grand theory that adequately explains variation in juvenile punishment across courts and the communities they inhabit.

Instead, the present study takes Dixon (1995)'s tripartite approach as a helpful theoretical framework for guiding the study. According to this approach, there are three theoretical frameworks by which justice system outcomes might be understood. First is political theory, where outcomes are driven primarily by socioeconomic factors such as race and class (similar to conflict theory). Second is legal theory, where outcomes are driven primarily by legal characteristics of each case (similar to consensus theory). Third is organizational theory, where outcomes are driven primarily by organizational factors specific to each court considered as its own natural ecosystem.[2] Dixon's (1995) framework provides a useful way of dividing up the field, as most variables that influence juvenile court processes could be broadly considered legal, sociopolitical, or organizational. With that in mind, we turn to consideration of organizational perspectives on juvenile justice processing.

Organizational Perspectives

Organizational theory provides a perspective on court decision-making that neither consensus nor conflict approaches clearly anticipate:

> Repudiating the Weberian perception of the organization of sentencing as a technically rational machine, as well as the Marxian perception of it as a political machine, the organizational maintenance perspective depicts the organization of sentencing as a natural system … Because a complex network of ongoing informal relationships among court actors is formed, a cooperative effort to efficiently dispose of cases evolves, with effects not envisioned by the substantive political [i.e., conflict] or formal legal [i.e., consensus] models.
>
> (Dixon, 1995, p. 1162)

An organizational perspective is not inconsistent with sociopolitical perspectives, however. For instance, it could be that substantive "politics are institutionalized in organizational practices" (Dixon, 1995, p. 1163). Nevertheless, paying attention to organizational context can help move beyond the more simplistic consensus-conflict framing that has been criticized by many scholars, and to consider the context of the juvenile justice system beyond sociopolitical factors.[3]

Rational Goals, Functional Systems, and Institutional Approaches

Feeley (1973) presents one of the first systematic accounts of an organizational approach to the criminal justice system. He argues that most early criminal justice system research assumed a "rational goal" model of decision-making. If one adopts this rational goal model of criminal justice, the main focus becomes the formal rules of the system. Following Weber (1954), this focus sees the modern U.S. criminal justice system as a rational organization that is "de-personalized, rule-bound, and hierarchically structured" to produce "highly predictable, rationalized, and efficient results" (Feeley, 1973, pp. 409–410). The movement to minimize discretion in criminal justice is a paradigmatic example of the influence of this rational goal model of the organization.

Analysis by rational goal model theorists will tend either to assess interrelationships among formal rules or to compare the rules to empirical descriptions of the system in order to "identify and measure discrepancies between reality and ideal" (Feeley, 1973, p. 409). This tends to be the perspective taken by legal scholars—examining the formal rules of the system—as well as social scientists—focusing on the empirical realities of the administration of justice and whether it is consistent with formal rules. Such an approach may often adopt a consensus sociopolitical perspective—the goals of the system reflect widely shared social norms—although a rational goal approach could similarly adopt a conflict perspective. For example, according to the minority threat hypothesis (discussed below), criminal justice agents respond to a threatening minority population by increasing social control. Given their purported discriminatory goals, such enhanced social control would reflect a rational approach.

Feeley (1973) finds fault in this analytical approach, however, due to the underlying narrowness of the "goal model" in contrast to what he calls the "functional systems" model. With the functional systems model, greater emphasis is placed on *explaining* the behavior of organizational actors rather than *evaluating* this behavior in light of organizational goals. In other words, formal rules are no longer the primary focus on analysis. Important here is who makes decisions and what constraints and incentives they face. As Sowell (1996) observes,

> [W]hen social processes are described in terms of their hoped-for results, this obscures the more fundamental question as to just what they actually do—and circumvents questions as to whether doing such things is likely to lead to the result expected or proclaimed.
>
> (p. x)[4]

The goals that organizational actors pursue may also be personal or sub-group goals, shifting the focus toward informal "rules of the game," such as norms arising out of courtroom workgroups. Correspondingly, the roles assumed by organizational actors are essentially local adaptations to their particular environments, workloads, and the personal goals of other actors in the system. The upshot, Feeley (1973) argues, is that while the rational goal model takes the perspective of "the *rational organization* pursuing its single set of goals," functional systems models take the perspective of "the set of *rational individuals* who comprise the system … pursuing their various individual goals" (p. 413).

Fundamentally, this reframing involves the following insight: organizations only act through individual persons who are autonomous agents that respond to signals in their local environments (i.e. incentives), and who have their own goals that may not be perfectly aligned with abstract organizational goals. This more methodologically individualist perspective bears some resemblance to the "public choice" field of economics. According to public choice, political behavior is not assumed to be solely (or even primarily) the pursuit of publicly stated goals, but rather of many short-term goals based on individual (i.e. economic and political) self-interest (see Buchanan, 2000; Buchanan & Tullock, 1962). Similarly, the functional systems model posits that organizational goals will not be automatically followed by organizational actors. Instead, conflicts between formal organizational goals and goals of individual rational actors will occur in the mere presence of formal rules.[5] Instead, there must be local, sometimes complex, incentives for individual actors to pursue organizational goals while complying with formal rules. Two such incentives are the norm of professionalism—i.e. informal social control—and appellate procedure—i.e. formal social control—neither of which are powerful enough to ensure perfect unity of goals as envisioned by the rational goal model.

While Feeley (1973) contrasts the *rational goal model* of organizational behavior with the *functional systems model*—preferring the latter as more realistic—a third organizational approach is the *institutional model*. This more recent approach in organizational theory focuses on how "organizations interact with their social, political, and economic environments in producing outcomes" (Snipes & Maguire, 2007, p. 38). Like the functional systems approach, institutional theory posits that organizations will act in ways that are difficult to explain via the rational goal model, but unlike the functional systems approach the focus is not limited to relationships among individual system actors. Instead, there is greater emphasis on institutional realities such as the institution's responses to changes in its social and political context. The institution must act to further its own survival, sometimes in ways that are in conflict with the rational goals of the organization as well as the goals of individual system actors. As Crank and Bowman (2008) observe,

> [T]he institutional theory of organizations, popular in the study of police and correctional organizations, argues that the behavior and values carried by criminal justice organizations [are grounded] in the value structures of principal audiences, especially those in local communities, not in immanent notions of human behavior.
>
> (p. 570)

For example, Zimring and Hawkins (1991) provide a public choice account of the scale of imprisonment, highlighting the misaligned incentives of different levels of state governments that determine penal policy:

> Since localities do not contribute to central state correctional budgets, the marginal cost of an extra prisoner may be zero at the local level of

> government, where the decision to confine is made. Thus, a perceived marginal benefit from imprisonment in excess of zero is likely to result in a decision to imprison, even though the total marginal cost to all levels of government far exceeds the perceived benefit of imprisonment.
>
> (pp. 211–212)

The result is a "correctional free lunch" (p. 212). Recently, a natural experiment from California supports the notion that prison is over-used when costs are not internalized (Ouss, 2020). As Mears (2017) describes it, the institutional actors who make imprisonment decisions do not have "skin in the game" (p. 222). This represents a public choice interpretation of institutions within the larger correctional system. The same might be true of the juvenile justice system and the goals (and incentives) of various institutional actors within that system. The organizational perspective—whether in terms of rational goals, functional systems, or institutional context—thus proposes a third set of variables related to the incentives of individual decision-makers within a specific context: for our purposes, the political economy of the juvenile court.

Applying sociopolitical and organizational frameworks to the juvenile justice system, we might reasonably expect that legal, sociopolitical, and organizational variables will be associated with juvenile justice outcomes, but different theories will tend to emphasize one class at the expense of the others.[6] Dixon (1995) writes:

> Taken alone, none of these sentencing theories can fully explain variations in sentencing across courts. Since each perspective begins with the assumption that courts operate with a unitary system of sentencing, some rationality of sentencing is stressed with the exclusion or diminution of others. An alternative and less-utilized approach to the study of sentencing, the contextual approach, provides an analytical tool for capturing variations in sentencing processes across courts. A contextual perspective on sentencing maintains that the sentencing of individuals in a given court is influenced by the political, social, and organizational context of the court.
>
> (p. 1164)

When only case-level variables are under examination, their operationalization and interpretation may depend crucially on a theoretical lens. Lynch (2019), for example, provides a critique of one dominant theoretical lens—focal concerns—due to its exclusive focus on individual (psychological) decision-making without consideration of social context. As Lynch (2019) observes: "Put simply, in a large body of sentencing research, focal concerns has become an individual-level, common-sense psychological theory of judging" that ignores how "sentencing happens as a socio-legal practice in the real-world context of criminal courts" (pp. 6, 8).

A contextual approach to understanding the juvenile justice system can provide more understanding of the complex system by assessing legal, socio-political, and organizational variables simultaneously—and at various levels of explanation. This vertical expansion of our theoretical understanding of juvenile justice can also be accompanied by a horizontal expansion also inspired by organizational theory, focusing on distinct phases of the juvenile justice system and how those phases interact with their organizational contexts: loose versus tight coupling.

Loose and Tight Coupling

An organizational, systems perspective on criminal and juvenile justice suggests that certain stages of processing may be more "loosely" or "tightly" coupled based on the relationships among various system actors. As a result, it may be that contextual influences on juvenile court processing are *not* uniform across different stages of processing. As described in Chapter 2, some stages of processing may allow for greater discretion than others due to differing organizational constraints and differential emphasis on individualized consideration versus formal rules.

Hagan (1989) first adapted this terminology from organizational theorists and applied it to the criminal justice system: "In connotative terms, loose coupling is meant to evoke the image of entities (e.g., court systems) that are responsive to one another, while still maintaining independent identities and some evidence of physical or logical separateness" (p. 119). As Ulmer (2019) observes, the distinction between tight and loose coupling has at least two meanings in organizational sociology. First, coupling might refer to the manner in which formal institutional norms correspond to actual, everyday practice. Second, coupling may refer to how different stages of processing are connected and intertwined: tightly (i.e. interdependent with high levels of coordination) or loosely (i.e. largely independent and with less coordination). A central insight from this perspective is that tightly coupled systems will be more responsive to explicit rules and organizational norms, while loosely coupled systems may be more willing to circumvent such rules and norms via "localized adaptation" (Ulmer, 2019, p. 488).

Empirically, loosely coupled systems can be characterized by sharing few predictive independent variables, substantial differences in the influence of shared predictive variables, and overall weak influence of shared variables compared to non-shared variables. Hagan (1989) argues that the criminal justice system is a loosely coupled system where subsystems are highly independent, "characterized by unexpected evidence of randomness and inconsistency in the influence of legal and extralegal variables" as well as "low levels of explained variance in outcomes across subsystems" (p. 129). More recently, Ulmer (2019, p. 496) observes that while the same focal concerns may characterize all stages of criminal justice processing, "the meaning, relative emphasis and priority, and situational interpretation of them are embedded in local legal and organizational cultures and surrounding sociopolitical contexts."

Following Hagan (1989) and others, Bishop, Leiber, and Johnson (2010) have developed a structural-processual perspective as a means of explaining variation in outcomes across different stages of the juvenile justice system (see also Engen, Steen, & Bridges, 2002). They argue that it is important to consider how stages of processing may differ: "From an organizational perspective, the juvenile justice system is a collection of bureaucracies whose representatives participate in decisions about appropriate responses to offenders" (Bishop et al., 2010, p. 216). As we saw in the previous chapters, this includes law enforcement (the source of most referrals), intake officers (usually part of the probation department), prosecutors, and juvenile court judges. Some stages are "loosely coupled" because they are less formal and discretion is thereby greater, for example intake and judicial disposition, while "tightly coupled" stages are more formal and legalistic and involve less discretion, for example petition and adjudication.

While Bishop and colleagues (2010) were largely guided by focal concerns theory and applied this organizational framework to case-level factors, it can also be employed to examine the differential impact of contextual factors on different stages of juvenile court processing. As noted in Chapter 2, there are a variety of important points of contact in the juvenile justice system before judicial disposition, including arrest, referral, detention, formal petition of delinquency, and waiver to adult court.

With all this in mind, the following section explores the more specific contextual theories that will guide our examination of juvenile justice processing in the present study.

Contextual Theories of Juvenile Justice

The contextual hypotheses in the present study predict that contextual variables reflecting sociopolitical and organizational context, the dominant theoretical perspectives discussed above, will be associated with juvenile court outcomes. Notably, contextual effects may differ across decision points in a loosely coupled system, so contextual or institutional effects may be present at some individual stage(s) but not at others. Moreover, since juvenile justice actors have more discretion due to the *parens patriae* orientation of the juvenile justice system, we might expect even greater variation across community contexts compared to the criminal justice system. Three guiding perspectives are as follows: community threat hypotheses (conflict theory), social disorganization (consensus theory), and the political economy of the juvenile court (organizational theory).

Community Threat

Community threat perspectives predict more punitive outcomes in communities with larger minority populations, greater poverty, or other structural threats (see Tittle & Curran, 1988).[7] Blalock (1967) first developed a social conflict perspective known as the minority threat hypothesis. This original formulation predicts that as a racial or ethnic minority group grows relative to the dominant group, those in power may begin to feel threatened and discriminate against the minority group (in order to maintain power). Specifically, Blalock (1967) suggested that a growing minority population might threaten the dominant group primarily as an economic threat or a political threat—resulting in discrimination against the (growing) threat to economic or political power. While Blalock (1967) did not explicitly address discrimination within the criminal justice system, others have extended the hypothesis. In the criminal justice system context, Liska (1992) posited a general social threat perspective—"the greater the number of acts and people threatening to the interests of the powerful, the greater the level of crime control" (p. 165)—that can include the symbolic threat of a growing minority population. In the juvenile justice context, Tittle and Curran (1988) observed, "differential sanctioning of members of a minority or other group within a given political jurisdiction should reflect the degree of threat that particular minority or group constitutes for elites in that area" (p. 32).

Minority threat has subsequently become one of the most frequently tested macro-social theories in criminal and juvenile justice, evaluating the prediction that minority percentage in the population will be associated with more punitive treatment, most often tested in terms of sentencing outcomes (see Feldmeyer & Cochran, 2018). Although the majority of this research tests the *racial* threat hypothesis (i.e. examining Black population size), the same strategy has also been employed more recently to examine the *ethnic* threat hypothesis—examining Hispanic population size (see, e.g., Caravelis, Chiricos, & Bales, 2011; Feldmeyer, Warren, Siennick, & Neptune, 2015).

While minority threat is the most often examined community threat explanation for racial disparities in juvenile justice, other community threats have also emerged in extant research. Most similar to minority threat is the "economic threat" perspective, which poses the same basic conflict hypothesis but for socioeconomic class rather than race and ethnicity. The economic threat hypothesis posits that economically disadvantaged communities are perceived as more threatening by court actors and that this translates into harsher sentencing as a form of social control (Britt, 2000; Tittle & Curran, 1988). For example, Sampson and Laub's (1993) contextual theory of urban inequality is influenced by the minority threat perspective described above, but adds specific focus on concentrated disadvantage: their theory posits that "underclass Black males are viewed as a threatening group to middle-class populations and thus will be subjected to increased formal social control by the juvenile justice system."

Social Disorganization

Dating back to the early insights of Shaw and McKay (1942), social disorganization theory posits that structural factors such as greater concentrated disadvantage, ethnic heterogeneity, and residential mobility impede social integration and contribute to the breakdown of informal social control (see Pratt & Cullen, 2005). Although typically envisaged as a theory of *neighborhood* processes, we might imagine that this breakdown creates the need for greater formal social control, presenting a non-conflict explanation for the relationship between structural variables and more punitive court outcomes at the county level.

Social disorganization taps into similar mechanisms as community threat, but from a *consensus* rather than *conflict* perspective. This creates some ambiguity with interpreting empirical evidence. Notably, findings of a positive relationship between more punitive court outcomes and community threat may be equally compatible with a social disorganization perspective (see Chamlin & Cochran, 2000). Specifically, a larger minority presence is likely associated with increased social disorganization and greater need for formal social control. But while community threat focuses on threatening demographic characteristics and changes, social disorganization focuses also on other indicators that are more directly linked to breakdowns in informal social control (see Sampson & Groves, 1989). Unlike community threat, social disorganization is largely untested as an explicit consensus explanation for variation in juvenile court outcomes, in contrast to conflict theory (i.e. community threat).

Political Economy

Juvenile court outcomes can also be examined from a contextual approach that takes an organizational perspective, rather than the conflict perspective assumed by community threat hypotheses or the consensus perspective assumed by social disorganization hypotheses. Organizational theorists tend to focus on variables specific to the local culture of the court, what Worden (2007) refers to as "workgroup theory." Typically, such approaches focus on organizational variables that involve either court structure—including staffing, caseload, resources, and role specialization or routinization (e.g. bureaucratic structure)—or local legal culture—including substantive (political or ideological) norms, procedural norms, case delay norms, and norms about criminal behavior.

One such organizational theory of juvenile justice processing is proposed by Hasenfeld and Cheung (1985, p. 803), who apply a political economy framework to the juvenile court. Following Wamsley and Zald (1973), political here refers to "the structure and process of the uses of authority and power to affect definitions of goals, directions, and major parameters for the organizational economy" while economy refers to "the combination of factors of production, the arrangement of division of labor, allocation of resources for task accomplishment, and maximization of efficiency" that produce organizational outputs (pp. 18–19). Hasenfeld and Cheung (1985) focus specifically on the decision for judicial versus non-judicial handling of a case (the regulation of inputs to the juvenile justice system) and the final judicial disposition for adjudicated cases (the regulation of outputs of the system) but their framework can be applied to other decision points as well. According to their theory, the juvenile court as a "people-processing organization" is influenced by four sets of structural variables: the external polity, the external economy, the internal polity, and the internal economy.

First, the external polity "refers to the exchanges between the organization and external units 'for control over legitimation, resource base, goal definitions, and the channels for exertion of influence'" (p. 805). Hasenfeld and Cheung (1985) predict that juvenile court outcomes would vary according to the prestige and legitimation of the juvenile court, operationalized as whether judges are elected or appointed (i.e. how political context may influence judges).[8] Specifically, they argue that elected judges are more focused on establishing "their legitimation in the community both through responsiveness to diverse constituencies and by elevating the importance of the court in the local youth service network" (p. 94). As a result, they should be more likely to divert cases to informal processing as a way to maintain "organizational flexibility." Second, elected judges will be more sensitive to crime control concerns of the general public, and thus more likely to commit "dangerous" youth.

Second, the external economy "refers to conditions which affect the supply of resources to the court and the demand for its services" (p. 805). This involves the economic resources available to the court, which should be expected to influence how courts process cases. The economic status of the surrounding community and the volume and seriousness of cases would both be expected to influence court outcomes. Specifically, the authors argue that wealthier communities will have lower judicial handling rates and lower commitment rates due to having more court resources available for informal processing and more outside resources for treatment (i.e. parents who can afford non-punitive treatment for referred youth). Tittle and Curran (1988) refer to this as the "value dominance hypothesis": juvenile courts in wealthier counties will exhibit more "middle class values" and hence a more lenient approach to juvenile delinquency among the "middle class" youth (p. 32).

Third, the internal polity "refers to the internal structure of authority and the dominant elite values and goals" (p. 805). Some juvenile court judges can be expected to be more child-focused and rehabilitative (i.e. progressive), while others will be more focused on community safety and punitively oriented (i.e. conservative). The authors predicted that judges with more punitive orientations would have higher rates of judicial handling and commitment rates.

Fourth, the authors proposed that the internal economy of the juvenile court "refers to the ways the organizational tasks are accomplished and encompasses the production system, the rules governing it, and the resources allocated to it" (p. 805). This involves the internal structure of the court, including the level of bureaucratization and due process orientation, as well as the available resources. Here, urbanism was used as a proxy for this bureaucratization and routinization of the court. Others have suggested that due to lower informal social control (e.g. collective efficacy) in urban neighborhoods, urban courts tend to be more tightly coupled, routinized, and due process oriented (Feld, 1991; Worden, 2007), especially in the post-*Gault* era.[9] As such, the formal legalism of urban courts should be expected to produce less discretion. While Hasenfeld and Cheung (1985) predicted that this greater due process-oriented urbanism would be associated with *lower* commitment rates. Feld (1991) argues that greater formalism in the juvenile court will actually translate into *more* punitive outcomes. As we saw in Chapter 1, Feld refers to this as the "criminalization" of the juvenile court.

Conclusion

A systems approach to understanding the juvenile justice system requires that we consider system outcomes in their social contexts. Contextual variation in the punitiveness of loosely coupled outcomes—ranging from intake processing to final disposition—may be due to differences in sociopolitical context (e.g. community threat), differences in social disorganization and the need for informal social control, or differences in organizational characteristics (e.g. political economy). Importantly, we may find that different juvenile court outcomes vary across communities and states according to different contextual factors, which would provide evidence of the loosely coupled systems hypothesis. In the following chapter, we will review the empirical research literature on these contextual approaches to understanding juvenile justice.

Notes

1 It is worth observing that when conflict theory is re-conceptualized as involving conflict between mainstream society and the underclass (or marginalized groups), it appears less distinct from a consensus, functionalist perspective, which posits that the community finds solidarity in punishing violators of its mainstream norms—for example, by members of the underclass. Thus, norm violators (according to consensus theory) are largely made up or persons who can also be described as the powerless (according to conflict theory). This presents challenges for establishing a clear conceptual dichotomy between these sociopolitical perspectives.

2 In a more comprehensive catalogue of criminal justice theory, for example, Kraska (2006) identifies the following eight theoretical frameworks by which we might explain variation in punishment in the criminal justice system more generally: (1) rationalism-legalism, (2) systems theory, (3) crime control versus due process, (4) politics, (5) social construction of reality, (6) growth complex, (7) oppression, and (8) late modernity. Some of these theories fit neatly under what Dixon (1995) calls "legal theory" (e.g. "rationalism-legalism"), "political theory" (e.g. "oppression"), or "organizational theory" (e.g. "growth complex"), whereas others combine insights from legal, political, and organizational perspectives (e.g. "systems theory," "late modernity").

3 One problem with sociopolitical perspectives may be the "animistic fallacy":

> Perhaps the simplest and most psychologically satisfying explanation of any observed phenomena is that it happened that way because someone wanted it to happen that way. ... Some events are in fact the result of purposeful activity toward the goal achieved, but the general presumption that this *must* be the case can be classified as "the animistic fallacy."
>
> (Sowell, 1996, pp. 97–98)

4 Sowell (1996) goes on to observe that "the most basic decision is *who* makes the decision, under what constraints, and subject to what feedback mechanisms" (p. 17).

5 On this point, Sowell (1996) observes that "[m]uch criticism of 'incompetent bureaucrats' implicitly assumes that those in the bureaucracy are pursuing the assigned goal but failing to achieve it due to lack of ability. In fact, they may be responding very rationally and ably to the set of incentives facing them" (p. 15).

6 As Worden (2007) argues, the three dominant theoretical perspectives on courts and communities are each informed by a different academic discipline: representational theory is largely informed by political science, conflict theory is largely informed by sociology, and local courtroom workgroup theory is largely informed by organizational science.

7 Conflict theory may also predict less social control in areas that are heavily populated by these disadvantaged groups, what Liska and Chamlin (1984, p. 384) call "benign neglect." As a result, minority threat is often operationalized as a curvilinear relationship between minority presence and punitive outcomes, such that outcomes become more punitive as the minority presence increases up to a point at which social control actually decreases.

8 There is some historical evidence that elected state judiciaries act differently than appointed judges, specifically exercising more power than judges appointed by the legislature (Stuntz, 2011). Others have similarly argued that elected judges will tend to be more punitive. For example, "the pressures of upcoming re-election and retention election campaigns make judges more punitive toward defendants" (Berry, 2015, p. 1). Contrasting the US courts with European courts, Lacey (2008) argues,

> [A] system like that of US states in which judges are elected is one in which one key barrier between popular demands for punishment and sentencing is, if not removed, seriously weakened. This becomes important under conditions in which criminal justice is highly politicised.
>
> (p. 94)

9 As Feld (1991, 1999) suggests, urbanization could be considered from an organizational perspective in light of *In Re Gault*, 387 U.S. 1 (1967), where the Supreme Court of the United States first extended some basic due process protections to defendants in juvenile court. It has been suggested that urban courts place more emphasis on due process rights (reflecting a "post-Gault" organizational approach), while rural courts place more emphasis on individualized consideration of the child's needs (reflecting a "pre-Gault" organizational approach).

References

Bernard, T. J., & Engel, R. S. (2001). Conceptualizing criminal justice theory. *Justice Quarterly*, *18*(1), 1–30.

Berry, K. (2015). *How judicial elections impact criminal cases*. New York, NY: Brennan Center for Justice, New York University.

Bishop, D. M., Leiber, M. J., & Johnson, J. (2010). Contexts of decision making in the juvenile justice system: An organizational approach to understanding minority overrepresentation. *Youth Violence and Juvenile Justice*, *8*(3), 213–233.

Blalock, H. M. (1967). *Toward a theory of minority group relations*. New York, NY: Wiley.

Britt, C. L. (2000). Social context and racial disparities in punishment decisions. *Justice Quarterly*, *17*(4), 707–732.

Buchanan, J. M. (2000). *The collected works of James M. Buchanan: Politics as public choice (Volume 13)*. Indianapolis, IN: Liberty Fund, Inc.

Buchanan, J. M., & Tullock, G. (1962). *The calculus of consent: Logical foundations of constitutional democracy*. Ann Arbor, MI: The University of Michigan Press.

Caravelis, C., Chiricos, T., & Bales, W. (2011). Static and dynamic indicators of minority threat in sentencing outcomes: A multi-level analysis. *Journal of Quantitative Criminology*, *27*(4), 405–425.

Chamlin, M. B., & Cochran, J. K. (2000). Race riots and robbery arrests: Toward a direct test of the threat hypothesis. *Social Pathology*, *6*(2), 83–101.

Crank, J. P., & Bowman, B. A. (2008). What is good criminal justice theory? *Journal of Criminal Justice*, *36*(6), 563–572.

Dennett, D. C. (2013). *Intuition pumps and other tools for thinking*. New York, NY: W.W. Norton & Company.

Dixon, J. (1995). The organizational context of criminal sentencing. *American Journal of Sociology*, *100*(5), 1157–1198.

Duffee, D. E., & Allen, E. (2007). Criminal justice, criminology, and criminal justice theory. In D. E. Duffee & E. R. Maguire (Eds.), *Criminal justice theory: Explaining the nature and behavior of criminal justice* (pp. 1–26). New York, NY: Routledge.

Durkheim, E. (1964). *The division of labor in society*. New York, NY: Free Press.

Engen, R. L., Steen, S., & Bridges, G. S. (2002). Racial disparities in the punishment of youth: A theoretical and empirical assessment of the literature. *Social Problems*, *49*(2), 194–220.

Feld, B. C. (1991). Justice by geography: Urban, suburban, and rural variations in juvenile justice administration. *The Journal of Criminal Law and Criminology*, *82*(1), 156–210.

Feeley, M. M. (1973). Two models of the criminal justice system: An organizational perspective. *Law & Society Review*, 7(3), 407–426.

Feldmeyer, B., & Cochran, J. C. (2018). Racial threat and social control: A review and conceptual framework for advancing racial threat theory. In J. D. Unnever, S. L. Gabbidon, & C. Chouhy. (Eds.), *Building a black criminology: Race, theory, and crime* (pp. 283–316). New York, NY: Routledge.

Feldmeyer, B., Warren, P. Y., Siennick, S. E., & Neptune, M. (2015). Racial, ethnic, and immigrant threat: Is there a new criminal threat on state sentencing? *Journal of Research in Crime and Delinquency*, *52*(1), 62–92.

Hagan, J. (1989). Why is there so little criminal justice theory? Neglected macro-and micro-level links between organization and power. *Journal of Research in Crime and Delinquency*, *26*(2), 116–135.

Hasenfeld, Y., & Cheung, P. P. (1985). The juvenile court as a people-processing organization: A political economy perspective. *American Journal of Sociology*, *90*(4), 801–824.

Kraska, P. B. (2006). Criminal justice theory: Toward legitimacy and an infrastructure. *Justice Quarterly*, *23*(2), 167–185.

Lacey, N. (2008). *The prisoner's dilemma: Political economy and punishment in contemporary democracies*. Cambridge, UK: Cambridge University Press.

Liska, A. E. (1992). *Social threat and social control*. Albany, NY: SUNY Press.

Lynch, M. (2019). Focally concerned about focal concerns: A conceptual and methodological critique of sentencing disparities research. *Justice Quarterly*, *36*(7), 1148–1175.

Mears, D. P. (1998). The sociology of sentencing: Reconceptualizing decisionmaking processes and outcomes. *Law & Society Review, 32*(3), 667–724.

Mears, D. P. (2017). *Out-of-control criminal justice: The systems improvement solution for more safety, justice, accountability, and efficiency*. Cambridge, UK: Cambridge University Press.

Myers, M. A., & Talarico, S. M. (1987). *The social contexts of criminal sentencing*. New York, NY: Springer-Verlag.

Ouss, A. (2020). Misaligned incentives and the scale of incarceration in the United States. *Journal of Public Economics, 191*, 104285.

Pratt, T. C., & Cullen, F. T. (2005). Assessing macro-level predictors and theories of crime: A meta-analysis. *Crime & Justice, 32*, 373–450.

Sampson, R. J., & Groves, W. B. (1989). Community structure and crime: Testing social-disorganization theory. *American Journal of Sociology, 94*(4), 774–802.

Sampson, R. J., & Laub, J. H. (1993). Structural variations in juvenile court processing: Inequality, the underclass, and social control. *Law & Society Review, 27*(2), 285–311.

Shaw, C., & McKay, H. (1942). *Juvenile delinquency and urban areas*. Chicago, IL: The University of Chicago Press.

Sowell, T. (1996). *Knowledge and decisions*. New York, NY: Basic Books.

Snipes, J. B., & Maguire, E. R. (2007). Foundations of criminal justice theory. In David E. Duffee and Edward R. Maguire (eds.), *Criminal Justice Theory: Explaining the Nature and Behavior of Criminal Justice* (pp. 27–50). New York, NY: Routledge.

Stuntz, W. (2011). *The collapse of American criminal justice*. Cambridge, MA: Harvard University Press.

Tittle, C. R., & Curran, D. A. (1988). Contingencies for dispositional disparities in juvenile justice. *Social Forces, 67*(1), 23–58.

Ulmer, J. T. (2019). Criminal courts as inhabited institutions: Making sense of difference and similarity in sentencing. *Crime & Justice, 48*, 483–522.

Wamsley, G, L., & Zald, M. N. (1973). *The political economy of public organizations: a critique and approach to the study of public administration*. Lexington, MA: Lexington Books.

Weber, M. (1954). *Max Weber on law in economy and society* (trans. Max Rheinstein). Cambridge, MA: Harvard University Press.

Worden, A. (2007). Courts and communities: Toward a theoretical synthesis. In D. E. Duffee & E. R. Maguire (Eds.), *Criminal justice theory: Explaining the Nature and behavior of criminal justice* (pp. 181–216). New York, NY: Routledge.

Zimring, F. E., & Hawkins, G. (1991). *The scale of imprisonment*. Chicago, IL: The University of Chicago Press.

Chapter 4

Exploring the Influence of Community Characteristics

A Review of the Literature

Almost 30 years ago, Barry Feld (1991) made an important observation about juvenile justice research:

> Studies which analyze and interpret aggregated data without accounting for contextual and structural characteristics may systematically mislead and obscure, rather than clarify. Both theoretically and operationally, it is necessary to refine the relationships between social structure and justice administration.
>
> (p. 208)

In the intervening several decades, scholars have emphasized the importance of considering macro-social context, but empirical tests of contextual effects have been limited. Specifically, only in the past decade or so has multilevel modeling become prominent in testing contextual influences on juvenile court processing outcomes across courts. By treating individual cases as nested within macro-social units such as courts or counties, this statistical approach avoids several issues that faced older research looking into macro-social influences on court processing. For purposes of testing contextual hypotheses, multilevel models are necessary for two primary reasons. First, single-level regression models do not account for the "statistical dependencies that occur among clusters of hierarchically organized data" (Johnson, 2010, p. 622). As a result of this clustering, standard errors will be underestimated and hypothesis tests "will therefore be too liberal" (p. 622). Second, tests of contextual hypotheses with single-level models utilize the wrong degrees of freedom. For research testing contextual hypotheses with county-level data, for example, the correct sample size is at the county-level (i.e. level-2) rather than the case-level (i.e. level-1). If the (larger) level-1 sample size is used to test such contextual hypotheses, the statistical power of the tests is greatly exaggerated. For both these reasons, tests of contextual hypotheses that do not employ multilevel modeling are more likely to commit Type I errors, rejecting the null hypothesis when doing so is not inferentially warranted.

While multilevel research in juvenile justice has begun to address these important macro-social questions through increasingly sophisticated analyses that control for many extraneous influences, this research is dwarfed by similar research in the criminal justice context. This matters since juvenile court outcomes are arguably *more* likely to be affected by social context due to the more informal nature of the juvenile court and the greater discretion of juvenile court actors (see Sampson & Laub, 1993). The following chapter presents a summary of extant multilevel research on juvenile justice outcomes and contextual factors that may influence variation in outcomes across macro-social units. In so doing, I focus on community factors tested in the present study: minority threat, economic threat, urbanism, political context, social disorganization measures, and organizational factors.

Minority Threat

Minority threat is one of the most frequently tested contextual hypotheses in criminology and criminal justice. Although the majority of the minority threat literature has tested racial and ethnic threat in the context of criminal justice outcomes such as arrests and sentencing (Feldmeyer & Cochran, 2018), it also represents the most tested contextual hypothesis in juvenile justice research. As described in Chapter 3, minority threat draws upon conflict theory and posits that minorities are subjected to greater social control because they are perceived as a threat to those in power.

In an early macro-level study, Sampson and Laub (1993) found that measures of racial inequality and underclass poverty were significantly related to juvenile justice outcomes—especially secure detention and out-of-home placements—supporting their "symbolic threat" hypothesis. Additionally, these contextual factors interacted significantly with race and gender, suggesting "that underclass Black males are viewed as a threatening group to middle-class populations and thus will be subjected to increased formal social control by the juvenile justice system" (p. 306). Other early research also found significant relationships between contextual indicators of racial threat and juvenile justice outcomes (see, e.g., Leiber & Jamieson, 1995; Tittle & Curran, 1988; but see Frazier, Bishop, & Henretta, 1992). As noted above, a major limitation of this research is that it did not employ multilevel modeling to capture the nested, hierarchical nature of the data.

More recent multilevel research provides limited support for the minority threat hypothesis in the context of juvenile justice processing. In one of the earliest such studies, Armstrong and Rodriguez (2005) examined 8,289 juvenile referrals across 65 counties in a Northeastern state (in 1990) and found that juvenile offenders were 14 percent more likely to be detained in counties with 1 percent larger Black population (OR = 1.14). In a more recent multilevel study, Peck and colleagues (2019) examined the influence of percent Black and percent Hispanic on juvenile court outcomes for 302,531 juvenile referrals across 67 counties in a Northeast state from 2000 to 2010. They found that odds of intake were 11 percent higher in counties with 1 percent larger Black population (OR = 1.11), but did not find any relationship between percent Hispanic and intake processing. Elsewhere, in a study of 1,164 juvenile referrals in South Carolina, Lowery and colleagues (2018) found that odds of confinement were higher in counties with higher percent Black (i.e. static racial threat) as well as counties with an increase in percent Black over time (i.e. dynamic racial threat). Looking at 58,550 juvenile referrals from 4,390 communities in Florida between 2010 and 2015, Maroun (2019) found lower odds of diversion (OR = .97) and higher odds of residential placement (OR = 1.01) for juveniles from zip codes with higher percent Black. For juveniles from zip codes with higher percent Hispanic, however, Maroun (2019) found higher odds of diversion (OR = 1.02) and lower odds of adjudication (OR = .97) and placement (OR = .96). Taking a more aggregate approach, Andersen and Oullette (2019) performed a national test of minority threat hypotheses, examining self-reported outcomes for 451 juveniles who reported being arrested prior to their 18th birthday. (These juveniles were from 207 counties across 42 states and Washington, D.C.) The authors found that juveniles were more likely to receive formal petition as well as secure placement in counties with higher percent Black, although percent Black was not associated with adjudication and percent Hispanic was not associated with any outcomes.

Most research, however, has found no significant relationship between measures of minority threat and various juvenile court outcomes, including intake (Leiber & Peck, 2019; Leiber, Peck, & Rodriguez, 2016; Peck, Leiber, & Beaudy-Cyr, 2019), detention (Lowery & Smith, 2020; Thomas, Moak, & Walker, 2013; Zane, Mears, & Welsh, 2020), petition (Freiburger & Jordan, 2011; Maume, Toth, & Spears, 2006; Zane et al., 2020), adjudication (Hayes-Smith & Hayes-Smith, 2009; Leiber et al., 2016; Leiber, Donnelly, & Wu, 2020; Maroun, 2019; Peck et al., 2019; Zane et al., 2020), and placement (Bray et al., 2005; Leiber et al., 2016, 2020; Leiber & Peck, 2019; Zane et al., 2020). Some research has even found a negative relationship. For example, in a study of 87,739 juvenile referrals across 67 counties in a Southern state (in 2009–2010), Leiber and Peck (2019) found that odds of intake processing were 7 percent lower in counties with 1 percent higher Hispanic population (OR = .93).

Economic Threat

Similar to minority threat, the economic threat hypothesis posits that economically disadvantaged communities are perceived as more threatening by court actors and that this translates into harsher sentencing as a form of social control (Tittle & Curran, 1988). According to this perspective, higher economic threat—usually measured as poverty, unemployment, income inequality, or concentrated disadvantage—should be positively associated with harsher juvenile court outcomes. As mentioned above, Sampson and Laub (1993) found that in addition to racial inequality, measures of "underclass" poverty were significantly related to detention and placement outcomes. Some other early research corroborated this association between economic measures and juvenile justice outcomes (Leiber & Jamieson, 1995), while others found no relationship (Frazier et al., 1992).

More recent research that employs multilevel modeling to assess the economic threat hypothesis has reached similarly mixed results. Several studies have found a significant relationship between economic community indicators and juvenile justice outcomes. Using 345 residential zip codes (instead of counties) as the level-2 unit of analysis, Rodriguez (2010) examined the influence of structural disadvantage on juvenile court outcomes for 23,156 juvenile referrals in Arizona. The author found that odds of detention were higher for juveniles from more disadvantaged communities, although structural disadvantage was not associated with odds of diversion, petition, or judicial placement. Elsewhere, Rodriguez (2013) similarly looked at the relationship between concentrated disadvantage and correctional confinement for 2,152 juveniles who were adjudicated delinquent in Phoenix, Arizona. Of the 37 zip codes making up Phoenix, the author found that juveniles from more disadvantaged zip codes were more likely to be committed. In a study of 8,901 adjudicated delinquents across 133 counties in Virginia from 2012 to 2017, Lowery and Smith (2020) found that odds of preadjudication detention were 60 percent higher in counties with greater concentrated disadvantage (OR = 1.60). In another study, Maroun (2019) found that odds of diversion (OR = 1.16) and adjudication (OR = 1.41) were higher for juveniles from communities in Florida (i.e. zip codes) with more structural disadvantage. Finally, in their national test of minority threat, Andersen and Oullette (2019) also found that judicial placement was more likely in counties with greater concentrated disadvantage, although disadvantage was not associated with odds of petition or adjudication.

Other research has found no significant relationship between economic measures and juvenile court outcomes such as intake (Leiber et al., 2016; Leiber & Peck, 2019; Peck et al., 2019; Rodriguez, 2007), detention (Thomas et al., 2013; Rodriguez, 2007, 2010; Zane et al., 2020), petition (Zane et al., 2020), adjudication (Hayes-Smith & Hayes-Smith, 2009; Leiber et al., 2016; Peck et al., 2019; Rodriguez, 2010; Zane et al., 2020), and placement (Leiber et al., 2016; Leiber & Peck, 2019; Maroun, 2019; Peck et al., 2019; Rodriguez, 2010; Zane et al., 2020). Still others have found a significant but *negative* relationship between economic context and juvenile court outcomes such as petition to juvenile court (Freiburger & Jordan, 2011) and residential placement (Lowery, Burrow, & Kaminski, 2018). In these studies, punitive outcomes are more likely in *less* disadvantaged contexts.

Urbanism

In addition to community threats, commentators have long postulated that courts may differ considerably from urban to rural contexts (Feld 1991, 1993, 1999). Specifically, Feld (1991) found that urban courts were more punitive, consistent with his hypothesis that urban courts were more tightly coupled and due process oriented, guided more by just deserts philosophy and "the principle of the offense."

Empirical support for this proposition from multilevel research, however, is quite limited. Andersen and Oullette (2019) found that odds of petition were higher in urban courts, while odds of adjudication and placement were not associated with county urbanism. In another study, Rodriguez (2010) examined 23,156 juvenile referrals in Arizona in 2000 and found that odds of detention and petition were higher for juveniles *from* more urban zip codes (although this study did not assess the urbanism of the court itself). Other research has found no significant relationship between urbanism and juvenile court outcomes such as detention (Armstrong & Rodriguez, 2005; Leiber & Peck, 2019; Lowery & Smith, 2020; Zane et al., 2020), intake (Peck et al., 2019), petition (Freiburger & Jordan, 2011; Zane et al., 2020), adjudication (Peck et al., 2019; Rodriguez, 2010; Zane et al., 2020), and placement (Bray et al., 2005; Leiber & Peck, 2019; Peck et al., 2019; Rodriguez, 2010; Zane et al., 2020). Lowery and colleagues (2018) found that odds of secure confinement were *lower* in more urban counties, contrary to Feld's (1991) hypotheses.

Other Contextual Characteristics

While most macro-social research has focused on minority threat, economic threat, and urbanism, some research has also examined the relationship between juvenile court outcomes and several other contextual variables (often used as control variables in the above analyses). These include crime levels, youth population density, residential mobility, community wealth, political context, and region of country.

Community crime rates have been used as a contextual control variable in many of the above studies examining community threats, with the expectation that higher crime rates would be associated with more punitive outcomes. Early research was mixed, with some indicating a significant positive relationship between crime and juvenile court outcomes (see, e.g., Leiber & Jamieson, 1995) and others indicating no relationship (Frazier et al., 1992). Perhaps surprisingly, most recent multilevel research has found no relationship between crime rates and juvenile court outcomes such as detention (Armstrong & Rodriguez, 2005; Thomas et al., 2013; Zane et al., 2020), intake (Leiber et al., 2016; Leiber & Peck, 2019; Peck et al., 2019), adjudication (Hayes-Smith and Hayes-Smith, 2009; Leiber et al., 2016; Peck et al., 2019; Rodriguez, 2007; Thomas et al., 2013; Zane et al., 2020), and placement (Leiber et al., 2016; Leiber & Peck, 2019; Lowery et al., 2018; Peck et al., 2019; Zane et al., 2020).

A few recent multilevel studies have examined additional contextual factors related to social disorganization, positing that greater social disorganization will be associated with more punitive outcomes. Such studies have largely failed to find any relationship between juvenile court outcomes and indicators of social disorganization such as residential stability (Lowery & Smith, 2020; Peck et al., 2019) and youth population (Lowery et al., 2018; Peck et al., 2019), however.

Some studies have also looked at community wealth, possibly as a proxy for juvenile justice system resources. Maume and colleagues (2006) looked at 39,764 juvenile referrals across 28 counties in Missouri (in 1994) and found that cases were more likely to be formally processed in counties with higher median wealth. Contrary to this, Peck and colleagues (2019) found that odds of formal intake processing were slightly lower in counties with greater wealth. Elsewhere, Lowery and Smith (2020) found that wealthier counties were slightly less likely to detain juvenile offenders, while others have found no relationship between community wealth and juvenile court outcomes (Leiber & Peck, 2019).

In addition, a few studies have examined the effect of political context on juvenile court outcomes, also with limited support for any contextual influences. Leiber and Peck (2019) examined juvenile court referrals in one Southern state and found that odds of secure placement were higher in counties with a higher percent who voted for the Republican Party in the 2008 U.S. Presidential election. They found no association between political context and intake processing, however. Elsewhere, others have found no association between political context and intake, petition, adjudication, or disposition outcomes (Peck et al., 2019; Zane et al., 2020).[1]

Region of country has also served as a control variable in two recent multilevel studies.[2] In a survey of 172 counties across 16 states, Leiber and Peck (2014) found that petition was significantly less likely in Northeastern counties and more likely in Southern counties (compared to Midwestern counties).[3] Detention, on the other hand, was significantly more likely in the Northeast, and placement was less likely in the South and West. Even more recently, in a study of 37 counties across three states, Leiber and colleagues (2016) found that formal intake processing was least likely in the Northeast and most likely in the Midwest, adjudication of delinquency was most likely in the Northeast, and secure placement was most likely in the Midwest.[4] In their national test of minority threat across 207 counties in 42 states, Andersen and Oullette (2019) found that odds of placement were significantly greater in the West than in the Northeast, while other regions were not associated with placement odds and region was unrelated to petition and adjudication outcomes.

Finally, several other contextual factors have been assessed in the criminal justice context but have not yet been evaluated with respect to the juvenile justice system. For present purposes, the most important are ethnic heterogeneity (e.g. Britt, 2000; Fearn, 2005), judicial selection (e.g. Carmichael, 2010), and other organizational features of the court. Britt (2000) suggested that ethnic heterogeneity (an indicator of social disorganization) might be associated with increased social control via harsher court outcomes—although no significant findings emerged (see also Fearn, 2005). Carmichael (2010) also found that judicial elections were associated with longer sentences compared to judges selected by appointment (see also Hall, 1992; Huber & Gordon, 2004). Some research has also looked more closely at judicial characteristics and opinions. In an early example, Johnson (2006) examined whether personal characteristics of the judge (e.g. age, gender, race/ethnicity) and professional experience were associated with sentencing outcomes. More recently, Ulmer and Johnson (2017) utilized survey data for federal judges to assess whether departures from the federal sentencing guidelines were a function of judges' perceptions. They found that departures were more likely where the legitimacy and coercive power of the guidelines were perceived by judges to be lower, suggesting that court culture matters. (They also found that case processing pressure was unrelated to guidelines departure, although departures were more likely in larger courts.) Others have also looked at organizational features of the court such as court size, caseload, trial rate, and available jail space (Johnson, 2005; Ulmer & Johnson, 2004). One common finding involves caseload pressure, which several studies have found to be negatively associated with sentencing severity (Ulmer & Bradley, 2006; Ulmer & Johnson, 2004). Most recently, Arazan and colleagues (2019) examined imprisonment and sentence length decisions for 382,262 criminal defendants across 67 counties in Florida from 1999 to 2002. Using multilevel modeling, the authors found that prison sentences were less likely, and sentences were shorter, in courts with more caseload pressure and higher trial rates—after controlling for case-level characteristics as well as county demographics. As noted, these types of organizational factors have not yet been assessed with respect to juvenile justice processing.

Conclusion

Multilevel research on contextual influences on juvenile court outcomes has produced mixed findings—*without a single contextual factor being consistently associated with more punitive treatment across studies*. One possible explanation for this is that different studies use different contextual measures, look at different outcomes, and draw samples from different jurisdictions. This can make comparison across studies quite difficult. In light of this, the present study seeks to make several contributions. First, while a large research literature is devoted to testing minority threat, the current study provides a robust test of several contextual influences, including community threats, social disorganization, and political economy. Second, most studies that use multilevel modeling to examine contextual influences on juvenile court processing are limited to one state. As Britt (2000) points out, this leaves open the possibility that most findings are idiosyncratic to particular jurisdictions—and potentially leads to contradictory research findings across different jurisdictions.

Notes

1 Additionally, in an examination of sentencing outcomes for juveniles waived to *criminal* court, Carmichael (2010) found that greater political conservatism (measured as the percentage of Republicans in the state legislature) was associated with increased sentence length. In a subsequent study, Carmichael and Burgos (2012) found that the number of juveniles sentenced to life in prison was higher in states with a larger Republican Party presence in the legislature and in states with a more conservative public. Elsewhere, Carmichael (2011) found that juvenile prison admission rates were *not* associated with Republican Party's control of state legislatures, however.

2 Others have suggested that sentencing practices may vary across states due to regional cultures that vary in punitive orientation (see Feld, 1991; Krisberg, Litsky, & Schwartz, 1984; Mears, 2006), including the suggestion that the Deep South in the United States is especially punitive (Eason, 2010). Of course, this higher punitive orientation may not be due to a regional culture, but due to regional differences in poverty, crime, or other factors associated with incarceration rates.

3 Counties were grouped into Northeast, Midwest, South, and West (with Midwest as the reference category).

4 The three states were referred to as Northeast, Midwest, and Southwest (with Southwest as the reference category).

References

Andersen, T. S., & Oullette, H. M. (2019). Juvenile court outcomes following youth's first arrest: a national test of the racial and ethnic threat hypothesis. *Crime & Delinquency*, *65*(2), 183–214.

Arazan, C. L., Bales, W. D., & Blomberg, T. G. (2019). Courtroom context and sentencing. *American Journal of Criminal Justice, 44*(1), 23–44.

Armstrong, G. S., & Rodriguez, N. (2005). Effects of individual and contextual characteristics on preadjudication detention of juvenile delinquents. *Justice Quarterly, 22*(4), 521–539.

Bray, T. M., Sample, L. L., & Kempf-Leonard, K. (2005). Justice by geography: Racial disparity and juvenile courts. In D. F. Hawkins & K. Kempf-Leonard (Eds.), *Our children, their children: Confronting racial and ethnic differences in American juvenile justice* (pp. 270–290). Chicago, IL: The University of Chicago Press.

Britt, C. L. (2000). Social context and racial disparities in punishment decisions. *Justice Quarterly, 17*(4), 707–732.

Carmichael, J. T. (2010). Sentencing disparities for juveniles sentenced to adult prisons: An individual and contextual analysis. *Journal of Criminal Justice, 38*(4), 747–757.

Carmichael, J. T. (2011). Punishing juvenile offenders as adults: An analysis of the social and political determinants of juvenile prison admissions across the United States. *Sociological Focus, 44*(2), 102–123.

Carmichael, J. T., & Burgos, G. (2012). Sentencing juvenile offenders to life in prison: The political sociology of juvenile punishment. *American Journal of Criminal Justice, 37*(4), 602–629.

Eason, J. (2010). Mapping prison proliferation: Region, rurality, race and disadvantage in prison placement. *Social Science Research, 39*(6), 1015–1028.

Fearn, N. E. (2005). A multilevel analysis of community effects on criminal sentencing. *Justice Quarterly, 22*(4), 452–487.

Feld, B. C. (1991). Justice by geography: Urban, suburban, and rural variations in juvenile justice administration. *The Journal of Criminal Law and Criminology, 82*(1), 156–210.

Feld, B. C. (1993). Criminalizing the American juvenile court. *Crime & Justice, 17*, 197–280.

Feld, B. C. (1999). *Bad kids: Race and the transformation of the juvenile court*. New York, NY: Oxford University Press.

Feldmeyer, B., & Cochran, J. C. (2018). Racial threat and social control: A review and conceptual framework for advancing racial threat theory. In J. D. Unnever, S. L. Gabbidon, & C. Chouhy. (Eds.), *Building a black criminology: Race, theory, and crime* (pp. 283–316). New York, NY: Routledge.

Frazier, C. E., Bishop, D. M., & Henretta, J. C. (1992). The social context of race differentials in juvenile justice dispositions. *Sociological Quarterly, 33*(3), 447–458.

Freiburger, T. L., & Jordan, K. L. (2011). A multilevel analysis of race on the decision to petition a case in the juvenile court. *Race & Justice, 1*(2), 185–201.

Hall, M. G. (1992). Electoral politics and strategic voting in state supreme courts. *The Journal of Politics, 54*(2), 427–446.

Huber, G. A., & Gordon, S. C. (2004). Accountability and coercion: Is justice blind when it runs for office? *American Journal of Political Science, 48*(2), 247–263.

Krisberg, B., Litsky, P., & Schwartz, I. (1984). Youth in confinement: Justice by geography. *Journal of Research in Crime and Delinquency, 21*(2), 153–181.

Leiber, M. J., & Jameison, K. M. (1995). Race and decision making within juvenile justice: The importance of context. *Journal of Quantitative Criminology, 11*(4), 363–388.

Hayes-Smith, J., & Hayes-Smith, R. (2009). Race, racial context, and withholding adjudication in drug cases: A multilevel examination of juvenile justice. *Journal of Ethnicity in Criminal Justice*, 7(3), 163–185.

Johnson, B. D. (2005). Contextual disparities in guidelines departures: Courtroom social contexts, guidelines compliance, and extralegal disparities in criminal sentencing. *Criminology, 43*(3), 761–796.

Johnson, B. D. (2006). The multilevel context of criminal sentencing: Integrating judge- and county-level influences. *Criminology, 44*(2), 259–298.

Johnson, B. D. (2010). Multilevel analysis in the study of crime and justice. In A. R. Piquero & D. Weisburd (Eds.), *Handbook of quantitative criminology* (pp. 615–648). New York, NY: Springer.

Leiber, M. J., & Peck, J. H. (2014). *Race/Ethnicity, juvenile court processing and case outcomes: Fluctuation or stability?* Washington, D. C.: National Institute of Justice.

Leiber, M. J., Peck, J. H., & Rodriguez, N. (2016). Minority threat and juvenile court outcomes. *Crime & Delinquency, 62*(1), 54–80.

Leiber, M. J., & Peck, J. H. (2019). Clarifying the theoretical tents of the symbolic threat perspective. *Justice Quarterly, 37*(6), 1040–1066.

Leiber, M. J., Donnelly, E. A., & Lu, Y. (2020). What context matters and at what level? A test of racial/ethnic threat, symbolic threat, and structural inequality perspectives in juvenile court decision-making. *Crime & Delinquency, 66*(2), 234–261.

Lowery, P. G., Burrow, J. D., & Kaminski, R. J. (2018). A multilevel test of the racial threat hypothesis in one state's juvenile court. *Crime & Delinquency, 64*(1), 53–87.

Lowery, P. G., & Smith, J. C. (2020). The impact of concentrated affluence and disadvantage on the pre-adjudication detention decision: a status characteristics approach. *Crime & Delinquency, 66*(6–7), 915–948.

Maroun, R. (2019). *Contextual characteristics in juvenile sentencing: Examining the impact of concentrated disadvantage on youth court outcomes*. New York, NY: Routledge.

Maume, M. O., Toth, R. C., & Spears, J. W. (2006). Race in context: The impact of structural factors on racial differences in juvenile court processing. *International Review of Modern Sociology, 32*(2), 53–73.

Mears, D. P. (2006). Exploring state-level variation in juvenile incarceration rates: Symbolic threats and competing explanations. *The Prison Journal, 86*(4), 470–490.

Peck, J. H., Leiber, M. J., & Beaudry-Cyr, M. (2019). Expanding the applicability of Sampson and Laub's theory of inequality and social control: A multilevel examination. *Criminal Justice and Behavior, 46*(6), 902–919.

Rodriquez, N. (2007). Juvenile court context and detention decisions: Reconsidering the role of race, ethnicity, and community characteristics in juvenile court processes. *Justice Quarterly, 24*(4), 629–656.

Rodriquez, N. (2010). The cumulative effect of race and ethnicity in juvenile court outcomes and why preadjudication detention matters. *Journal of Research in Crime and Delinquency, 47*(3), 391–413.

Rodriquez, N. (2013). Concentrated disadvantage and the incarceration of youth: Examining how context affects juvenile justice. *Journal of Research in Crime and Delinquency*, *50*(2), 189–215.

Sampson, R. J., & Laub, J. H. (1993). Structural variations in juvenile court processing: Inequality, the underclass, and social control. *Law & Society Review*, *27*(2), 285–311.

Tittle, C. R., & Curran, D. A. (1988). Contingencies for dispositional disparities in juvenile justice. *Social Forces*, *67*(1), 23–58.

Thomas, S. A., Moak, S. C., & Walker, J. T. (2013). The contingent effect of race in juvenile court detention decisions: The role of racial and symbolic threat. *Race & Justice*, *3*(3), 239–265.

Ulmer, J. T., & Bradley, M. S. (2006). Variation in trial penalties among serious violent offenses. *Criminology*, *44*(3), 631–670.

Ulmer, J. T., & Johnson, B. (2004). Sentencing in context: A multilevel analysis. *Criminology*, *42*(1), 137–178.

Ulmer, J. T., & Johnson, B. D. (2017). Organizational conformity and punishment: Federal court communities and judge-initiated guidelines departures. *Journal of Criminal Law and Criminology*, *107*(2), 253–292.

Zane, S. N., Mears, D. P., & Welsh, B. C. (2020). How universal is disproportionate minority contact? An examination of racial and ethnic disparities in juvenile justice processing across four states. *Justice Quarterly*, *37*(5), 817–841.

Chapter 5

Data, Methods, and Analytical Approach

Research Hypotheses

The present study is oriented around the following research question: Do juvenile justice outcomes vary according to community and system characteristics? For each of five major juvenile court outcomes, a series of hypotheses predict that contextual factors will directly influence juvenile justice outcomes. In most cases, *positive* outcomes represent *more punitive* (i.e. exclusionary) treatment. Exceptions are diversion (at the petition stage) and judicial release (at the disposition stage), which represent more treatment-oriented (i.e. inclusionary) outcomes. Diversion is a unique outcome since it may appear more punitive than outright case dismissal, but also reflects the non-punitive, treatment-oriented alternative mission of the traditional juvenile court. For this reason, the direction of hypotheses differs from other outcomes. Similarly, judicial release is considered less punitive than community supervision, and the direction of hypotheses differs from other outcomes. Contextual factors have been selected based on extant research on macro-social context in juvenile and criminal court processing, and the directionality of hypotheses is based on theory (see Chapter 3) and prior findings (see Chapter 4). Hypotheses can be broken down into three categories corresponding to underlying theoretical frameworks: community threat, social disorganization, and political economy.

First, it is predicted that more punitive juvenile court outcomes will be more likely in the presence of greater community threats: racial threat, ethnic threat, economic threat, and inequality threat. Specifically:

> H_{1A}: **Detention** will be more likely than release in the presence of greater community threats. That is, percent Black, increase in percent Black, percent Hispanic, increase in percent Hispanic, concentrated disadvantage, increase in concentrated disadvantage, income inequality, and increase in income inequality, will be positively associated with odds of detention.

H_{1B}: **Formal petition** will be more likely than dismissal in the presence of greater community threats. That is, percent Black, increase in percent Black, percent Hispanic, increase in percent Hispanic, concentrated disadvantage, increase in concentrated disadvantage, income inequality, and increase in income inequality, will be associated with higher odds of petition. **Diversion**, on the other hand, will be less likely than dismissal in the presence of greater community threats. That is, percent Black, increase in percent Black, percent Hispanic, increase in percent Hispanic, concentrated disadvantage, increase in concentrated disadvantage, income inequality, and increase in income inequality, will be negatively associated with odds of diversion.

H_{1C}: **Waiver** to criminal court will be more likely in the presence of greater community threats. That is, percent Black, increase in percent Black, percent Hispanic, increase in percent Hispanic, concentrated disadvantage, increase in concentrated disadvantage, income inequality, and increase in income inequality, will be positively associated with odds of waiver.

H_{1D}: **Adjudication of delinquency** will be more likely in the presence of greater community threats. That is, percent Black, increase in percent Black, percent Hispanic, increase in percent Hispanic, concentrated disadvantage, increase in concentrated disadvantage, income inequality, and increase in income inequality, will be positively associated with odds of adjudication.

H_{1E}: **Secure placement** will be more likely than community supervision in the presence of greater community threats. That is, percent Black, increase in percent Black, percent Hispanic, increase in percent Hispanic, concentrated disadvantage, increase in concentrated disadvantage, income inequality, and increase in income inequality, will be positively associated with odds of placement. **Judicial release**, on the other hand, will be less likely than community supervision in the presence of greater community threats. That is, percent Black, increase in percent Black, percent Hispanic, increase in percent Hispanic, concentrated disadvantage, increase in concentrated disadvantage, income inequality, and increase in income inequality, will be negatively associated with odds of release.

Second, it is predicted that more punitive juvenile court outcomes will be more likely in the presence of greater social disorganization. Specifically:

H_{2A}: **Detention** will be more likely than release in the presence of greater social disorganization. That is, crime rates, juvenile arrest rates, ethnic heterogeneity, residential mobility, and youth population density will be positively associated with odds of detention.

H_{2B}: **Formal petition** will be more likely than dismissal in the presence of greater social disorganization. That is, crime rates, juvenile arrest rates, ethnic heterogeneity, residential mobility, and youth population density will be positively associated with odds of petition. **Diversion**, on the other hand, will be less likely than dismissal in the presence of greater social disorganization. That is, crime rates, juvenile arrest rates, ethnic heterogeneity, residential mobility, and youth population density will be negatively associated with odds of diversion.

H_{2C}: **Waiver** to criminal court will be more likely in the presence of greater social disorganization. That is, crime rates, juvenile arrest rates, ethnic heterogeneity, residential mobility, and youth population density will be positively associated with odds of waiver.

H_{2D}: **Adjudication of delinquency** will be more likely in the presence of greater social disorganization. That is, crime rates, juvenile arrest rates, ethnic heterogeneity, residential mobility, and youth population density will be positively associated with odds of adjudication.

H_{2E}: **Secure placement** will be more likely than community supervision in the presence of greater social disorganization. That is, crime rates, juvenile arrest rates, ethnic heterogeneity, residential mobility, and youth population density will be positively associated with odds of placement. **Judicial release**, on the other hand, will be less likely than community supervision in the presence of greater social disorganization. That is, crime rates, juvenile arrest rates, ethnic heterogeneity, residential mobility, and youth population density will be negatively associated with odds of dismissal.

Third, it is predicted that aspects of the political economy of the juvenile court will be associated with punitive outcomes. Elected judges (i.e. external polity) are expected to be more responsive to punitive community demands and thus more punitive and less aligned with the original, treatment-oriented vision of the juvenile court. Community wealth (i.e. external economy) is expected to be negatively associated with punitive treatment, as greater resources within and outside the court support the original mission of the juvenile court. Political conservatism (i.e. internal polity) is expected to be positively associated with punitive treatment, as conservatism is associated with the "get tough" approach to juvenile crime (Feld, 2003). And urbanism acts as a proxy for bureaucratization (i.e. internal economy), which is expected to be positively associated with punitive treatment as a more tightly coupled, routinized court is expected to follow the Weberian rational legal model, producing less individualized treatment. Specifically:

> H_{3A}: **Odds of detention** will be positively associated with elected judges, political conservatism, and urbanism, while negatively associated with community wealth.
>
> H_{3B}: **Odds of petition** will be positively associated with elected judges, political conservatism, and urbanism, while negatively associated with community wealth. On the other hand, **odds of diversion** will be negatively associated with elected judges, political conservatism, and urbanism, while positively associated with community wealth.
>
> H_{3C}: **Odds of waiver** to criminal court will be positively associated with elected judges, political conservatism, and urbanism, while negatively associated with community wealth.
>
> H_{3D}: **Odds of adjudication of delinquency** will be positively associated with elected judges, political conservatism, and urbanism, while negatively associated with community wealth.
>
> H_{3E}: **Odds of secure placement** will be positively associated with elected judges, political conservatism, and urbanism, while negatively associated with community wealth. On the other hand, **odds of judicial release** will be negatively associated with elected judges, political conservatism, and urbanism, while positively associated with community wealth.

Data and Sample

Data for this study were obtained through the National Juvenile Court Data Archive (NJDCA), a research organization maintained by the National Center for Juvenile Justice in Pittsburgh, Pennsylvania, and supported by a grant from the Office of Juvenile Justice and Delinquency Prevention, U.S. Department of Justice. The restricted data were originally collected by the following agencies: Administrative Office of the Courts, Alabama; Judicial Branch, Connecticut; Office of State Court Administrator, Missouri; Oregon Youth Authority; South Carolina Department of Juvenile Justice; Texas Juvenile Justice Department; and Administrative Office of the Courts, Utah.[1] I cleaned and coded the state-level data according to a consistent methodology so it could be merged into a multistate dataset with shared variables.

The main dataset consists of juvenile case referrals disposed in 2010 across seven states. Specifically the final sample consists of all non-dependency juvenile court referrals in seven states—Alabama, Connecticut, Missouri,

Oregon, South Carolina, Texas, and Utah—for which final disposition was entered in 2010. These states were not selected randomly, but based on data availability for the research questions. Specifically, states were selected if they collected data for each of five outcomes to serve as dependent variables: preadjudication detention, petition of delinquency, adjudication of delinquency, judicial disposition, and waiver to criminal court. Only seven states collected data for each of these five outcomes. The year 2010 was selected as the most recent year for which accurate contextual (i.e. county-level) measures could be created by using the most recent decennial Census data. In addition, a dataset was created for 2000 with the same states except for Oregon, using the same methodology and generating the same case-level measures. This 2000 dataset is used for supplemental analysis, examining whether the same contextual variables are predictive of outcomes over time.

The original 2010 dataset consisted of 303,297 referral cases across 546 counties in 7 states. The original dataset contained 47,102 dependency referrals (15.5 percent); dropping these cases resulted in a sample of 256,195 cases across 542 counties. Counties with fewer than 10 referrals were also dropped from the analysis (n = 218) due to concerns with the reliability of these estimates, resulting in a sample of 255,977 cases across 494 counties. Next, observations were dropped for case-level missing data (n = 7,763) which was not imputed because it could not be assumed that data was missing at random. (For instance, about half of the missing data involved apparent mis-coding of "age.") This resulted in a sample of 248,214 cases across 494 counties. Additionally, counties were dropped from the analysis if the county-level variables had low reliability values according to the coefficient of variation (CV) described below; this dropped 19 counties (and 1,485 cases) and resulted in a final sample size of 246,729 cases nested within 475 counties. Referrals serve as the unit of analysis at level-1, while counties serve as the unit of analysis at level-2. Referrals could be duplicate persons in some cases, but due to anonymity of referrals this could only be roughly estimated based on birth date, race, gender, county location, and in some instances, case identifiers. On the basis of these characteristics, there were an estimated 173,103 unique youth among the 246,729 referrals.

The original 2000 dataset consisted of 382,500 referral cases across 507 counties in 6 states. The original dataset contained 42,451 dependency referrals (11 percent); dropping these cases resulted in a sample of 340,049 cases across 507 counties. Counties with fewer than 10 referrals were also dropped from the analysis (n = 170) due to concerns with the reliability of these estimates, resulting in a sample of 339,879 cases across 472 counties. Next, observations were dropped for case-level missing data (n = 34,755). This resulted in a sample of 305,124 cases across 467 counties. Additionally, counties were dropped from the analysis if the county-level variables had low reliability values according to the CV; this dropped 23 counties (and 3,483 cases) and resulted in a final sample size of 301,641 cases nested within 444 counties. Referrals serve as the unit of analysis at level-1, while counties serve as the unit of analysis at level-2. As with 2010, referrals could be duplicate persons in some cases. On the basis of the characteristics listed above, there were an estimated 199,249 unique juveniles among the 301,641 referrals.

The final samples described above are for the detention outcome (i.e. the full sample), as sample size varied based on the dependent variable, with fewer observations as referrals traveled further into the juvenile justice system. Specifically, the petition sample was smaller than the detention sample because some cases were detained (or released) but were missing values on the petition outcome (i.e. cases still pending). Similarly, the waiver and adjudication samples were smaller than the petition sample because only petitioned cases could be waived or adjudicated delinquent. In turn, only cases that were adjudicated delinquent received a judicial disposition. The samples sizes were thus as follows. For 2010: preadjudication detention (N_1 = 246,729; N_2 = 475); petition of delinquency (N_1 = 241,921; N_2 = 475); judicial waiver (N_1 = 85,545; N_2 = 464); adjudication of delinquency (N_1 = 93,730; N_2 = 465); and judicial disposition (N_1 = 65,960; N_2 = 462). For 2000: preadjudication detention (N_1 = 301,641; N_2 = 444); petition of delinquency (N_1 = 272,032; N_2 = 443); judicial waiver (N_1 = 97,469; N_2 = 439); adjudication of delinquency (N_1 = 109,747; N_2 = 439); and judicial disposition (N_1 = 79,573; N_2 = 435).[2]

The multistate case-level datasets were merged with county-level datasets including measures for the contextual variables of interest in the present research. Several sources were utilized to construct the measures of interest. First, the decennial Census, a full population enumeration collected every ten years (most recent in 2010 at the time of writing), was used to create several measures, including racial and ethnic threat. Second, some measures were created using the 2000 long-form Census sample questionnaire and the 2010 American Community Survey (ACS), a questionnaire that replaced the long-form sample questionnaire after 2000. The ACS provides more detailed information than long-form Census questionnaire, but does so for a smaller sample. For that reason, one-year estimates, three-year estimates, and five-year estimates are available for each year, with a tradeoff of precision versus reliability. To include reliable estimates for the largest number of counties, five-year estimates were used to create several level-2 variables. Each estimate is accompanied by a margin of error (90 percent confidence interval) that was transformed into a CV to determine whether a county should be dropped. The CV is the ratio of the standard error to the value of the estimate (Spielman, Folch, & Nagle, 2014). A CV>.40 indicates a low-quality estimate, while a CV<.12 indicates a high-quality estimate. The choice was made to drop counties with low-quality estimates but retain medium-quality estimates. Dropping counties with low-quality estimates (CV>.40) from the final sample resulted in the exclusion of counties as described above.

Third, some measures were based on data from Uniform Crime Reports (UCR), an FBI database that contains aggregated official crime and arrest statistics for the entire U.S. population. Fourth, Dave Leip's Atlas of U.S. Presidents provides a reliable source of information on state and county election contests for U.S. president (from 1789 to 2018), U.S. senate (from 1990 to 2018), and state governors (from 1990 to 2018). Last, Ballotpedia is a website that provides state and county information on judges, including judicial selection procedures.

Measures

Dependent Variables

Table 5.1 summarizes the measurement of case-level variables. The dependent variables were juvenile justice outcomes at five stages: preadjudication detention, petition of delinquency, judicial waiver, adjudication of delinquency, and judicial disposition.[3] Preadjudication detention was coded as "1" for detention and "0" for release pending adjudication. In 2010, 22.8 percent of referrals were detained prior to the petition decision (n = 56,277), while 22.6 percent of referrals were detained in 2000 (n = 68,114). Over time, then, the proportion of detained cases was largely unchanged. Across states, however, use of detention varied widely: detained referrals ranged from a high of 41.6 percent in Texas (in 2010) to 11.1 percent in Oregon (in 2010), and from 37.7 percent in Texas to 9.3 percent in Missouri in 2000 (see Appendices A, B).

Petition was measured as a multinomial variable with three categories: (1) release, (2) diversion (i.e. informal processing), and (3) formal petition of delinquency. In 2010, approximately 41.3 percent of referrals received formal petition (n = 99,877), while 36.8 percent were diverted (n = 88,971) and 21.9 percent were released (n = 53,072). In 2000, approximately 43.7 percent of referrals received formal petition (n = 118,922), while 33.5 percent were diverted (n = 91,245) and 22.7 percent were released (n = 61,865). Over time, the proportion of cases that were formally versus informally processed remained largely unchanged, with use of diversion increasing slightly. Across states, there was variation in the proportion of referred cases that were formally petitioned, informally diverted, or dismissed. In 2010, formal petition ranged from a high of 69.2 percent in Utah to a low of 20.4 percent

Table 5.1 Case-level descriptive statistics

Variables	*2010*		*2000*	
	%	*n*	%	*n*
Detention				
Detained	22.81	56,277	22.58	68,114
Released	77.19	190,453	77.42	233,527
Total	100.00	246,729	100.00	301,641
Petition				
Petition filed	41.28	99,877	43.72	118,922
Diverted	36.78	88,971	33.54	91,245
Dismissed	21.94	53,073	22.74	61,865
Total	100.00	241,921	100.00	272,032
Waiver				
Transferred	1.05	899	.98	956
Retained	98.95	84,646	99.02	96,513
Total	100.00	85,545	100.00	97,469
Adjudication				
Delinquent	71.33	66,861	72.52	79,588
Not delinquent	28.67	26,870	27.48	30,159
Total	100.00	93,730	100.00	109,747
Disposition				
Placement	13.76	9,074	17.37	13,825
Community supervision	78.29	51,640	78.48	62,447
Released/diverted	7.95	5,247	4.15	3,301
Total	100.00	65,960	100.00	79,573
Race/ethnicity				
White	46.61	115,010	53.97	162,797
Black	26.63	65,716	25.70	77,509
Hispanic	23.85	58,847	17.91	54,025
Other race/ethnicity	2.90	7,157	2.42	7,310
Total	100.00	246,729	100.00	301,641
Sex				
Male	68.40	168,760	70.23	211,852
Female	31.60	77,970	29.77	89,789
Total	100.00	246,729	100.00	301,641
Age				
7–9	1.05	2,598	1.51	4,560
10	.90	2,227	1.50	4,518
11	1.93	4,763	2.86	8,614
12	4.87	12,006	6.00	18,100
13	9.77	24,106	11.29	34,050
14	16.28	40,156	17.87	53,905
15	23.83	58,784	23.83	71,883
16	28.62	70,621	24.66	74,378
17	11.73	28,939	9.00	27,132

(continued)

Table 5.1 Cont.

Variables	*2010*		*2000*	
	%	*n*	%	*n*
18–20	1.03	2,529	1.50	4,498
Total	100.00	246,729	100.00	301,641
Offense type				
Violent	16.84	41,556	15.95	48,103
Property	27.31	67,382	28.39	85,639
Drug/alcohol	13.43	33,145	10.09	30,440
Weapon	1.28	3,161	1.35	4,079
Probation violation	6.83	16,841	6.74	20,342
Status	16.93	41,760	19.97	60,225
Other	17.38	42,884	17.66	52,813
Total	100.00	246,729	100.00	301,641

in Missouri, diversion ranged from a high of 62.3 percent in Missouri to a low of 12.2 percent in Connecticut, and dismissal ranged from a high of 46.7 percent in Oregon to a low of 1.7 percent in Utah (see Appendix A). In 2000, formal petition ranged from a high of 66.3 percent in Utah to a low of 18.3 percent in Missouri, diversion ranged from a high of 48.2 percent in Missouri to a low of 6.2 percent in Connecticut, and dismissal ranged from a high of 35 percent in South Carolina to a low of 6.8 percent in Utah (see Appendix B).

Transfer to criminal court via judicial waiver was also coded as a binary measure, with "1" for judicial waiver and "0" for juvenile court processing. For states that utilized blended sentencing, a criminal sentence from a juvenile court judge was treated as transfer to adult court. States differed in waiver eligibility. In the majority of the states under investigation, waiver eligibility began at age 14. Exceptions were Missouri, where the age of eligibility was 12, and Oregon, where it was 15. Waiver eligibility was also based on felony versus misdemeanor status in many states, although this could not be precisely determined in the present analysis. Status offenders were treated as not waiver-eligible, however. Among petitioned, waiver-eligible cases, approximately 1.1 percent were transferred to criminal court in 2010 (n = 899) and approximately 1 percent were transferred in 2000 (n = 956). Again, we see about the same proportion over time. Across states, however, there was variation in the proportion of petitioned, waiver-eligible cases that were transferred to criminal court. In 2010, waiver ranged from a high of 3.2 percent in Oregon to a low of .04 percent in Utah (see Appendix A). In 2000, waiver ranged from a high of 2 percent in Missouri to a low of .2 percent in South Carolina (see Appendix B).

Adjudication was coded as a binary variable with "1" for delinquency and "0" for not delinquent. (Not delinquent includes judicial diversion, e.g. a suspended sentence). Among petitioned cases that were not transferred to the criminal justice system, approximately 71.3 percent were adjudicated delinquent in 2010 (n = 66,861) and approximately 72.5 percent were adjudicated delinquent in 2000 (n = 79,588). Again, we can see that the overall proportions remained about the same over time. Across states, there was variation in the proportion of petitioned cases that were adjudicated delinquent, however. In 2010, adjudication of delinquency ranged from a high of 93.6 percent in South Carolina to a low of 44.8 percent in Alabama (see Appendix A). In 2000, adjudication of delinquency ranged from a high of 92.6 percent in South Carolina to a low of 55.7 percent in Connecticut (see Appendix B).

Lastly, judicial disposition was measured as a multinomial variable with three categories: (1) judicial release or diversion (including a suspended sentence), (2) community supervision (i.e. probation), or (3) secure placement (i.e. commitment to residential facility). In 2010, approximately 13.8 percent of these cases received secure placement (n = 9,074), while approximately 78.3 percent received community supervision (n = 51,640) and 8 percent were released (n = 5,247). In 2000, approximately 17.4 percent of these cases received secure placement (n = 13,825), while approximately 78.5 percent received community supervision (n = 62,447) and 4.2 percent were released (n = 3,301). Unlike the stability over time observed for other outcomes, there is a notable decrease in secure placement and increase in judicial release over time—with approximately the same proportion of cases receiving probation. Across states, there was also variation in the proportion of delinquent cases that were committed, placed on probation, or released. In 2010, placement ranged from a high of 35.8 percent in Missouri to a low of 6.3 percent in Texas, community supervision ranged from a high of 89.8 percent in Texas to a low of 57.3 percent in Missouri, and judicial release ranged from a high of 26.4 percent in Oregon to a low of 3.4 percent in Utah (see Appendix A). In 2000, placement ranged from a high of 35 percent in Missouri to a low of 10 percent in Utah, community supervision ranged from a high of 90 percent in Utah to a low of 56.7 percent in South Carolina, and judicial release ranged from a high of 23.2 percent in South Carolina to a low of .3 percent in Texas and 0 in Utah (see Appendix B).

Case-Level Variables

The first case-level independent variable included in the analytical models was the race or ethnicity of the juvenile defendant. This was a categorical measure of Black, Hispanic (non-White), Other (Asian, American

Indian, etc.), and White (reference category). Six of seven state juvenile justice systems reported race and ethnicity in mutually exclusive categories that could be re-coded into a factor variable with these four categories. Utah reported 15 racial/ethnic categories, including those for mixed race and ethnic background. To create mutually exclusive racial/ethnic categories, these mixed designations were not treated as separate groups, but were recoded into the four categories based on the following classification hierarchy: Hispanic, Black, Other, and White. So, for example, a referral originally coded as "Black-Hispanic" was recoded as Hispanic, a referral originally coded as "American Indian—Not Hispanic" was coded as Other, and so on. The designation "mixed race—cannot determine" (*n* = 7) was also recoded as Other. This recoding only applied to a small minority of the Utah sample (*n* = 214; .6 percent) and a vanishingly small proportion of the overall sample (.07 percent). In 2010, the full sample consisted of 46.6 percent White youth (*n* = 115,010), 26.6 percent Black youth (*n* = 65,716), 23.9 percent Hispanic youth (*n* = 58,847), and 2.9 percent Other youth (*n* = 7,157). In 2000, the full sample consisted of 54 percent White youth (*n* = 162,797), 25.7 percent Black youth (*n* = 77,509), 17.9 percent Hispanic youth (*n* = 54,025), and 2.4 percent Other youth (*n* = 7,310). Most notably, youth referred to the juvenile justice system became less White and more Hispanic over time.

Sex was measured as a binary variable coded as "1" for male and "0" for female. The majority of referrals were male: in 2010, males made up 68.4 percent of the sample (*n* = 168,760), while in 2010, males made up 70.2 percent of the sample (*n* = 211,852). Age was measured as a continuous variable ranging from 7 to 20.[4] While most states did not specify a lower age of jurisdiction, it was assumed that they followed the common law lower age of 7, and referrals coded as age 0–6 were not included in the analysis.[5] The upper age of jurisdiction ranged from 15 to 17 across states, but all states had extended jurisdiction to age 20.[6] In 2010, the mean (SD) age at referral was 14.9 (1.7), while in 2000 the mean (SD) age was 14.6 (1.8).

Offense type was measured as a series of seven dummy variables for each type of offense: violent, property, drug/alcohol, weapons, probation violation, status offense, and other offenses (mostly public order and traffic offenses). To ensure the same measure was used across dependent variables (i.e. different stages of processing), initial charges were used rather than charges at petition, adjudication, or disposition. These categories were recoded based on lists of offense codes in each jurisdiction, ranging from 655 offense values in South Carolina to 4,197 offense values in Texas. While myriad categories could have been created, six broad categories were ultimately selected since specific offenses can encompass different behaviors in different jurisdictions. In 2010, 16.8 percent of offenses were violent (*n* = 41,556), 27.3 percent were property offenses (n = 67,382), 13.4 percent were drug or alcohol offenses (n = 33,145), 1.3 percent were non-violent weapon offenses (n = 3,161), 6.8 percent were probation violations (n = 16841), 16.9 percent were status offenses (n = 41,759), and 17.4 percent were other offenses (n = 42,884). In 2000, 16 percent of offenses were violent (n = 48,103), 28.4 percent were property offenses (n = 85,639), 10.1 percent were drug or alcohol offenses (n = 30,440), 1.4 percent were non-violent weapon offenses (n = 4,079), 6.7 percent were probation violations (n = 20,342), 20 percent were status offenses (n = 60,225), and 17.7 percent were other offenses (n = 52,813). Finally, in addition to serving as a dependent variable in the first analytical phase of study, preadjudication detention also served as a control variable for the petition, waiver, adjudication, and disposition analyses.

Notably, prior record was *not* included as a case-level control variable because it was missing for three states—Missouri, Oregon, and Texas—that did not provide this information. As such, approximately 60 percent of referrals—and, more importantly, 70 percent of counties—were missing prior record. Dropping these observations was not desirable given the main goal of the study to examine the relationship between context and major juvenile court outcomes.[7] Additionally, one of the chief strengths of the dataset is the large number of level-2 units to provide sufficient statistical power for multilevel analysis with 20 level-2 variables (see Britt & Weisburd, 2010). Moreover, the main focus of the present study is on *contextual* effects, not case-level effects, which should thus be interpreted with caution due to omitted variable bias.

Contextual Variables

Table 5.2 summarizes the measurement of contextual-level variables. The present study includes measures for 20 contextual-level variables for each of the included counties (i.e. level-2 variables). These 20 variables were placed into three groups, each testing a particular contextual theory. The first group of eight variables measures community threat; the second group of eight variables measures social disorganization; and the third group of four variables measures the organizational context of the juvenile court in terms of its political economy. In addition to the 20 explanatory variables of interest, "south" is included as a level-3 (i.e. state) variable, following Census definitions for region. Forty three percent of states were in the South in 2010, while 50 percent were in the South in 2000 (without Oregon). Descriptive statistics for contextual variables are based on counties rather than referrals (i.e. sample sizes of N = 475 [2010] and N = 444 [2000]), and grand mean centering and standardization of contextual variables were performed at the county level.

Table 5.2 County-level descriptive statistics

2010[a]	Mean	Std. Dev.	Min	Max
Community threat				
Percent Black	11.83	16.03	.10	83.20
Change in percent Black	.10	1.37	-6.40	6.40
Percent Hispanic	15.42	20.18	.51	95.74
Change in percent Hispanic	2.98	2.67	-2.84	16.94
Concentrated disadvantage (CD)	0	1.71	-3.47	7.19
Change in CD	0	.84	-5.04	2.89
Gini index (0–1)	.44	.03	.34	.58
Change in Gini index	-.01	.03	-.14	.08
Social disorganization				
Crime rate (per 1,000)	28.51	13.7	.99	104.33
Change in crime rate	-4.23	11.52	-92.43	33.56
Juvenile crime rate (per 1,000)	4.42	3.17	.2	21.34
Change in juvenile crime rate	-2.77	3.99	-23.93	8.49
Ethnic heterogeneity (0–1)	.35	.17	.03	.73
Residential mobility (% moved)	15.53	4.61	4.08	41.34
Youth population density (%)	24.47	3.43	14.5	37.4
Change in youth population (%)	-1.9	1.38	-7.7	2.4
Political economy				
Judicial elections	.83	.37	0	1
Median income (× $1,000)	42.13	10.15	20.08	81.27
Conservative voting majority	14.45	28.41	-75.62	79.08
Population density (per sq/mi) (×100)	1.41	3.74	.01	51.58
Region[b]				
South	.43	.53	0	1
2000[c]				
Community threat				
Percent Black	12.45	16.11	0	85.2
Percent Hispanic	14.63	20.54	.29	97.54
Concentrated disadvantage	0	1.69	-3.5	10.45
Gini index (0–1)	.45	.04	.34	.59
Social disorganization				
Crime rate (per 1,000)	32.98	20.98	0	166.88
Juvenile crime rate (per 1,000)	7.06	5.29	.3	31.42
Ethnic heterogeneity (0–1)	.34	.17	.03	.69
Youth population density (%)	26.64	3.51	15.9	39.3
Political economy				
Judicial elections	.81	.39	0	1
Median income (× $1,000)	33.56	7.96	16.5	70.83
Conservative voting majority	17.72	31.4	-78.57	83.27
Population density (per sq/mi) (× 100)	1.25	3.66	.01	56.23
Region[d]				
South	.50	.55	0	1

Notes
a N = 475
b N = 7
c N = 444
d N = 6

Community Threat

The community threat hypotheses to be tested are minority threat (racial and economic) and economic threat (poverty and inequality). Racial and ethnic threat were measured as four variables created from the decennial Census 2010 and 2000. First, *static* racial threat was measured as the percentage of Black residents in the county population. A quadratic term was also included to test for non-linear effects. In 2010, the mean (SD) percent Black was 11.8 (16.0), ranging from .1 to 83.2 percent. In 2000, the mean (SD) percent Black was 12.5 (16.1), ranging from 0 to 85.2 percent. Second, *dynamic* racial threat was measured as the change in racial composition (from 2000 to 2010). This variable was only included in the analysis of 2010 data, with a mean (SD) of .1 (1.4) percent and range from -6.4 to 6.4 percent. Third, static ethnic threat was measured as the percentage of Hispanic residents in the county (quadratic term also included). In 2010, the mean (SD) percent Hispanic was 15.4 (20.2), ranging from .5 to 95.7 percent. In 2000, the mean (SD) percent Hispanic was 14.6 (20.5), ranging from .3 to 97.5 percent. Fourth, *dynamic* ethnic threat was measured as the change in Hispanic composition (from 2000 to 2010). This variable was only included in the analysis of 2010 data, with a mean (SD) of 3.0 (2.8) percent and range from -2.8 to 16.9 percent.

Economic threat was also measured as four variables, based on ACS 2010 five-year estimates. First, a measure of concentrated disadvantage was included as a proxy for economic threat. To separate economic threat from racial threat, the present paper follows Rodriguez (2013) in operationalizing concentrated disadvantage without any racial or ethnic component. Principal components analysis was used to create a measure of concentrated disadvantage based on percent unemployed, percent of families using supplemental nutrition assistance program (SNAP), percent of households below poverty, and percent female-headed households (α = .73).[8] Principal components analysis suggested a one factor solution with all factor loadings above .44 and a first eigenvalue of 2.92 (all others below .55), indicating that approximately 73 percent of the variance among the items was accounted for by the first factor. For the 2000 construct, α = .72. Principal components analysis suggested a one factor solution with all factor loadings above .44 and a first eigenvalue of 2.87 (all others below .68), indicating that approximately 72 percent of the variance among the items was accounted for by the first factor. In 2010, the mean (SD) value for concentrated disadvantage was 0 (1.7), with a range from -3.5 (low disadvantage) to 7.2 (high disadvantage). In 2000, the mean (SD) value for concentrated disadvantage was 0 (1.7), ranging from -3.5 (low disadvantage) to 10.5 (high disadvantage).

Second, a dynamic measure of concentrated disadvantage was measured as the change in concentrated disadvantage from 2000 to 2010; this represents the extent to which a county became more or less disadvantaged over time. The mean (SD) value of change in disadvantage was 0 (.8), ranging from -5.0 (decreasing disadvantage) to 2.9 (increasing disadvantage). Third, a measure of income inequality is measured using the traditional Gini index, which measures the distribution of income from completely equal (0) to completely unequal (1). In 2010, the mean (SD) Gini value was .44 (.03), ranging from .34 to 58; in 2000, the mean (SD) Gini value was .45 (.04), ranging from .34 to .59. Fourth, a dynamic measure of income inequality was measured as the change in the Gini index score, representing how much inequality increased over time. The mean (SD) value for change in income inequality was -.01 (.03), ranging from -.14 (decreasing inequality) to .08 (increasing inequality). Newly standardized measures of concentrated disadvantage and economic inequality were created for each sample corresponding to different dependent variables, as well as for each state-specific analysis.

Social Disorganization

Social disorganization was measured in terms of crime rates, ethnic heterogeneity, residential mobility, and youth population density. First, total crime was measured as an average for total index crime rates reported to police for the years 2009–2011 (for 2010) and 1999–2001 (for 2000). The mean (SD) index crime rate was 28.5 (13.7) per 1,000 residents in 2010 (ranging from 1.0 to 104.3), and 33.0 (21.0) per 1,000 residents in 2000 (ranging from 0 to 166.9). Second, a measure of the *change* in total crime rates from 2000 to 2010 was included to assess whether an increase in crime rates over time was associated with juvenile court outcomes. (This was not included in the 2000 models.) The mean (SD) change in crime rates was -4.2 (11.5), indicating an average decline in crime consistent with the national trends, ranging from -92.4 to 33.6 (per 1,000 residents).

Third, the juvenile crime rate was measured as the number of juvenile *arrests* per 1,000 residents. (UCR includes juvenile arrests rather than reported crime as criminal offenders cannot be reliably identified as juvenile until an arrest is made.) Total juvenile arrests are used instead of juvenile index arrests as there are fewer juvenile crimes than total crimes, and many counties had no felony arrests for juveniles. As with total index crime, juvenile arrest rates for the years 2009–2011 were averaged for a more reliable estimate. The mean (SD) juvenile crime rate was 4.4 (3.2) per 1,000 residents in 2010 (ranging from .2 to 21.3), and 7.1 (5.3) per 1,000 residents in 2000 (ranging from .3 to 31.4). Fourth, a measure of the *change* in juvenile arrest rates from 2000 to 2010 was included. (Not included for 2000 models.) The mean (SD) change in juvenile crime rates was -2.8 (3.2), ranging from -23.9 to 8.5 (per 1,000 residents).

Fifth, ethnic heterogeneity was calculated as the proportion of the population that identified as White, Black, Hispanic, Asian American, Native American, Hawaiian/Pacific Islander, Other, or Mixed Race. Following Britt (2000), a variable was created with a minimum value (0) reflecting no heterogeneity and a maximum value (1) reflecting equal proportions of racial/ethnic groups in the county population.[9] In 2010, the mean (SD) value for ethnic heterogeneity was .35 (.17), ranging from .03 (low heterogeneity) to .73 (high heterogeneity). In 2000, the mean (SD) value for ethnic heterogeneity was .34 (.17), ranging from .03 to .69. A newly standardized measure of ethnic heterogeneity was created for each sample corresponding to different dependent variables, as well as for each state-specific analysis. Sixth, residential mobility was measured as the percentage of county residents that moved in the past five years.[10] The mean (SD) value for residential mobility was 15.5 (4.6) percent, ranging from 4.1 to 41.3 percent. Seventh, youth population density was measured as the proportion of the county population that was in the age range of 15–18. The mean value (SD) for youth population density in 2010 was 24.5 (3.4), ranging from 14.5 to 37.4; in 2000, the mean value (SD) was 26.6 (3.5), ranging from 15.9 to 39.3. Last, a measure of the *change* in youth density from 2000 to 2010 was included. The mean (SD) change in youth population was -1.9 (1.4), ranging from -7.7 to 2.4.

Political Economy

Four contextual variables were used to measure the political economy of the juvenile court. First, the "external polity" of the court was operationalized as a binary variable indicating whether juvenile court judges were elected or appointed, where election was coded as "1." This includes partisan and nonpartisan elections, while appointment includes executive appointment as well as legislative election (since voters do not directly select judges in legislative elections). A slight majority of states selected juvenile court judges by election rather than appointment. Judges were appointed in Connecticut, South Carolina, and Utah, as well as in the cities of St. Louis and Springfield, Missouri and Jackson county, Missouri. Other Missouri counties, along with Alabama, Texas, and Oregon, used judicial elections. In 2010, 83 percent of included counties had judicial elections, while in 2000, 81 percent of counties had judicial elections.

Second, the external economy of the court was operationalized using the proxy of county median income, based on ACS 2010 five-year estimates. For ease of interpretation of coefficients, median income was divided by 1,000 so that a coefficient unit-change represents an additional $1,000 in median income. In 2010, the mean (SD) value of median income was 42.1 (10.2), or $42,130. This ranged from 20.1 (i.e. $20,100) to 81.3 (i.e. $81,270). In

2000, the mean (SD) value of median income was 33.6 (9), or $33,560. This ranged from 16.5 (i.e. $16,500) to 70.8 (i.e. $70,830).

Third, the "internal polity" of the court was measured using the political party of county voting as a proxy. Following Greenberg and West (2001), gubernatorial voting was used rather than presidential or senatorial voting (i.e. national elections) because the state executive determines crime policy.[11] The present study measures "conservative" using the difference in the percentage of citizens voting Republican versus Democrat in the most recent Gubernatorial election, which was in the year 2008 in Missouri and Utah and in the year 2010 in the other five states. For the 2000 data, the most recent election was in the year 1998 in Alabama, Connecticut, South Carolina, and Texas and in the year 2000 in Missouri and Utah. In 2010, the mean (SD) value for conservative was 14.5 (28.4), a 14.5 percent Republican majority, ranging from -75.6 (i.e. 76 percent Democrat majority) to 79.1 (i.e. 79 percent Republican majority). In 2000, the mean (SD) value for conservative was 17.7 (31.4), ranging from -78.6 to 83.3.

Finally, "internal economy" was operationalized using the proxy of urbanism, measured as population density. Rather than create a binary category for urban-versus-rural based on Census designation, this was operationalized as a continuous measure ranging from low (i.e. rural) to high (i.e. urban) population density for each county. For ease of interpretation of coefficients, population density was divided by 100 so that a unit-change in coefficients represents 100 persons per square mile. In 2010, the mean (SD) value for population density was 1.4 (3.7), or 141 persons per square mile, ranging from .01 (i.e. 10 persons) to 51.6 (i.e. 5,158 persons). In 2000, the mean (SD) value for population density was 1.3 (3.7), or 125 persons per square mile, ranging from .01 (i.e. 10 persons) to 56.2 (i.e. 5,623 persons).

State-Level Descriptive Statistics

In addition to the main three-level hierarchical models estimated for 2010 data (presented in Chapter 6) and 2000 data (presented in Chapter 7), two-level hierarchical models were estimated for each state—Alabama, Connecticut, Missouri, Oregon, Texas, South Carolina, and Utah—across the five outcomes of interest for the year 2010. Several variables were no longer included in these state-specific models: (1) election was dropped because it is a state-level variable in every state other than Missouri, (2) dynamic variables (i.e. change over time) were not included, and (3) region was no longer included. State-level case data is mentioned in the discussion above, and contextual variables are described below (see Appendix C).

First, community threat measures varied across states. First, in 2010, mean percent Black ranged from .8 in Utah to 36.9 in South Carolina, while in 2000 percent Black ranged from .5 in Utah to 37.6 in South Carolina. Second, in 2010, percent Hispanic ranged from 2.4 in Missouri to 31.7 in Texas, while in 2000 percent Hispanic ranged from 1.5 in Missouri to 27.9 in Texas. Third, the mean value of concentrated disadvantage was 0 for each state as a result of recreating the construct for each specific sample (by state, year, and dependent variable). Variation in concentrated disadvantage, as indicated by the value of the standard deviation, was highest in Connecticut (1.93) and lowest in Oregon (1.47) in 2010, and highest in Oregon (1.94) and lowest in Missouri (1.70) in 2000. Fourth, income inequality in 2010 ranged from .40 in Utah to .46 in Alabama and South Carolina, while in 2000 Gini scores ranged from .40 in Utah to .47 in Alabama.

Measures of social disorganization also varied across states. First, average index crime rates in 2010 ranged from 23.5 (per 1,000) in Utah to 44.2 in South Carolina; in 2000, index crime rates ranged from 29.1 in Texas to 47.6 in South Carolina. Second, juvenile arrest rates in 2010 ranged from 1.5 (per 1,000) in Alabama to 7.8 in Utah, while in 2000 juvenile arrest rates ranged from 2.4 in Alabama to 16.0 in Utah. Third, ethnic heterogeneity in 2010 ranged from .15 in Missouri to .48 in South Carolina; similarly, in 2000, this ranged from .13 in Missouri to .46 in South Carolina. Fourth, residential mobility in 2010 ranged from 12.7 percent in Connecticut to 18.8 percent in Texas. Fifth, youth population density in 2010 ranged from 22 percent in Oregon to 31.9 percent in Utah; in 2000, this ranged from 24.4 percent in Connecticut to 33.1 percent in Utah.

Finally, aspects of political economy also varied across states systems. First, the median county income ranged from $37,000 in Alabama to $68,900 in Connecticut in 2010, and from $30,600 in Alabama to $54,400 in Connecticut in 2000. Second, in 2010 the conservative majority ranged from -4.5 (indicating a slight Democrat voting majority) in South Carolina to 61 in Utah (indicating a large Republican majority). In 2000, the conservative majority ranged from -17.8 in Alabama to 40.3 in Texas. Fourth, average population density ranged from 90 persons per square mile in Alabama to 7,200 persons per square mile in Connecticut in 2010; in 2000, similarly, average population density ranged from 90 in Alabama to 6,900 in Connecticut.

Multicollinearity Diagnostics

As noted in Chapter 4, the present study tests more contextual hypotheses than any prior research on juvenile court outcomes. The downside to this, of course, is that many of these contextual variables are themselves related, posing possible multicollinearity concerns. Correlations among variables ranged from weak to moderate, with most under .5. Several correlations exceeded

.5, however: concentrated disadvantage and median income (r = -.76), change in percent Hispanic and ethnic heterogeneity (r = .58), percent Black and heterogeneity (r = .55), heterogeneity and population density (r = .54), and concentrated disadvantage and conservative majority (r = -.53). Collinearity tests revealed that when a model was estimated with all 21 level-2 variables, the mean variance inflation factor (VIF) was 4.12, with VIF values as high as 10.92 (percent Hispanic).[12] VIFs indicate how much of the variance of a coefficient is inflated by linear dependence with other variables in the model. Thus, high VIFs correspond to standard errors being inflated. As a result, including variables with high VIFs in the model is not recommended. At VIF = 2.5, the variance of the coefficient is 150 percent larger than it would be if completely uncorrelated with other variables in the model (Allison, 2012).[13] The present study uses VIF < 2.5 as a benchmark for concerns with multicollinearity, and makes note of variables with VIF > 2.5 as having moderately high dependence on other variables in the model.

Since seven variables had VIF values greater than 5, I estimated three separate models for each outcome, corresponding to the theoretical perspectives being tested: (1) community threat model, (2) social disorganization model, and (3) political economy model. In these reduced models, multicollinearity no longer presented any substantial concerns: for community threat, mean VIF = 1.89 (all VIFs < 3.1); for social disorganization, mean VIF = 1.35 (all VIFs < 1.75); and for political economy, mean VIF = 1.25 (all VIFs < 1.5). For the 2000 models, multicollinearity also did not pose any concerns: for community threat, mean VIF = 1.85 (all VIFs < 2.3); for social disorganization, mean VIF = 1.26 (all VIFs <1.5); and for political economy, mean VIF = 1.20 (all VIFs < 1.5). Additionally, no within-model correlations exceeded .5 in the reduced models.

With specific states, level-2 samples were smaller and collinearity concerns were higher. As noted above, dynamic variables (i.e. change from 2000 to 2010) were dropped from the models, resulting in models with VIFs < 2.5 for most variables. Several variables exceeded VIF = 2.5, however, and are as follows: in Alabama, percent Black (VIF = 2.55); in Missouri, conservative majority (VIF = 3.72) and urbanism (VIF = 3.67); in Oregon, youth population density (VIF = 3.52), conservative majority (VIF = 3.39), and urbanism (VIF = 3.39); in South Carolina, percent Black (VIF = 2.73); in Texas, percent Hispanic (VIF = 4.64) and concentrated disadvantage (VIF = 3.79); and in Utah, percent Hispanic (VIF = 4.69), percent Black (VIF = 3.83), crime rates (VIF = 5.96), ethnic heterogeneity (VIF = 4.78), conservative majority (VIF = 2.99), and urbanism (VIF = 3.71). As such, coefficients corresponding to these particular variables should be interpreted with caution, and the Utah models in particular should be interpreted with caution given the small sample size and high collinearity.

Analytical Strategy

The contextual research hypotheses are tested via estimation of a series of multilevel models (see Johnson, 2010). For binary outcomes (i.e. detention, adjudication, waiver), hierarchical logistic regression was used. For categorical outcomes (i.e. petition, disposition), hierarchical multinomial logistical regression was employed. Three-level hierarchical models were estimated for each outcome, with different sample sizes corresponding to each level. The main limiting feature of a multilevel design is the sample size at the highest level of the model. In the present case, this is seven states (and six states for the 2000 data). The sample size at each level determines the statistical power of the tests for that level (see Snijders, 2005). As such, the main level of interest for our hypotheses is level-2, the county. This ranges from $N_2 = 475$ for detention to $N_2 = 462$ for judicial disposition. Despite the main focus being at the county level (i.e. level-2), three-level models were estimated to account for the fact that counties were nested within state juvenile justice systems. Only one variable was included at the highest level of analysis—South—which served only as a control variable.

The analyses proceeded as follows. First, the main multistate analyses were estimated, testing whether community threat, social disorganization, and political economy were associated with juvenile court outcomes. The results are presented in Chapter 6. Second, the analyses were repeated for a similar 2000 dataset with the same level-1 measures and many of the same level-2 measures. (Dynamic indicators were no longer included as demographic estimates for 1990 were less reliable.) The main difference is that the 2000 data did not include Oregon. Here, the sample size ranged from $N_2 = 444$ for detention to $N_2 = 435$ for judicial disposition. These analyses served as a kind of replication of the original study, assessing whether any contextual hypotheses supported in the 2010 data were also supported in the (independent) 2000 data. The results are presented in Chapter 7. Third, the analyses were repeated for each state using two-level hierarchical models. These supplemental analyses were used to explore whether the contextual hypotheses were better supported for some states than others. Connecticut was excluded from state-level analyses due to low power to test the contextual analyses ($N_2 = 8$). Additionally, state-specific analyses employed reduced models to reflect the smaller level-2 sample, ranging from $N_2 = 22$ (Utah) to $N_2 = 189$ (Texas). On theoretical grounds, the decision was made to drop "dynamic" variables (i.e. change from 2000 to 2010). These analyses can be thought of as breaking down the main results from Chapter 6, especially whether findings from the main analysis are corroborated by state-specific models. The results are presented in Chapter 8.

All analyses were performed using hierarchical linear modeling software (HLM 7.1), with two-sided alpha = .05. Given the number of tests performed, however, there is some concern that statistically significant relationships will be spurious (see Shaffer, 1995). Bonferroni corrections would require α/N for tests of statistical significance. In the present case, this would imply .05/20 = .0025 as the corrected *p*-value threshold. This is probably an overly strict criterion, so I make note of it but take a different approach. Namely, I employ two conventions. First, estimates were interpreted in terms of confidence intervals, indicating the range of values consistent with the data (where lower confidence bounds can be interpreted as the most conservative estimate of the effect size). Second, exact *p*-values were reported in the text for each contextual variable of interest (where $p < .10$), allowing the reader to interpret the statistical significance of the estimate beyond the designated alpha threshold. This encourages the interpretation of evidence that goes beyond binary thinking (see Sweeten, 2020).[14] For consistency with standard conventions, however, tables report *p*-values at .10, .05. .01, and .001 levels.

The approach to testing hypotheses that I adopt is the frequentist, neo-Popperian "severe testing" methodology advocated by Mayo (2018): hypotheses that survive "severe testing" provide evidence for the alternative hypothesis. These hypotheses are interpreted as "well probed"— providing corroboration of the hypothesis—rather than "probable" (Mayo, 2018, p. 201). This expands upon the basic falsificationist insight that scientific explanations must be capable of being rejected by the data. As Zimring and Hawkins (1991) put it, an "empirically meaningful" hypothesis "must also constitute a denial of whatever would be incompatible with its truth" (p. 27). Put more bluntly: "If there is nothing a hypothesis excludes, it explains nothing" (p. 27).

Notes

1 These agencies and the National Center for Juvenile Justice bear no responsibility for the analyses or interpretations presented therein.

2 It is worth nothing that the non-random reduction in sample size across stages of processing raises the possibility of selection bias (see Elwert & Winship, 2014). Although it has become commonplace to use the Heckman two-step procedure to account for potential selection effects when looking at sequential criminal justice outcomes (see Heckman, 1979), doing so is only proper when valid exclusion restrictions are included (Bushway, Johnson, & Slocum, 2007). Here, no exclusion restrictions could be identified.

3 Because it is necessary to create exclusive categories (here and elsewhere), a juvenile defendant who is coded as being dismissed or diverted at the petition or adjudication stage is dropped from later stages (e.g. disposition). This reflects that the juvenile defendant exited the juvenile justice system prior to the relevant dispositional stage. However, the practice of diversion (at the petition or, in some cases, adjudication stage) does allow for many non-petitioned or non-adjudicated juvenile defendants to receive dispositions such as probation or out-of-home placement (see Mears et al., 2016a). Since these are included as "0" in the earlier models, it would be misleading and conceptually confusing to include them in final disposition models.
4 Age was measured at time of referral rather than time of disposition. As such, while the majority of cases were referred during the same year as the final disposition (2010), some cases involve referrals from earlier years.
5 Texas had a lower age of jurisdiction of 10 in 2010, so cases under age 10 in Texas were dropped.
6 Cases coded as older than 20 were also not included in the analysis.
7 Missing cases were not imputed since it could not be assumed that they were "missing at random"—and thus could be ignored (see Brame, Turner, & Paternoster, 2010). Listwise deletion of cases with missing data "is the method that is the most robust to violation of the MAR assumption among the independent variables in a regression analysis" (p. 283). Here, this was not desirable for reasons noted in the text.
8 Formerly referred to as "food stamps," SNAP is the largest form of public assistance income supplement (i.e. welfare) in the United States—a $75 billion program which served 15 percent of the population in 2012. For the 2000 data, "percent receiving cash public assistance income" was used instead since the SNAP program was created in 2008. Due to welfare reforms, cash public assistance was less common by 2010 and SNAP was used instead (see Schuck, 2017).
9 Specifically, the following equation was used: heterogeneity = 1 – ([proportion White]^2 +[proportion Black]^2 + [proportion Hispanic]^2 + [proportion American Indian]^2 + [proportion Asian]^2 + [proportion Hawaiian/Pacific Islander]^2 + [proportion Other]^2 + [proportion Mixed Race]^2).
10 The measure of residential mobility was based on ACS five-year estimates of "same residence" for past year; there was no comparable measure in the 2000 long-form Census data, so there is no 2000 measure.
11 One might argue that senatorial voting is more consistent with political ideology since national elections are less tied to idiosyncratic local- and state-level voting patterns. Nevertheless, on the whole it stands to reason that gubernatorial voting presents a more appropriate measure of county-level politics than national elections.
12 For the 2000 data, the mean VIF in the full model was 3.26, with a high VIF of 6.69 (percent Black) and six variables with VIF values greater than 2.5.
13 Since VIF = ($1/1-R^2$), the measure can also be interpreted in terms of the R^2 value of the coefficient of interest with other variables in the model. For example: at VIF = 2.5, R^2 = .60; at VIF = 5, R^2 = .80; at VIF = 10, R^2 = .90 (Allison, 2012).

14 It also addresses the possibility of *p*-hacking, evidenced by *p*-values just below the alpha threshold being more common than lower *p*-values (see Wooditch et al., 2020). As Ioannidis (2018) puts it, "[m]ost claims supported with P values slightly below .05 are probably false (ie, the claimed associations and treatment effects do not exist)" (p. 1429; see also Ioannidis, 2005).

References

Allison, P. (2012). When can you safely ignore multicollinearity. *Statistical Horizons*, *5*(1), 1–2.

Brame, R., Turner, M. G., & Paternoster, R. (2010). Missing data problems in criminological research. In A. R. Piquero & D. Weisburd (Eds.), *Handbook of quantitative criminology* (pp. 273–288). New York, NY: Springer.

Britt, C. L. (2000). Social context and racial disparities in punishment decisions. *Justice Quarterly*, *17*(4), 707–732.

Britt, C. L., & Weisburd, D. (2010). Statistical power. In A. R. Piquero & D. Weisburd (Eds.), *Handbook of quantitative criminology* (pp. 313–332). New York, NY: Springer.

Bushway, S. D., Johnson, B. D., & Slocum, L. A. (2007). Is the magic still there? The use of the Heckman two-step correction for selection bias in criminology. *Journal of Quantitative Criminology*, *23*(2), 151–178.

Elwert, F., & Winship, C. (2014). Endogenous selection bias: The problem of conditioning on a collider variable. *Annual Review of Sociology*, *40*, 31–53.

Greenberg, D., & West, V. (2001). State prison populations and their growth, 1971–1991. *Criminology*, *39*(3), 615–654.

Heckman, J. J. (1979). Sample selection bias as a specification error. *Econometrica: Journal of the Econometric Society*, *47*(1), 153–161.

Ioannidis, J. P. A. (2005). Why most published research findings are false. *PLoS Medicine*, *2*(8), e124.

Ioannidis, J. P. A. (2018). The proposal to lower p-value thresholds to .005. *JAMA*, *319*(14), 1429–1430.

Johnson, B. D. (2010). Multilevel analysis in the study of crime and justice. In A. R. Piquero & D. Weisburd (Eds.), *Handbook of quantitative criminology* (pp. 615–648). New York, NY: Springer.

Mayo, D. G. (2018). *Statistical inference as severe testing: How to get beyond the statistics wars*. Cambridge, UK: Cambridge University Press.

Rodriguez, N. (2013). Concentrated disadvantage and the incarceration of youth: Examining how context affects juvenile justice. *Journal of Research in Crime and Delinquency*, *50*(2), 189–215.

Schuck, P. (2017). *One nation undecided: Clear thinking about five hard issues that divide us*. Princeton, NJ: Princeton University Press.

Shaffer, J. P. (1995). Multiple hypothesis testing. *Annual Review of Psychology*, *46*(1), 561–584.

Spielman, S. E., Folch, D., & Nagle, N. (2014). Patterns and causes of uncertainty in the American Community Survey. *Applied Geography*, *46*, 147–157.

Sweeten, G. (2020). Standard errors in quantitative criminology: Taking stock and looking forward. *Journal of Quantitative Criminology*, *36*(2), 263–272.

Wooditch, A., Fisher, R., Woo, X., & Johnson, N. J. (2020). *P*-value problems? An examination of evidential value in criminology. *Journal of Quantitative Criminology*, *36*(2), 305–328.

Zimring, F. E., & Hawkins, G. (1991). *The scale of imprisonment*. Chicago, IL: The University of Chicago Press.

Chapter 6

Multistate Findings, 2010

Variation in Juvenile Justice Outcomes

The contextual research hypotheses are motivated by explaining variance in juvenile court outcomes across counties and states. As such, the first step in the analysis is to assess whether juvenile court outcomes vary significantly across counties and states by estimating empty three-level hierarchical models (i.e. variance component models) for each outcome, with cases nested within counties (level-2) nested within states (level-3). Here, intraclass correlation was calculated for each level of the model. Since multilevel logit models do not include a level-1 variance term, intraclass correlation was estimated as follows: $\rho = \psi/(\psi + \pi^2/3)$. This assumes that the level-1 variance follows the logistic distribution. The formula for level-3 intraclass correlation is $\rho= (\psi^3)/(\psi^2 + \psi^3 + \pi^2/3)$; the formula for level-2 intraclass correlation is $\rho= (\psi^2)/(\psi^2 + \psi^3 + \pi^2/3)$. Results (not shown) indicated that *all* juvenile court outcomes varied significantly across counties as well as states.

For detention, the level-2 variance component (ψ^2) was .74 ($p < .001$) and level-3 variance component (ψ^3) was .49 ($p < .001$). At level-2, the corresponding intraclass correlation (ρ^2) was.16; at level-3, $\rho^3 = .11$. This indicates that before any predictors were added to the model, approximately 11 percent of the variation in detention outcomes was attributable to between-state differences, while 16 percent was due to between-county differences within states.

For formal petition, there are two comparisons of interest: diversion (versus dismissal) and petition (versus dismissal). For diversion, $\psi^2 = 1.34$ ($p < .001$) and $\psi^3 = 1.77$ ($p < .001$), with $\rho^2 = .21$ and $\rho^3 = .28$, respectively. This indicates that before any predictors were added to the model, approximately 28 percent of the variation in diversion was attributable to between-state differences, while 21 percent was due to between-county differences within states. For petition, $\psi^2 = 1.16$ ($p < .001$) and $\psi^3 = 1.41$ ($p < .001$), with $\rho^2 = .20$ and $\rho^3 = .24$. This indicates that before any predictors were added to the model, approximately 24 percent of the variation in petition was attributable to between-state differences, while 20 percent was due to between-county differences.

For waiver to criminal court, $\psi^2 = 1.48$ ($p < .001$) and $\psi^3 = 1.47$ ($p < .001$), with $\rho^2 = .24$ and $\rho^3 = .24$. This indicates that before any predictors were added to the model, approximately 24 percent of the variation in waiver outcomes was attributable to between-state differences, while 24 percent was due to county-level differences. For adjudication of delinquency, $\psi^2 = 1.29$ ($p < .001$) and $\psi^3 = 1.39$ ($p < .001$), with $\rho^2 = .22$ and $\rho^3 = .23$. This indicates that before any predictors were added to the model, approximately 23 percent of the variation in adjudication outcomes was attributable to between-state differences, while 22 percent was due to between-county differences.

Finally, for judicial disposition there are two comparisons of interest: judicial release (versus community supervision) and residential placement (versus community supervision). For release, $\psi^2 = 1.40$ ($p < .001$) and $\psi^3 = .90$ ($p < .001$), with $\rho^2 = .25$ and $\rho^3 = .16$. This indicates that before any predictors were added to the model, approximately 16 percent of the variation in judicial release was attributable to between-state differences, while 25 percent was due to between-county differences. For placement, $\psi^2 = .49$ ($p < .001$) and $\psi^3 = .50$ ($p < .001$) with $\rho^2 = .12$ and $\rho^3 = .12$. This indicates that before any predictors were added to the model, approximately 12 percent of the variation in secure placement was attributable to between-state differences, while 12 percent was due to between-county differences.

In sum, juvenile court outcomes varied significantly across counties and states, with 12–25 percent of the variation in these outcomes attributable to county-level differences and 11–28 percent attributable to state-level differences. The most variation was observed at *diversion*, while the least variation was observed at *judicial placement*.

Contextual Effects

Table 6.1 reports on the results of a series of three-level hierarchical regression models estimating odds ratios and 95 percent confidence intervals for each outcome of interest. The findings are discussed below for each outcome.

Detention

For the detention decision, the sample consisted of 246,729 juvenile referrals nested within 475 counties nested within seven states. As noted in the prior chapter, about 22.8 percent of referrals were detained ($n = 56,277$).

Table 6.1 Multistate analyses, year 2010

		Petition[b]		*Waiver*[c]	*Adjudication*[d]	*Disposition*[e]	
	Detention[a]	*Diversion*[f]	*Petition*[f]			*Release*[g]	*Placement*[g]
Fixed effects	OR (95% CI)	OR (95% CI)	OR (95% CI)	OR (95% CI)	OR (95% CI)	OR (95% CI)	OR (95% CI)
Intercept	.10 (.05, .20)	4.47† (.80, 25.16)	3.23 (.64, 16.32)	.00*** (.00, .02)	2.59* (.53, 12.70)	.09** (.02, .36)	.08*** (.03, .19)
Level-1 variables							
Black[h]	1.34*** (1.30, 1.38)	.80*** (.77, .83)	1.09*** (1.06, 1.13)	1.30*** (1.14, 1.49)	1.09*** (1.05, 1.14)	.91* (.83, .99)	1.16*** (1.08, 1.25)
Hispanic[h]	1.23*** (1.19, 1.27)	1.04* (1.00, 1.08)	1.28*** (1.23, 1.33)	1.22** (1.05, 1.42)	1.11*** (1.06, 1.16)	.86** (.78, .96)	1.12** (1.04, 1.21)
Other race/ethnicity[h]	1.07† (.99, 1.15)	.92* (.85, 1.00)	.98 (.91, 1.07)	.89 (.65, 1.22)	.98 (.90, 1.07)	1.05 (.89, 1.24)	1.02 (.88, 1.17)
Male	1.41*** (1.37, 1.44)	.79*** (.77, .81)	1.34*** (1.30, 1.37)	1.91*** (1.67, 2.18)	1.22*** (1.18, 1.26)	.95 (.88, 1.02)	1.40*** (1.32, 1.49)
Age	1.10*** (1.09, 1.11)	.95*** (.94, .96)	1.06*** (1.06, 1.07)	1.95** (1.85, 2.05)	1.01** (1.00, 1.02)	1.06*** (1.04, 1.09)	1.20*** (1.18, 1.22)
Violent offense[i]	1.94*** (1.88, 2.00)	.45*** (.47, .51)	.77*** (.75, .80)	3.27*** (2.88, 3.72)	.84*** (.80, .88)	1.05 (.95, 1.15)	1.45*** (1.34, 1.57)
Drug/alcohol offense[i]	.86*** (.82, .89)	1.30*** (1.24, 1.36)	1.47*** (1.40, 1.54)	.57*** (.46, .69)	.93** (.88, .98)	.96 (.86, 1.06)	.70*** (.63, .78)

Weapon offense[i]	2.08*** (1.92, 2.25)	.78*** (.69, .89)	1.41*** (1.26, 1.58)	1.40* (1.00, 1.95)	.92 (.82, 1.04)	.88 (.69, 1.11)	.87 (.72, 1.06)
Probation violation[i]	3.49*** (3.35, 3.62)	.45*** (.42, .48)	.98 (.92, 1.03)	.22** (.16, .28)	.90*** (.84, .95)	.98 (.85, 1.14)	4.46*** (4.12, 4.84)
Status offense[i]	.30*** (.28, .31)	.34*** (.33, .36)	.22*** (.21, .23)	1.04 (.82, 1.31)	.55*** (.52, .59)	5.53*** (4.86, 6.29)	2.09*** (1.88, 2.33)
Other offense[i]	.92*** (.89, .95)	.66** (.64, .69)	.65*** (.62, .68)	1.19* (1.03, 1.38)	.68*** (.65, .71)	1.39*** (1.27, 1.55)	1.72*** (1.59, 1.86)
Detention	–	.42*** (.40, .43)	2.98*** (2.88, 3.08)	2.05*** (1.85, 2.28)	1.88*** (1.81, 1.95)	.75*** (.69, .81)	2.71*** (2.57, 2.86)
Level-2 variables							
Community threat model							
Percent Black	1.00 (.98, 1.02)	1.00 (.97, 1.02)	1.02 (.99, 1.04)	1.03 (.99, 1.06)	.98 (.96, 1.01)	1.02 (.99, 1.06)	1.01 (.98, 1.03)
Percent Black (squared)	1.00 (1.00, 1.00)	1.00 (1.00, 1.00)	1.00 (1.00, 1.00)	1.00* (1.00, 1.00)	1.00 (1.00, 1.00)	1.00 (1.00, 1.00)	1.00 (1.00, 1.00)
Change in percent Black	1.03 (.96, 1.09)	.99 (.91, 1.08)	.95 (.88, 1.03)	.96 (.86, 1.06)	1.06 (.97, 1.15)	1.02 (.91, 1.14)	.96 (.90, 1.03)
Percent Hispanic	1.00 (.98, 1.03)	1.00 (.97, 1.03)	1.00 (.97, 1.03)	.98 (.94, 1.03)	1.00 (.96, 1.03)	1.01 (.97, 1.06)	1.00 (.97, 1.03)
Percent Hispanic (squared)	1.00 (1.00, 1.00)	1.00 (1.00, 1.00)	1.00 (1.00, 1.00)	1.00 (1.00, 1.00)	1.00 (1.00, 1.00)	1.00 (1.00, 1.00)	1.00 (1.00, 1.00)
Change in percent Hispanic	.99 (.94, 1.04)	.98 (.91, 1.05)	1.00 (.94, 1.07)	.99 (.88, 1.11)	1.03 (.95, 1.10)	.98 (.88, 1.10)	.99 (.92, 1.06)
Concentrated disadvantage (CD)[j]	1.08 (.90, 1.29)	1.16 (.90, 1.50)	1.03 (.81, 1.30)	1.11 (.80, 1.54)	1.19 (.92, 1.54)	.96 (.68, 1.35)	1.05 (.86, 1.28)

(*continued*)

Table 6.1 Cont.

	Detention[a]	Petition[b]		Waiver[c]	Adjudication[d]	Disposition[e]	
		Diversion[f]	Petition[f]			Release[g]	Placement[g]
Change in CD[i]	.99 (.89, 1.11)	.94 (.80, 1.11)	.91 (.79, 1.06)	.94 (.76, 1.16)	.85* (.72, 1.00)	1.23† (.99, 1.53)	1.04 (.91, 1.18)
Gini index (0–1)[j]	1.09 (.95, 1.24)	.93 (.78, 1.12)	.93 (.79, 1.10)	1.28* (1.02, 1.60)	.86† (.72, 1.02)	1.01 (.80, 1.26)	.90 (.78, 1.03)
Change in Gini index[j]	.99 (.89, 1.11)	1.01 (.86, 1.18)	1.03 (.89, 1.19)	.73** (.58, .91)	1.04 (.89, 1.22)	.94 (.75, 1.18)	1.03 (.90, 1.18)
Social disorganization model							
Crime rate (per 1,000)	1.00 (1.00, 1.01)	1.00 (.99, 1.01)	.99 (.98, 1.00)	1.00 (.99, 1.02)	.99† (.98, 1.00)	1.00 (.99, 1.02)	1.00 (.99, 1.01)
Change in crime rate	1.00 (.99, 1.00)	1.00 (.99, 1.01)	1.01 (1.00, 1.02)	1.00 (.99, 1.02)	1.00 (.99, 1.01)	1.00 (.99, 1.01)	1.00 (.99, 1.00)
Juvenile arrest rate (per 1,000)	1.01 (.97, 1.04)	1.05† (1.00 1.10)	1.04† (.99, 1.09)	.97 (.91, 1.04)	1.03 (.98, 1.08)	1.05 (.99, 1.11)	.95** (.91, .98)
Change in juvenile arrest rate	1.01 (.98, 1.03)	.99 (.95, 1.02)	.99 (.96, 1.02)	.99 (.95, 1.05)	.97† (.93, 1.00)	1.02 (.97, 1.06)	1.00 (.97, 1.02)
Ethnic heterogeneity (0–1)[j]	.95 (.84, 1.09)	.99 (.82, 1.19)	1.16† (.98, 1.37)	1.22 (.96, 1.54)	.98 (.81, 1.17)	1.31* (1.04, 1.64)	1.12 (.97,1.29)
Residential mobility (% moved)	1.01 (.99, 1.04)	.98 (.95, 1.01)	.98 (.96, 1.01)	.93*** (.89, .97)	1.00 (.97, 1.03)	.92*** (.88, .96)	.97* (.95, 1.00)
Youth population %	.99 (.96, 1.02)	.96† (.92, 1.01)	.96† (.92, 1.00)	.93* (.87, 1.00)	.99 (.95, 1.04)	.94† (.89, 1.00)	1.00 (.96, 1.04)
Change in youth population %	1.02 (.96, 1.10)	1.06 (.96, 1.17)	1.05 (.96, 1.15)	1.14† (.99, 1.31)	.99 (.89, 1.09)	1.09 (.96, 1.25)	1.05 (.96, 1.14)

Political economy model							
Judicial elections	1.19	3.93*	1.41	1.42	1.53	1.21	.52†
	(.59, 2.41)	(1.10, 14.04)	(.44, 4.51)	(.44, 4.58)	(.47, 5.04)	(.38, 3.79)	(.26, 1.02)
Median income (×1,000)	1.00	1.00	1.00	.98*	.99	1.01	1.00
	(.99, 1.01)	(.98, 1.01)	(.98, 1.01)	(.96, 1.00)	(.98, 1.01)	(.99, 1.03)	(.99, 1.01)
Conservative voting majority	1.00	1.00	1.00	1.00	1.01*	.99*	1.00
	(1.00, 1.00)	(1.00,1.01)	(1.00, 1.01)	(.99, 1.01)	(1.00, 1.01)	(.98, 1.00)	(.99, 1.00)
Population density (per sq/mi) (×100)	1.01	.98	.98	1.02	.99	1.00	.98†
	(.98, 1.03)	(.95, 1.02)	(.95, 1.01)	(.98, 1.05)	(.95, 1.02)	(.96, 1.03)	(.96, 1.00)
Level-3 variables							
South	1.91	.59	.65	.72	1.04	.46	.34†
	(.64, 5.72)	(.04, 8.12)	(.06, 7.63)	(.07, 7.03)	(.09, 11.64)	(.05, 4.01)	(.09, 1.27)
Random effects							
Random intercept variance component, level-2	.75***	1.42***	1.16***	1.40***	1.28***	1.40***	.57***
	(.87)	(1.19)	(1.08)	(1.18)	(1.13)	(1.19)	(.75)
Intraclass correlation (ρ), level-2	.17	.22	.20	.24	.21	.24	.13
Random intercept variance component, level-3	.26***	1.69***	1.49***	1.21***	1.43***	1.08***	.40***
	(.51)	(1.30)	(1.22)	(1.10)	(1.20)	(1.04)	(.63)
Intraclass correlation (ρ), level-3	.06	.26	.25	.21	.24	.19	.09

Note: Estimates for three separate models presented: community threat, social disorganization, and political economy. Random effects and control variable coefficients are based on the community threat model.

a N_1 = 246,729; N_2 = 475; N_3 = 7.
b N_1 = 241,921; N_2 = 475; N_3 = 7.
c N_1 = 85,545; N_2 = 464; N_3 = 7.
d N_1 = 93,730; N_2 = 465; N_3 = 7.
e N_1 = 65,960; N_2 = 462; N_3 = 7.
f Reference category: Dismissal.
g Reference: Community supervision.
h Reference: White.
i Reference: Property offense.
j Standardized.
† p <.10; * p <.05; ** p <.01; *** p <.001 (two tailed).

Community threats were not significantly associated with variation in detention outcomes. First, odds of detention were not associated with racial threat as measured by percent Black (OR = 1.00; 95% CI: .98–1.02) or change in percent Black (OR = 1.03; 95% CI: .93–1.09) in the surrounding county. Second, odds of detention were not associated with ethnic threats as measured by percent Hispanic (OR = 1.00; 95% CI: .98–1.03) or change in percent Hispanic (OR = .99; 95% CI: .94–1.04). Third, odds of detention were not associated with economic threats as measured by concentrated disadvantage (OR = 1.08; 95% CI: .90–1.29), change in concentrated disadvantage (OR = .99; 95% CI: .89–1.11), income inequality (OR = 1.09; 95% CI: .95–1.24), or change in income inequality (OR = .99; 95% CI: .89–1.11).

Similarly, social disorganization was not significantly associated with detention outcomes. First, odds of detention were not associated with crime rates (OR = 1.00; 95% CI: 1.00–1.01), changes in crime rates (OR = 1.00; 95% CI: .99–1.00), juvenile arrest rates (OR = 1.01; 95% CI: .97–1.04), or changes in juvenile arrests (OR = 1.01; 95% CI: .98–1.03). Similarly, odds of detention were not associated with ethnic heterogeneity (OR = .95; 95% CI: .84–1.09), residential mobility (OR = 1.01; 95% CI: .99–1.04), youth population density (OR = .99; 95% CI: .96–1.02), or change in youth population (OR = 1.02; 95% CI: .96–1.10).

Finally, political economy was also not significantly associated with detention outcomes. First, judicial elections were not associated with odds of detention (OR = 1.19; 95% CI: .59–1.01). Second, community median income was not associated with odds of detention (OR = 1.00; 95% CI: .99–1.01). Third, conservativism was not associated with odds of detention (OR = 1.00; 95% CI: 1.00–1.00). Fourth, urbanism was not associated with odds of detention (OR = 1.01; 95% CI: .98–1.03).

In sum, there was no evidence that detention outcomes varied according to community threats, social disorganization, or political economy in the surrounding court and community.

Petition of Delinquency

For the petition decision, the sample consisted of 241,921 juvenile referrals nested within 475 counties nested within seven states. Petition is a categorical outcome with three possible outcomes; approximately 41.3 percent of cases received a petition of delinquency filed (*n* = 99,877), 36.8 percent were diverted to informal processing (*n* = 88,971), and 21.9 percent were dismissed (*n* = 53,073). Dismissal served as the reference category.

Community threats were not significantly associated with variation in petition or diversion outcomes. First, odds of petition (versus dismissal) were not associated with racial and ethnic threats: percent Black (OR = 1.02;

95% CI: .99–1.04), change in percent Black (OR = .95; 95% CI: .88–1.03), percent Hispanic (OR = 1.00; 95% CI: .97–1.03), or change in percent Hispanic (OR = 1.00; 95% CI: .94–1.07). Similarly, odds of diversion (versus dismissal) were not associated with racial and ethnic threats: percent Black (OR = 1.00; 95% CI: .97–1.02), change in percent Black (OR = .99; 95% CI: .91–1.08), percent Hispanic (OR = 1.00; 95% CI: .97–1.03), or change in percent Hispanic (OR = .98; 95% CI: .91–1.05). Second, odds of petition were not associated with economic threats: concentrated disadvantage (OR = 1.03; 95% CI: .81–1.30), change in concentrated disadvantage (OR = .91; 95% CI: .79–1.06), income inequality (OR = .93; 95% CI: .79–1.10), or change in income inequality (OR = 1.03; 95% CI: .89–1.19). Similarly, odds of diversion were not associated with economic threats: concentrated disadvantage (OR = 1.16; 95% CI: .90–1.50), change in concentrated disadvantage (OR = .94; 95% CI: .80–1.11), income inequality (OR = .93; 95% CI: .78–1.12), or change in income inequality (OR = 1.01; 95% CI: .86–1.18).

Several social disorganization indicators approached significant associations with petition and diversion (relative to dismissal), while others did not. First, odds of petition (versus release) were 4 percent higher in counties with 1 percent higher juvenile crime rates (OR = 1.04; 95% CI: .99–1.09; $p = .09$), and odds of diversion were likewise 5 percent higher (OR = 1.05; 95% CI: 1.00–1.10; $p = .07$). In each case, the lower bound of the confidence interval (OR = .99 and 1.00, respectively) indicates that juvenile arrest rates may only be trivially associated with odds of petition and diversion, however. Second, odds of petition were 16 percent higher in counties with a one standard deviation increase in ethnic heterogeneity (OR = 1.16; 95% CI: .98–1.37; $p = .08$), while there was no observed relationship between ethnic heterogeneity and odds of diversion (OR = .99; 95% CI: .82–1.19). Additionally, the lower bound of the confidence interval (OR = .98) indicates that ethnic heterogeneity may only be trivially associated with odds of petition. Third, odds of petition were 4 percent lower in counties with 1 percent greater youth population (OR = .96; 95% CI: .92–1.00; $p = .07$), as were odds of diversion (OR = .96; 95% CI: .92–1.01; $p = .08$). Again, we can see that the upper bounds of the confidence intervals (OR = 1.00 and 1.01, respectively) indicate that the relationship between youth population and odds of petition and release may only be trivial. Odds of petition were not significantly associated with other indicators of social disorganization: crime rates (OR = .99; 95% CI: .98–1.00), changes in crime rates (OR = 1.01; 95% CI: 1.00–1.02), changes in juvenile arrest rates (OR = .99; 95% CI: .96–1.02), residential mobility (OR = .98; 95% CI: .96–1.01), or change in youth population (OR = 1.05; 95% CI: .96–1.15). Similarly, odds of diversion were not associated with crime rates (OR = 1.00; 95% CI: .99–1.01), changes in crime rates (OR = 1.00; 95% CI: .99–1.01), changes in juvenile arrests (OR = .99; 95% CI: .95–1.02), residential mobility (OR = .98; 95% CI: .95–1.01), or change in youth population (OR = 1.06; 95% CI: .96–1.17). It is also worth reiterating that the associations listed above approached but did not reach significance, meaning that the most conservative estimate of the association—the lower bound of the confidence interval—was not discernible from no association (i.e. OR = 1.00).

Finally, for political economy, odds of diversion were associated with external polity but not with external economy, internal polity, or internal economy. Specifically, odds of diversion were approximately four times higher in courts where judges were elected rather than appointed (OR = 3.93; 95% CI: 1.10–14.04; p = .04). The lower bound of this confidence estimate (OR = 1.10) indicates that judicial elections were at least associated with 10 percent greater odds of diversion. Judicial elections were not associated with odds of petition, however (OR = 1.41; 95% CI: .44–4.51). Second, community median income was not associated with odds of petition (OR = 1.00; 95% CI: .98–1.01) or diversion (OR = 1.00; 95% CI: .98–1.01). Third, conservativism was not associated with odds of petition (OR = 1.00; 95% CI: 1.00–1.01) or diversion (OR = 1.00; 95% CI: 1.00–1.01). Fourth, urbanism was not associated with odds of petition (OR = .98; 95% CI: .95–1.01) or diversion (OR = .98; 95% CI: .95–1.02).

In sum, there was limited evidence that petition outcomes varied according to community threats, social disorganization, or political economy in the surrounding court and community.

Waiver to Criminal Court

For the waiver decision, the sample consisted of 85,545 waiver-eligible petitioned juvenile offenders nested within 464 counties nested within seven states. As noted in the prior chapter, judicial waiver is a rare event, with about 1.1 percent of eligible petitioned cases being waived to criminal court in 2010 (n = 899).

The only community threats significantly associated with waiver were indicators of economic threat. Specifically, odds of waiver were 28 percent higher in counties with more income inequality by one standard deviation (OR = 1.28; 95% CI: 1.02–1.60; p = .04), but 27 percent lower in counties with a one standard deviation increase in income inequality from 2000 to 2010 (OR = .73; 95% CI: .58–.91; p = .01). Confidence interval bounds indicate that odds of waiver were at least 2 percent higher in counties with greater income inequality, and at least 9 percent lower in counties where income inequality had increased over the prior decade. Odds of waiver were not associated with other indicators of community threat, however. Specifically, odds of waiver were not associated with percent Black (OR = 1.03; 95% CI: .99–1.06), change in percent Black (OR = .96; 95% CI: .86–1.06), percent Hispanic (OR = .98; 95% CI: .94–1.03), change in percent Hispanic (OR = .99; 95% CI: .88–1.11), concentrated disadvantage (OR = 1.11; 95% CI: .80–1.54), or change in concentrated disadvantage (OR = .94; 95% CI: .76–1.16).

For social disorganization, several indicators were associated with waiver to criminal court. Odds of waiver were 7 percent lower in counties with 1 percent greater residential mobility (OR = .93; 95% CI: .87–1.00; $p <$ .001) and 7 percent lower in counties with 1 percent higher youth population density (OR = .93; 95% CI: .87–1.00; p = .04). Additionally, odds of waiver were 14 percent higher in counties with a 1 percent increase in youth population from 2000 to 2010 (OR = 1.14; 95% CI: .99–1.31; p = .06). In each case, however, confidence bounds indicate that the association may be trivial (OR = 1.00, 1.00, and .99, respectively). Other indicators of social disorganization were not associated with odds of waiver: crime rates (OR = 1.00; 95% CI: .99–1.02), changes in crime rates (OR = 1.00; 95% CI: .99–1.02), juvenile arrest rates (OR = .97; 95% CI: .91–1.04), changes in juvenile arrests (OR = .99; 95% CI: .95–1.05), or ethnic heterogeneity (OR = 1.22; 95% CI: .96–1.54).

Finally, for political economy, odds of waiver to criminal court were associated with external economy but not with external polity, internal polity, or internal economy. Specifically, odds of waiver were 2 percent lower in counties with higher median income by $1,000 (OR = .98; 95% CI: .96–1.00; p = .02), while odds of waiver were not associated with judicial elections (OR = 1.42; 95% CI: .44–4.58), conservatism (OR = 1.00; 95% CI: .99–1.01), or urbanism (OR = 1.02; 95% CI: .98–1.05). Notably, the upper confidence bounds indicate that median income may only be trivially associated with odds of waiver (OR = 1.00).

In sum, waiver to criminal court appeared to be weakly associated with several contextual variables: income inequality and change in inequality, residential mobility, youth population and change in youth population, and median income. As such, there was some evidence that waiver outcomes varied according to economic threat, social disorganization, and one aspect of political economy in the surrounding court and community.

Adjudication of Delinquency

For the adjudication decision, the sample consisted of 93,730 petitioned juvenile offenders nested within 465 counties nested within seven states. As noted in the prior chapter, approximately 71.3 percent were adjudicated delinquent in 2010 (n = 66,861).

Turning to the contextual hypotheses, the only community threats significantly associated with adjudication of delinquency were some indicators of economic threat. Odds of adjudication were 15 percent lower in counties where concentrated disadvantage had decreased by one standard deviation from 2000 to 2010 (OR = .85; 95% CI: .72–1.00; p = .05). Additionally, odds of adjudication were 14 percent lower in counties with one standard deviation higher income inequality (OR = .86; 95% CI: .72–1.02; p = .09), although this only approached significance and a null effect lies within the confidence bounds. For racial threat, odds of adjudication were not associated with percent Black (OR = .98; 95% CI: .96–1.01) or change in percent Black (OR = 1.06; 95% CI: .97–1.15). Similarly, for ethnic threat, odds of adjudication were not associated with percent Hispanic (OR = 1.00; 95% CI: .96–1.03) or change in percent Hispanic (OR = 1.03; 95% CI: .95–1.10). Additionally, another indicator of economic threat, concentrated disadvantage, was not associated with odds of adjudication (OR = 1.19; 95% CI: .92–1.54), nor was change in income inequality (OR = 1.04; 95% CI: .89–1.22).

For social disorganization, some indicators of crime rates approached significance. Specifically, odds of adjudication were 1 percent lower in counties with 1 percent higher crime rate (OR = .99; 95% CI: .98–1.00; p = .10) and 3 percent lower in counties where juvenile arrest rates had increased 1 percent from 2000 to 2010 (OR = .97; 95% CI: .93–1.00; p = .07). In each case, upper confidence bounds indicate that odds of adjudication may only be trivially associated with higher crime (OR = 1.00) and increased juvenile arrests (OR = 1.00). Additionally, odds of adjudication were not associated with change in crime rates (OR = 1.00; 95% CI: .99–1.01), juvenile arrest rates (OR = 1.03; 95% CI: .98–1.08), ethnic heterogeneity (OR = .98; 95% CI: .81–1.17), residential mobility (OR = 1.00; 95% CI: .97–1.03), youth population (OR = .99; 95% CI: .95–1.04), or change in youth population (OR = .99; 95% CI: .89–1.09).

Finally, for political economy, adjudication outcomes were associated with internal polity but not with external polity, external economy, or internal economy. Specifically, odds of adjudication were 1 percent higher in counties with 1 percent greater conservative voting majority (OR = 1.01; 95% CI: 1.00–1.01; p = .04), while odds of adjudication were not associated with judicial elections (OR = 1.53; 95% CI: .47–5.04), median income (OR = .99; 95% CI: .98–1.01), or urbanism (OR = .99; 95% CI: .95–1.02). Notably, lower confidence bounds indicate that conservatism may only be trivially associated with odds of adjudication (OR = 1.00).

In sum, there was limited evidence that adjudication outcomes varied according to community threats, social disorganization, or political economy in the surrounding court and community.

Judicial Disposition

For judicial disposition, the sample consisted of 65,729 juveniles who were adjudicated delinquent, nested within 462 counties nested within seven states. Disposition was treated as a categorical outcome with 3 possible outcomes; approximately 13.8 percent of these cases received residential placement (n = 9,074), while 78.3 percent received community supervision (n = 51,640) and 8 percent were released (n = 5,247). Community supervision serves as the reference category.

Community threats were not associated with judicial placement, while one indicator of economic threat approached a significant association with judicial release. Specifically, odds of release were 23 percent higher in counties where concentrated disadvantage had increased (by one standard deviation) from 2000 to 2010 (OR = 1.23; 95% CI: .99–1.53; p = .06). Lower confidence bounds indicate that concentrated disadvantage may only be trivially associated with odds of judicial release, however. Odds of judicial release were not associated with percent Black (OR = 1.02; 95% CI: .99–1.06), change in percent Black (OR = 1.02; 95% CI: .91–1.14), percent Hispanic (OR = 1.00; 95% CI: .97–1.06), change in percent Hispanic (OR = .98; 95% CI: .88–1.10), concentrated disadvantage (OR = .96; 95% CI: .68–1.35), income inequality (OR = 1.01; 95% CI: .80–1.26), or change in income inequality (OR = .94; 95% CI: .75–1.18). Odds of placement were similarly not significantly associated with percent Black (OR = 1.01; 95% CI: .98–1.04), change in percent Black (OR = .96; 95% CI: .90–1.03), percent Hispanic (OR = 1.00; 95% CI: .97–1.03), change in percent Hispanic (OR = .99; 95% CI: .92–1.06), concentrated disadvantage (OR = 1.05; 95% CI: .86–1.28), change in concentrated disadvantage (OR = 1.04; 95% CI: .91–1.18), income inequality (OR = .90; 95% CI: .78–1.03), or change in income inequality (OR = 1.03; 95% CI: .90–1.18).

Several social disorganization indicators were significantly associated with judicial dispositions, however. First, odds of placement were 5 percent lower in counties with a 1 percent higher juvenile arrest rate (OR = .95; 95% CI: .91–.98; p = .004) and 3 percent lower in counties with 1 percent higher residential mobility (OR = .97; 95% CI: .95–1.00; p = .03). Upper confidence bounds indicate that odds of placement were at least 2 percent lower in counties with higher juvenile arrests (OR = .98), while the association between residential placement and placement may only be trivial (OR = 1.00). Second, odds of release were 31 percent higher in counties with one standard deviation higher ethnic heterogeneity (OR = 1.31; 95% CI: 1.04–1.64; p = .02), while odds of release were 8 percent lower in counties with 1 percent higher residential mobility (OR = .92; 95% CI: .88–.96; $p < .001$) and 6 percent lower in counties with a 1 percent greater youth population (OR = .94; 95% CI: .89–1.00; p = .06). Confidence bounds indicate that odds of release were at least

4 percent higher in counties with greater heterogeneity (OR = 1.04) and at least 4 percent lower in counties with more residential mobility (OR = .96), while the association with youth population density may only be trivial (OR = 1.00). Additionally, odds of placement were not associated with crime rate (OR = 1.00; 95% CI: .99–1.01), change in crime rates (OR = 1.00; 95% CI: .99–1.00), change in juvenile arrest rate (OR = 1.00; 95% CI: .97–1.06), ethnic heterogeneity (OR = 1.12; 95% CI: .97–1.29), youth population (OR = 1.00; 95% CI: .96–1.04), or change in youth population (OR = 1.05; 95% CI: .96–1.14). Similarly, odds of release were not associated with crime rate (OR = 1.00; 95% CI: .99–1.02), change in crime rates (OR = 1.00; 95% CI: .99–1.01), juvenile arrest rate (OR = 1.05; 95% CI: .99–1.11), change in juvenile arrest rate (OR = 1.02; 95% CI: .97–1.06), or change in youth population (OR =1.09; 95% CI: .96–1.25).

Finally, several political economy factors were associated with judicial dispositions. Internal polity, as measured by conservative majority, was associated with odds of release, while internal economy, as measured by urbanism, was marginally associated with odds of placement. First, the odds of release (versus probation) were approximately 1 percent lower in counties with 1 percent higher conservative voting majority (OR = .99; 95% CI: .98–1.00; p = .01). The lower bound of this confidence estimate (OR = 1.00) indicates that conservatism may only be trivially associated with odds of release, however. Additionally, conservative majority was not associated with odds of placement (OR = 1.00; 95% CI: .99–1.00). Second, odds of placement (versus community supervision) were approximately 48 percent lower in counties with judicial elections (OR = .52; 95% CI: .26–1.02; p = .06) and 2 percent lower in counties with greater population density by 100 persons per square mile (OR = .98; 95% CI: .96–1.00; p = .08). In each case the upper bounds of the confidence limit (OR = 1.02 and 1.00, respectively) indicate that judicial elections and urbanism may only be trivially associated with odds of placement, however. Additionally, odds of release were not associated with judicial elections (OR = 1.21; 95% CI: .38–3.79) or with urbanism (OR = 1.00; 95% CI: .96–1.03). Finally, median income was not associated with odds of placement (OR = 1.00; 95% CI: .99–1.01) or odds of release (OR = 1.01; 95% CI: .99–1.03).

In sum, there was limited evidence that judicial disposition outcomes varied according to community threats, social disorganization, or political economy in the surrounding court and community.

Summary of Findings

Findings indicated that juvenile court outcomes varied significantly across counties and states. Variance component models indicated that approximately 12–25 percent of the variation in juvenile court outcomes was attributable to county-level differences and 11–28 percent was attributable to state-level differences. The most variation was observed for diversion, while the least variation was observed for judicial placement.

To explore whether variation in juvenile processing and sanctions could be explained by contextual influences on the juvenile court, the present study tested whether community threats, social disorganization, and political economy were associated with odds of detention, petition and diversion, waiver, adjudication, and placement and judicial release. The findings indicated limited support for the contextual hypotheses.

First, no contextual factors were significantly associated with odds of detention. Second, at the petition stage, odds of petition were positively associated with juvenile arrests and ethnic heterogeneity, and negatively associated with youth population density—all indicators of social disorganization. Notably, however, these associations approached but did not reach significance, meaning that associations could not inferred with high confidence (i.e. crossed OR = 1.00). Odds of diversion were also positively associated with juvenile arrests and negatively associated with youth population density (again, with associations only approaching significance). Odds of diversion were also strongly associated with judicial elections, however, which appears to be a robust effect indicating that *likelihood of diversion is considerably higher in states with elected rather than appointed judges*.

Third, odds of waiver were positively associated with income inequality (i.e. economic threat) and increased youth population (i.e. social disorganization), while negatively associated with increased income inequality, youth population size, and median income (i.e. external economy). This indicates that judicial waiver is more likely in communities with high income inequality that has remained constant over time (i.e. not increased), and less likely in counties with large youth populations that have remained constant over time (i.e. not increased). Judicial waiver is also less likely in more affluent communities. Several of these associations, however, were marginal (youth population, change in youth population, and median income). The most robust findings, in terms of their confidence bounds, involved the *positive association between waiver and income inequality*. Fourth, odds of adjudication were positively associated with conservatism (i.e. internal polity), and negatively associated with increased concentrated disadvantage and income inequality (i.e. economic threat) as well as crime rates and increased juvenile arrests (i.e. social disorganization). Notably, however, none of these associations were particularly robust in terms of confidence bounds.

Finally, at judicial disposition, odds of placement were negatively associated with juvenile arrests and residential mobility (i.e. social disorganization), as well as judicial elections (i.e. external polity) and urbanism (i.e. internal economy). The most robust of these associations involved juvenile arrests, indicating that *secure placement was less likely in counties with higher juvenile arrest rates*. Odds of release were positively associated with increased concentrated disadvantage (i.e. economic threat), as well as ethnic heterogeneity (i.e. social disorganization), while odds of release were negatively associated with youth population density (i.e. social disorganization) and conservatism (i.e. internal polity). The most robust of these associations involved ethnic heterogeneity, indicating that *judicial release was more likely in more heterogeneous counties.*

Chapter 7

Multistate Findings, 2000

Variation in Juvenile Justice Outcomes

As described in the last chapter, the contextual research hypotheses are motivated by unexplained variance in juvenile court outcomes across counties and states. As such, the first step in the analysis is to assess whether juvenile court outcomes vary significantly across counties and states by estimating empty three-level hierarchical models (i.e. variance component models) for each outcome, with cases nested within counties (level-2) nested within states (level-3). (For fuller explanation, see Chapter 6.)

For detention, the level-2 variance component (ψ^2) was .99 ($p<.001$) and the level-3 variance component (ψ^3) was .50 ($p<.001$). At level-2, the corresponding intraclass correlation (ρ^2) was .21; at level-3, $\rho^3 = .11$. This indicates that before any predictors were added to the model, approximately 11 percent of the variation in detention outcomes was attributable to between-state differences, while 21 percent was due to between-county differences within states. This represents the same proportion of variation in detention attributable to state-level differences as the 2010 data, but more variation in detention attributable to between-county differences.

For formal petition, there were two comparisons of interest: diversion (versus dismissal) and petition (versus dismissal). For diversion, $\psi^2 = 1.43$ ($p<.001$) and $\psi^3 = 1.31$ ($p<.001$), with $\rho^2 = .24$ and $\rho^3 = .22$. This indicates that before any predictors were added to the model, approximately 22 percent of the variation in diversion was attributable to between-state differences, while 24 percent was due to between-county differences within states. This is approximately the same amount of variation in diversion outcomes as observed in the 2010 data. For petition, $\psi^2 = 1.14$ ($p<.001$) and $\psi^3 = .94$ ($p<.001$), with $\rho^2 = .21$ and $\rho^3 = .18$. This indicates that before any predictors were added to the model, approximately 18 percent of the variation in petition was attributable to between-state differences, while 21 percent was due to between-county differences. This is slightly less variation in petition outcomes as observed in the 2010 data.

For waiver to criminal court, $\psi^2 = 1.24$ ($p<.001$) and $\psi^3 = 1.37$ ($p<.001$), with $\rho^2 = .21$ and $\rho^3 = .23$. This indicates that before any predictors were added to the model, approximately 23 percent of the variation in waiver outcomes was attributable to between-state differences, while 21 percent was due to between-county differences. This is approximately the same amount of variation in waiver outcomes as observed in the 2010 data.

For adjudication of delinquency, $\psi^2 = 1.05$ ($p<.001$) and $\psi^3 = .90$ ($p<.001$), with $\rho^2 = .20$ and $\rho^3 = .17$. This indicates that before any predictors were added to the model, approximately 17 percent of the variation in adjudication of delinquency was attributable to between-state differences, while 20 percent was due to between-county differences. This is approximately the same amount of county-level variation, and less state-level variation, compared to the 2010 data.

Finally, for judicial disposition there were two comparisons of interest: judicial release (versus community supervision) and secure placement (versus community supervision). For release, $\psi^2 = 2.07$ ($p<.001$) and $\psi^3 = 9.26$ ($p<.001$), with $\rho^2 = .14$ and $\rho^3 = .63$. This indicates that before any predictors were added to the model, approximately 63 percent of the variation in judicial release was attributable to between-state differences, while 14 percent was due to between-county differences. This is considerably more variation in judicial release attributable to state-level differences compared to the 2010 data. For secure placement, $\psi^2 = .45$ ($p<.001$) and $\psi^3 = .47$ ($p<.001$), with $\rho^2 = .11$ and $\rho^3 = .11$. This indicates that before any predictors were added to the model, approximately 11 percent of the variation in placement was attributable to between-state differences, while 11 percent was due to between-county differences. This is approximately the same amount of variation in placement outcomes as observed in the 2010 data.

In sum, juvenile court outcomes varied significantly across counties and states, with approximately 11–24 percent of the variation in these outcomes attributable to county-level differences and 11–63 percent attributable to state-level differences. As with 2010, the most variation was observed for *diversion*, while the least variation was observed for *judicial placement*.

Contextual Effects

Table 7.1 reports on the results of a series of three-level hierarchical regression models estimating odds ratios and 95 percent confidence intervals for each outcome of interest. The findings are discussed below for each outcome.

Table 7.1 Multistate analyses, year 2000

		Petition[b]		*Waiver*[c]	*Adjudication*[d]	*Disposition*[e]	
	Detention[a]	*Diversion*[f]	*Petition*[f]			*Release*[g]	*Placement*[g]
Fixed effects	OR (95% CI)	OR (95% CI)	OR (95% CI)	OR (95% CI)	OR (95% CI)	OR (95% CI)	OR (95% CI)
Intercept	.14**	1.60	1.91	.01**	2.98	.00*	.10**
	(.05, .40)	(.25, 10.13)	(.39, 9.21)	(.00, .06)	(.57, 15.54)	(.00, .17)	(.03, .33)
Level-1 variables							
Black[h]	1.34***	.95***	1.15***	1.84***	1.03	.84***	1.28***
	(1.30, 1.37)	(.92, .98)	(1.12, 1.18)	(1.64, 2.07)	(.99, 1.07)	(.76, .93)	(1.22, 1.35)
Hispanic[h]	1.21***	.93***	1.15***	1.44***	1.03	.48***	1.05
	(1.18, 1.26)	(.92, .98)	(1.10, 1.19)	(1.26, 1.66)	(.98, 1.08)	(.38, .61)	(.97, 1.13)
Other race/ethnicity[h]	1.10**	1.17***	1.16***	1.88***	.93	.78	.95
	(1.03, 1.17)	(1.07, 1.28)	(1.06, 1.27)	(1.52, 2.33)	(.84, 1.02)	(.55, 1.09)	(.82, 1.10)
Male	1.19***	.83***	1.34***	2.53***	1.17***	1.14**	1.39***
	(1.17, 1.22)	(.81, .85)	(1.31, 1.37)	(2.22, 2.89)	(1.13, 1.21)	(1.03, 1.25)	(1.32, 1.47)
Age	1.07***	.99**	1.09***	2.06***	1.00	1.07***	1.10***
	(1.06, 1.07)	(.98, 1.00)	(1.08, 1.10)	(1.97, 2.16)	(.99, 1.01)	(1.04, 1.11)	(1.08, 1.11)
Violent offense[i]	1.56***	.79***	.87***	2.23***	.78***	.77**	1.28***
	(1.52, 1.60)	(.76, .82)	(.84, .90)	(2.00, 2.49)	(.75, .82)	(.64, .93)	(1.21, 1.37)
Drug/alcohol offense[i]	1.24***	1.27***	1.33***	.84**	.98	1.11	.81***
	(1.20, 1.28)	(1.21, 1.33)	(1.27, 1.39)	(.74, .96)	(.93, 1.03)	(.89, 1.39)	(.75, .87)
Weapon offense[i]	1.77***	.90†	1.56***	1.06	1.18**	.54**	.71***
	(1.64, 1.90)	(.80, 1.01)	(1.41, 1.72)	(.82, 1.35)	(1.05, 1.33)	(.35, .84)	(.61, .84)
Probation violation[i]	4.39***	1.68***	1.70***	.06***	.98	1.26*	3.32***
	(3.40, 5.67)	(1.58, 1.79)	(1.61, 1.80)	(.04, .09)	(.93, 1.03)	(1.03, 1.53)	(3.11, 3.53)
Status offense[i]	.34***	1.30***	.49***	.38***	.63***	10.76***	1.43***
	(.33, .35)	(1.26, 1.34)	(.47, .51)	(.30, .47)	(.60, .66)	(9.36, 12.38)	(1.32, 1.56)
Other offense[i]	.95***	.91***	.65***	.70***	.66***	1.88***	1.20***
	(.92, .98)	(.88, .95)	(.63, .68)	(.62, .80)	(.63, .69)	(1.62, 2.18)	(1.12, 1.28)
Detention	–	.69***	3.61***	1.88***	2.00***	.50***	2.24***
		(.67, .72)	(3.49, 3.72)	(1.71, 2.06)	(1.93, 2.08)	(.43, .58)	(2.13, 2.34)

(continued)

Table 7.1 Cont.

		Petition[b]		Waiver[c]	Adjudication[d]	Disposition[e]	
	Detention[a]	Diversion[f]	Petition[f]			Release[g]	Placement[g]
Level-2 variables							
Community threat model							
Percent Black	1.01 (.99, 1.03)	.97* (.94, 1.00)	.98 (.96, 1.01)	1.00 (.97, 1.03)	.99 (.97, 1.01)	.97 (.93, 1.02)	1.00 (.99, 1.02)
Percent Black (squared)	1.00 (1.00, 1.00)	1.00* (1.00, 1.00)	1.00 (1.00, 1.00)	1.00 (1.00, 1.00)	1.00* (1.00, 1.00)	1.00 (1.00, 1.00)	1.00 (1.00, 1.00)
Percent Hispanic	1.01 (.99, 1.03)	1.01 (.98, 1.03)	1.01 (.99, 1.03)	1.00 (.96, 1.03)	1.02 (.99, 1.04)	1.05 (.97, 1.13)	1.00 (.98, 1.02)
Percent Hispanic (squared)	1.00 (1.00, 1.00)	1.00 (1.00, 1.00)	1.00 (1.00, 1.00)	1.00 (1.00, 1.00)	1.00 (1.00, 1.00)	1.00 (1.00, 1.00)	1.00 (1.00, 1.00)
Concentrated disadvantage (CD)[j]	1.06 (.87, 1.29)	1.04 (.82, 1.31)	1.04 (.83, 1.30)	1.27 (.94, 1.71)	1.32* (1.06, 1.63)	1.48 (.85, 2.56)	1.01 (.85, 1.20)
Gini index (0–1)[j]	1.03 (.90, 1.19)	1.11 (.93, 1.32)	1.08 (.92, 1.27)	1.03 (.83, 1.29)	.93 (.79, 1.08)	.93 (.65, 1.32)	.94 (.83, 1.07)
Social disorganization model							
Crime rate (per 1,000)	1.00 (1.00, 1.01)	1.00 (.99, 1.00)	1.00 (.99, 1.00)	1.00 (.99, 1.00)	.99* (.99, 1.00)	1.00 (.99, 1.01)	1.01* (1.00, 1.01)
Juvenile crime rate (per 1,000)	1.00 (.98, 1.03)	.99 (.97, 1.02)	.98 (.95, 1.01)	1.04* (1.00, 1.08)	1.03† (1.00, 1.05)	.96 (.89, 1.04)	.97** (.95, .99)
Ethnic heterogeneity (0–1)[j]	1.08 (.94, 1.24)	.99 (.83, 1.18)	1.02 (.98, 1.05)	1.00 (.81, 1.23)	1.06 (.91, 1.24)	1.06 (.95, 1.18)	1.06 (.94, 1.20)
Youth population %	1.00 (.96, 1.03)	1.03 (.99, 1.08)	1.01 (.98, 1.05)	.94* (.89, .99)	1.01 (.97 1.04)	1.05 (.74, 1.49)	1.03* (1.00, 1.07)
Political economy model							
Judicial elections	1.02 (.99, 1.05)	2.50† (.93, 6.76)	1.32 (.48, 3.61)	.49 (.12, 2.08)	1.75 (.56, 5.43)	.29 (.04, 2.32)	.93 (.44, 1.97)
Median income (×1,000)	1.00 (.99, 1.02)	.98* (.96, 1.00)	.98 (.97, 1.00)	.99 (.97, 1.01)	.99 (.98, 1.01)	.97 (.94, 1.01)	.99 (.98, 1.01)

Conservative voting majority	1.00 (1.00, 1.01)	1.01* (1.00, 1.01)	1.01** (1.00, 1.01)	1.00 (.99, 1.01)	1.01* (1.00, 1.01)	1.00 (.99, 1.02)	1.00 (1.00, 1.01)
Population density (per sq/mi) (×100)	1.23 (.52, 2.94)	.98 (.94, 1.01)	.99 (.96, 1.02)	.98 (.94, 1.01)	.99 (.96, 1.02)	1.00 (.94, 1.06)	.99 (.97, 1.01)
Level-3 variables							
South	1.07 (.25, 4.57)	.86 (.07, 11.47)	1.40 (.15, 12.63)	.67 (.02, 22.27)	1.01 (.10, 10.22)	15.97 (.02, 11366.8)	.82 (.16, 4.14)
Random effects							
Random intercept variance component, level-2	.98*** (.99)	1.39*** (1.18)	1.25*** (1.12)	1.37*** (1.17)	1.02*** (1.01)	2.00*** (1.41)	.47*** (.69)
Intraclass correlation (ρ), level-2	.21	.24	.23	.20	.24	.15	.11
Random intercept variance component, level-3	.36*** (.60)	1.21*** (1.10)	.87*** (.93)	2.29*** (1.51)	.98*** (.99)	7.85*** (2.80)	.48*** (.69)
Intraclass correlation (ρ), level-3	.08	.21	.16	.33	.19	.60	.11

Note: Estimates for three separate models presented: community threat, social disorganization, and political economy. Coefficients for case-level and state control variables are based on the community threat model.

a N_1 = 301,638; N_2 = 444; N_3 = 6.
b N_1 = 272,029; N_2 = 443; N_3 = 6.
c N_1 = 97,417; N_2 = 439; N_3 = 6.
d N_1 = 109,743; N_2 = 439; N_3 = 6.
e N_1 = 79,574; N_2 = 435; N_3 = 6.
f Reference category: Dismissal.
g Reference: Community supervision.
h Reference: White.
i Reference: Property offense.
j Standardized.
† p <.10; * p <.05; ** p <.01; *** p <.001 (two tailed).

Detention

For the detention decision, the sample consisted of 301,638 juvenile referrals nested within 444 counties nested within 6 states. As noted in Chapter 5, about 22.6 percent of referrals were detained (*n* = 68,114).

Community threats were not significantly associated with variation in detention outcomes. First, odds of detention were not associated with racial threat as measured by percent Black (OR = 1.01; 95% CI: .99–1.03) or with ethnic threat as measured by percent Hispanic (OR = 1.01; 95% CI: .99–1.03). Second, odds of detention were not associated with economic threat as measured by concentrated disadvantage (OR = 1.06; 95% CI: .87–1.29) or income inequality (OR = 1.03; 95% CI: .90–1.19). Similarly, social disorganization was not significantly associated with detention outcomes. First, odds of detention were not associated with crime rates (OR = 1.00; 95% CI: 1.00–1.01) or juvenile arrest rates (OR = 1.00; 95% CI: .98–1.03). Second, odds of detention were not associated with ethnic heterogeneity (OR = 1.08; 95% CI: .94–1.24) or youth population density (OR = 1.00; 95% CI: .96–1.03). Finally, political economy was also not significantly associated with detention outcomes. Specifically, odds of detention were not associated with judicial elections (OR = 1.02; 95% CI: .99–1.05), community median income (OR = 1.00; 95% CI: .99–1.02), conservative voting (OR = 1.00; 95% CI: 1.00–1.01), or urbanism (OR = 1.23; 95% CI: .52–2.94).

In sum, there was no evidence that detention outcomes varied according to community threats, social disorganization, or political economy in the surrounding court and community.

Petition of Delinquency

For the petition decision, the sample consisted of 272,029 juvenile referrals nested within 443 counties nested within 6 states. Petition was coded as a categorical outcome with 3 possible outcomes: approximately 43.7 percent of referrals received formal petition (*n* = 118,922), while 33.5 percent were diverted (*n* = 91,245) and 22.7 percent were dismissed (*n* = 61,865). Dismissal serves as the reference category.

Community threats were not significantly associated with variation in petition outcomes while indicators of racial threat were associated with variation in diversion outcomes. Specifically, odds of diversion (versus release) were 3 percent lower in counties with 1 percent higher Black population (OR = .97; 95% CI: .94–1.00; *p* = .02), with evidence that this was slightly non-linear (OR = 1.00; 95% CI: 1.00–1.00; *p* = .03). However, the upper bound of the confidence interval (OR = 1.00) indicates that racial threat may only be trivially associated with odds of diversion. For other community threats, there was no association with diversion or petition. First, odds of petition (versus dismissal) were not associated with percent Black (OR = .98; 95% CI: .96–1.01) or percent Hispanic (OR = 1.01; 95% CI: .99–1.03), while odds of diversion were not associated with percent Hispanic (OR = 1.01; 95% CI: .98–1.03). Second, odds of petition were not associated with economic threats: concentrated disadvantage (OR = 1.04; 95% CI: .83–1.30) or income inequality (OR = 1.08; 95% CI: .92–1.27). Similarly, odds of diversion were not associated with concentrated disadvantage (OR = 1.04; 95% CI: .82–1.31) or income inequality (OR = 1.11; 95% CI: .93–1.32).

Variation in petition and diversion were not associated with social disorganization. Specifically, odds of petition were not significantly associated with crime rates (OR = 1.00; 95% CI: .99–1.00), juvenile arrest rates (OR = .98; 95% CI: .95–1.01), ethnic heterogeneity (OR = 1.02; 95% CI: .98–1.05), or youth population (OR = 1.01; 95% CI: .98–1.05). Similarly, odds of diversion were not significantly associated with crime rates (OR = 1.00; 95% CI: .99–1.00), juvenile arrest rates (OR = .99; 95% CI: .97–1.02), ethnic heterogeneity (OR = .99; 95% CI: .83–1.18), or youth population (OR = 1.03; 95% CI: .99–1.08).

Finally, several aspects of political economy were significantly associated with diversion and petition outcomes. First, odds of diversion (versus dismissal) were approximately 2.5 times higher in courts where judges were elected rather than appointed (OR = 2.50; 95% CI: .93–6.76; $p = .07$). The lower bound of this confidence estimate (OR = .93), however, indicates that external polity may only be trivially associated with odds of diversion. Judicial elections were also not associated with odds of petition (OR = 1.32; 95% CI: .48–3.61). Second, odds of diversion were 2 percent lower in counties with a $1,000 higher median income (OR = .98; 95% CI: .96–1.00; $p = .03$). The upper bound of this confidence estimate (OR = 1.00), however, indicates that external economy may only be trivially associated with odds of diversion. Additionally, median income was not associated with odds of petition (OR = .98; 95% CI: .97–1.00). Third, odds of diversion were 1 percent higher in counties with a 1 percent greater conservative majority (OR = 1.01; 95% CI: 1.00–1.01; $p = .03$); similarly, odds of petition were 1 percent higher in counties with a 1 percent more conservatism (OR = 1.01; 95% CI: 1.00–1.01; $p = .01$). In both cases, however, the lower bounds of the confidence estimate (OR = 1.00) indicate that internal polity may only be trivially associated with odds of diversion and petition. Fourth, urbanism was not associated with odds of petition (OR = .99; 95% CI: .96–1.02) or diversion (OR = .98; 95% CI: .94–1.01).

In sum, there was limited evidence that petition outcomes varied according to community threats, social disorganization, or political economy in the surrounding court and community.

Waiver to Criminal Court

For the waiver decision, the sample consisted of 97,417 waiver-eligible petitioned juvenile offenders nested within 439 counties nested within 6 states. As noted in Chapter 5, judicial waiver is a rare event, with approximately 1 percent of eligible petitioned cases being waived to criminal court in 2000 (n = 956).

Community threats were not associated with waiver to criminal court. Specifically, odds of waiver were not associated with percent Black (OR = 1.00; 95% CI: .97–1.03), percent Hispanic (OR = 1.00; 95% CI: .96–1.03), concentrated disadvantage (OR = 1.27; 95% CI: .94–1.71), or income inequality (OR = 1.03; 95% CI: .83–1.29). For social disorganization, however, some indicators were associated with odds of waiver. Specifically, odds of waiver were 4 percent higher in counties with 1 percent higher juvenile arrest rates (OR = 1.04; 95% CI: 1.00–1.08; p = .03) and 6 percent lower in counties with 1 percent higher youth population density (OR = .94; 95% CI: .89–.99; p = .02). On the other hand, odds of waiver were not associated with crime rates (OR = 1.00; 95% CI: .99–1.00) or ethnic heterogeneity (OR = 1.00; 95% CI: .81–1.23). Finally, aspects of political economy were unrelated to variation in waiver outcomes. Specifically, odds of waiver were not associated with judicial elections (OR = .49; 95% CI: .12–2.08), median income (OR = .99; 95% CI: .97–1.01), conservatism (OR = 1.00; 95% CI: .99–1.01), or urbanism (OR = .98; 95% CI: .94–1.01).

In sum, there was little evidence that waiver outcomes varied according to community threats, social disorganization, or political economy in the surrounding court and community.

Adjudication of Delinquency

For the adjudication decision, the sample consisted of 109,743 petitioned juvenile offenders nested within 439 counties nested within six states. As noted in Chapter 5, approximately 72.5 percent were adjudicated delinquent in 2000 (n = 79,588).

The only community threats significantly associated with adjudication outcomes were some indicators of economic threat. Odds of adjudication were 32 percent higher in counties with one standard deviation higher concentrated disadvantage (OR = 1.32; 95% CI: 1.06–1.63; p = .01). Odds of adjudication were not associated with percent Black (OR = .99; 95% CI: .97–1.01), percent Hispanic (OR = 1.02; 95% CI: .99–1.04), or income inequality (OR = .93; 95% CI: .79–1.08), however.

For social disorganization, some indicators of crime were associated with adjudication outcomes. Specifically, odds of adjudication were 1 percent lower in counties with 1 percent higher crime rate (OR = .99; 95%

CI: .99–1.00; p = .02) and 3 percent higher in counties with 1 percent higher juvenile arrest rates (OR = 1.03; 95% CI: 1.00–1.05; p = .06). In each case, confidence bounds indicate that odds of adjudication may only be trivially associated with higher crime (OR = 1.00) and increased juvenile arrests (OR = 1.00), however. Further, odds of adjudication were not associated with ethnic heterogeneity (OR = 1.06; 95% CI: .91–1.24) or youth population (OR = 1.01; 95% CI: .97–1.04).

For political economy, adjudication outcomes were associated with internal polity but not with external polity, external economy, or internal economy. Specifically, odds of adjudication were 1 percent higher in counties with 1 percent greater conservative voting majority (OR = 1.01; 95% CI: 1.00–1.01; p = .02), while odds of adjudication were not associated with judicial elections (OR = 1.75; 95% CI: .56–5.43), median income (OR = .99; 95% CI: .98–1.01), or urbanism (OR = .99; 95% CI: .96–1.02). Notably, lower confidence bounds indicate that conservatism may only be trivially associated with odds of adjudication (OR = 1.00).

In sum, there was limited evidence that adjudication outcomes varied according to community threats, social disorganization, or political economy in the surrounding court and community.

Judicial Disposition

For judicial disposition, the sample consisted of 79,574 juveniles who were adjudicated delinquent, nested within 435 counties nested within 6 states. Disposition was treated as a categorical outcome with 3 possible outcomes; approximately 17.4 percent of delinquent cases received secure placement (n = 13,825), while 78.5 percent received community supervision (n = 62,447) and 4.2 percent were released (n = 3,301). Community supervision served as the reference category.

Turning to the contextual hypotheses, community threats were not significantly associated with judicial disposition. For racial threat, percent Black was not significantly associated with odds of placement (OR = 1.00; 95% CI: .99–1.02) or odds of release (OR = .97; 95% CI: .93–1.02). Similarly, for ethnic threat, percent Hispanic was not associated with odds of placement (OR = 1.00; 95% CI: .98–1.02) or odds of release (OR = 1.00; 95% CI: .97–1.13). For economic threat, concentrated disadvantage was not associated with odds of placement (OR = 1.01; 95% CI: .85–1.20) or odds of release (OR = 1.48; 95% CI: .85–2.56). Additionally, income inequality was not associated with odds of placement (OR = .94; 95% CI: .83–1.07) or odds of release (OR = .93; 95% CI: .65–1.32).

Several social disorganization indicators were significantly associated with placement outcomes, but not with judicial release. First, odds of placement were 1 percent higher in counties with a 1 percent higher crime rate (OR = 1.01; 95% CI: 1.00–1.01; p = .02), while odds of release were not associated with crime rates (OR = 1.00; 95% CI: .99–1.01). Second, odds of placement were 3 percent lower in counties with 1 percent higher juvenile arrests (OR = .97; 95% CI: .95–.99; p = .002), while odds of release were not associated with juvenile arrest rates (OR = .96; 95% CI: .89–1.04). Third, odds of placement were 3 percent higher in counties with a 1 percent larger youth population (OR = 1.03; 95% CI: 1.00–1.07; p = .02), while odds of release were not associated with youth population (OR = 1.05; 95% CI: .74–1.49). Confidence bounds indicate that odds of placement were at least 1 percent lower in counties with higher juvenile arrests (OR = .99), while the association between placement, on the one hand, and crime rates and youth population, on the other may only be trivial (OR = 1.00). Additionally, ethnic heterogeneity was not associated with odds of placement (OR = 1.06; 95% CI: .94–1.20) or odds of release (OR = 1.06; 95% CI: .95–1.18).

Finally, political economy factors were not significantly associated with judicial disposition. For external polity, judicial elections were not associated with odds of placement (OR = .93; 95% CI: .44–1.97) or odds of release (OR = .29; 95% CI: .04–2.32). For external economy, median income was not associated with odds of placement (OR = .99; 95% CI: .98–1.01) or odds of release (OR = .97; 95% CI: .94–1.01). For internal polity, conservative voting majority was not associated with odds of placement (OR = 1.00; 95% CI: 1.00–1.01) or odds of release (OR = 1.00; 95% CI: .98–1.02). Finally, for internal economy, urbanism was not associated with odds of placement (OR = .99; 95% CI: .97–1.01) or odds of release (OR = 1.00; 95% CI: .94–1.06).

In sum, there was limited evidence that judicial disposition outcomes varied according to community threats, social disorganization, or political economy in the surrounding court and community.

Summary of Findings

As with 2010, findings indicated that juvenile court outcomes in 2000 varied significantly across counties and states. Variance component models indicated that approximately 11–24 percent of the variation in these outcomes was attributable to county-level differences while 11–63 percent was attributable to state-level differences. As with the 2010 data, the most variation was observed at diversion and the least variation was observed for judicial placement.

To explore whether variation in juvenile processing and sanctions could be explained by contextual influences on the juvenile court, the present study tested whether community threat, social disorganization, and political economy were associated with odds of detention, petition and diversion, waiver, adjudication, and placement and release. As with the 2010 analyses, findings indicated limited support for the contextual hypotheses.

First, odds of detention were not associated with community threats, social disorganization, or political economy. Second, at the petition stage, odds of petition were positively associated with conservative voting majority (i.e. internal polity) but not with other indicators of political economy or with community threats or social disorganization factors. Odds of diversion were positively associated with judicial elections (i.e. external polity) and conservative voting majority (i.e. internal polity), and negatively associated with percent Black (i.e. racial threat) and median income (i.e. external economy). Notably, however, none of these associations were particularly robust in terms of confidence bounds.

Third, odds of waiver were positively associated with juvenile crime rates and negatively associated with youth population—both indicators of social disorganization—but not associated with community threats or political economy. Fourth, odds of adjudication were positively associated with concentrated disadvantage (i.e. economic threat), juvenile arrest rates (i.e. social disorganization), and conservatism (i.e. internal polity), and negatively associated with crime rates (i.e. social disorganization). The most robust of these findings involves economic threat, indicating high confidence that *concentrated disadvantage was positively associated with higher odds of adjudication.* Finally, at judicial disposition, odds of placement were positively associated with crime rates and youth population, and negatively associated with juvenile arrest rates—all indicators of social disorganization. Odds of release, however, were not associated with any contextual factors.

Chapter 8

State-Specific Results

County-Level Variation in Juvenile Justice Outcomes

We have seen that in the multistate samples, odds of juvenile court outcomes varied across counties. Is this equally true within individual states? Below, I report on the findings for each outcome, separately by state.

First, detention outcomes varied significantly across counties in each of the six states included in the state-specific analyses. In Alabama (N_1 = 30,293; N_2 = 65), the level-2 variance component (ψ^2) was 1.23 ($p < .001$), with corresponding intraclass correlation (ρ^2) of .27. In Missouri (N_1 = 40,580; N_2 = 111), ψ^2 = 1.06 ($p < .001$) with corresponding ρ^2 = .24. In Oregon (N_1 = 31,842; N_2 = 34), ψ^2 = .27 ($p < .001$) with corresponding ρ^2 = .08. In South Carolina (N_1 = 21,314; N_2 = 46), ψ^2 = .19 ($p < .001$) with corresponding ρ^2 = .06. In Texas (N_1 = 77,420; N_2 = 189), ψ^2 = .83 ($p < .001$) with corresponding ρ^2 = .20. In Utah, (N_1 = 33,015; N_2 = 22), ψ^2 = .10 ($p < .001$) with corresponding ρ^2 = .03. Overall, then, we observe that county-level variation in detention outcomes was highest in Alabama (27 percent) and lowest in Utah (3 percent).

Second, petition outcomes also varied significantly across counties in each of the six states. In Alabama (N_1 = 29,703; N_2 = 65), ψ^2 = 4.24 ($p < .001$) for diversion (ρ^2 = .56) and ψ^2 = 3.57 ($p < .001$) for petition (ρ^2 = .52). In Missouri (N_1 = 37,541; N_2 = 111), ψ^2 = 1.07 ($p < .001$) for diversion (ρ^2 = .25) and ψ^2 = 1.18 ($p < .001$) for petition (ρ^2 = .26). In Oregon (N_1 = 31,182; N_2 = 34), ψ^2 = .40 ($p < .001$) for diversion (ρ^2 = .11) and ψ^2 = .72 ($p < .001$) for petition (ρ^2 = .18). In South Carolina (N_1 = 21,129; N_2 = 46), ψ^2 = 1.02 ($p < .001$) for diversion (ρ^2 = .24) and ψ^2 = .53 ($p < .001$) for petition (ρ^2 = .14). In Texas (N_1 = 77,095; N_2 = 189), ψ^2 = 1.04 ($p < .001$) for diversion (ρ^2 = .24) and ψ^2 = .71 ($p < .001$) for petition (ρ^2 = .18). In Utah (N_1 = 33,006; N_2 = 22), ψ^2 = 1.26 ($p < .001$) for diversion (ρ^2 = .28) and ψ^2 = 1.04 ($p < .001$) for petition (ρ^2 = .24). Overall, then, we observe that county-level variation for diversion outcomes was highest in Alabama (56 percent) and lowest in Oregon (11 percent), while county-level variation in petition outcomes was highest in Alabama (52 percent) and lowest in South Carolina (14 percent).

Third, waiver outcomes also varied significantly across counties in each of the four states. In Alabama (N_1 = 15,356; N_2 = 65), the level-2 variance component (ψ^2) was 2.89 ($p < .001$), with corresponding intraclass correlation (ρ^2) of .47. In Missouri (N_1 = 7,195; N_2 = 105), $\psi^2 = .73$ ($p = .002$) with corresponding $\rho^2 = .18$. In Oregon (N_1 = 5,483; N_2 = 34), $\psi^2 = 1.07$ ($p < .001$) with corresponding $\rho^2 = .25$. In Texas (N_1 = 24,351; N_2 = 186), $\psi^2 = 1.15$ ($p < .001$) with corresponding $\rho^2 = .26$. Overall, then, we observe that county-level variation in waiver outcomes was highest in Alabama (47 percent) and lowest in Missouri (18 percent).

Fourth, adjudication outcomes also varied significantly across counties in each of the six states. In Alabama (N_1 = 17,327; N_2 = 65), the level-2 variance component (ψ^2) was 1.58 ($p < .001$), with corresponding intraclass correlation (ρ^2) of .32. In Missouri (N_1 = 7,534; N_2 = 105), $\psi^2 = .97$ ($p < .001$) with corresponding $\rho^2 = .23$. In Oregon (N_1 = 7,197; N_2 = 34), $\psi^2 = .81$ ($p < .001$) with corresponding $\rho^2 = .20$. In South Carolina (N_1 = 8,377; N_2 = 46), $\psi^2 = 1.20$ ($p < .001$) with corresponding $\rho^2 = .27$. In Texas (N_1 = 23,870; N_2 = 185), $\psi^2 = 1.76$ ($p < .001$) with corresponding $\rho^2 = .35$. In Utah, (N_1 = 22,824; N_2 = 22), $\psi^2 = .19$ ($p < .001$) with corresponding $\rho^2 = .06$. Overall, then, we observe that county-level variation in adjudication outcomes was highest in Texas (35 percent) and lowest in Utah (6 percent).

Fifth, judicial disposition outcomes also varied significantly across counties in each of the six states. In Alabama (N_1 = 7,648; N_2 = 65), $\psi^2 = 2.61$ ($p < .001$) for judicial release ($\rho^2 = .44$) and $\psi^2 = 1.92$ ($p < .001$) for placement ($\rho^2 = .37$). In Missouri (N_1 = 6,471; N_2 = 105), $\psi^2 = 2.81$ ($p < .001$) for judicial release ($\rho^2 = .46$) and $\psi^2 = .50$ ($p < .001$) for placement ($\rho^2 = .13$). In Oregon (N_1 = 6,089; N_2 = 34), $\psi^2 = .32$ ($p < .001$) for judicial release ($\rho^2 = .09$) and $\psi^2 = .34$ ($p < .001$) for placement ($\rho^2 = .09$). In South Carolina (N_1 = 7,809; N_2 = 46), $\psi^2 = 1.33$ ($p < .001$) for judicial release ($\rho^2 = .29$) and $\psi^2 = .28$ ($p < .001$) for placement ($\rho^2 = .08$). In Texas (N_1 = 17,867; N_2 = 182), $\psi^2 = 1.42$ ($p < .001$) for judicial release ($\rho^2 = .30$) and $\psi^2 = .32$ ($p < .001$) for placement ($\rho^2 = .09$). In Utah (N_1 = 17,058; N_2 = 22), $\psi^2 = .20$ ($p < .001$) for judicial release ($\rho^2 = .06$) and $\psi^2 = .08$ ($p < .001$) for placement ($\rho^2 = .02$). Overall, we observe that county-level variation in judicial release outcomes was highest in Missouri (46 percent) and lowest in Utah (6 percent), while county-level variation in placement was highest in Alabama (37 percent) and lowest in Utah (3 percent).

Findings from variance component models thus indicate significant variation in juvenile court outcomes across counties within all states, although this variation was not uniform. Across outcomes, we see the most county-level variation in Alabama, ranging from 27 percent variation in detention outcomes to 52 percent variation in petition and 56 percent variation in diversion outcomes. Alternatively, we observe the least county-level variation in Utah, ranging from 3 percent variation in detention and judicial placement outcomes (as well as 5 percent variation in adjudication outcomes) to 28 percent variation in diversion outcomes.

Contextual Effects

In what follows, this chapter reports on the findings from two-level hierarchical regression models testing the contextual research hypotheses for each state. Fewer contextual variables were included in the models compared to the full, multistate models reported in Chapter 6. These contextual factors varied considerably across states (see Appendix C).

For community threats, first, average percent Black at the county level ranged from .8 percent in Utah to 36.9 percent in South Carolina. Second, average percent Hispanic ranged from 2.4 percent in Missouri to 31.2 percent in Texas. Third, concentrated disadvantage at the county level was re-standardized for each state model. Prior to standardization, however, the mean county disadvantage raw score was highest in South Carolina (1.47) and lowest in Utah (-1.54). Fourth, income inequality was highest in Alabama and South Carolina (.46), and lowest in Utah (.40).

For social disorganization, first, average county crimes rates (per 1,000 persons) ranged from 23.5 in Utah to 44.2 in South Carolina. Second, average county juvenile arrest rates (per 1,000 persons) ranged from 1.5 in Alabama to 7.7 in Utah. Third, average county ethnic heterogeneity ranged from .15 in Missouri to .48 in South Carolina. Fourth, average residential mobility at the county level, measured as percent moved, ranged from 12.8 percent in Connecticut to 17.5 percent in Oregon. Fifth, average county youth population ranged from 22 percent in Oregon to 31.9 percent in Utah.

For political economy, first, median income (i.e. external economy) at the county level ranged from $36,970 in Alabama to $68,940 in Connecticut. Second, average conservative voting majority (i.e. internal polity) at the county level ranged from a 4.5 percent minority in South Carolina to a 61 percent majority in Utah. Third, average county population density (i.e. internal economy), measured as persons per square mile, ranged from 92 in Alabama to 723 in Connecticut.

Detention

Preadjudication detention varied considerably across states (see Appendix A). In 2010, the proportion of referrals that were detained by state was as follows: 41.6 percent in Texas (n = 32,239), 19.6 percent in Utah (n = 6,466), 18.1 percent in South Carolina (n = 3,853), 13 percent in Alabama (n = 3,934), 13 percent in Connecticut (n = 1,591), 11.5 percent in Missouri (n = 4,670), and 11.1 percent in Oregon. Table 8.1 reports the state-level findings for detention.

Community Threat

For community threat models, there was no evidence that percent Black (i.e. racial threat) or income inequality (i.e. inequality threat) was associated with detention in any state, while there was evidence that percent Hispanic (i.e. ethnic threat) was positively associated with detention in Missouri and Oregon, and evidence that concentrated disadvantage (i.e. economic threat) was positively associated with detention in Missouri.

First, percent Black was not significantly associated with odds of detention in any state, although the association approached significance for two states. Specifically, in counties with a 1 percent larger Black population, odds of detention were 4 percent lower in Missouri (OR = .96; 95% CI: .91–1.01; p = .09) and 5 percent higher in Texas (OR = 1.05; 95% CI: .99–1.11; p = .08). Second, percent Hispanic was positively associated with odds of detention in Missouri and Oregon, but not other states. Specifically, in counties with a 1 percent larger Hispanic population, odds of detention were 22 percent higher in Missouri (OR = 1.22; 95% CI: 1.04–1.44; p = .02), and the relationship appears curvilinear (OR = .99; 95% CI: .98–.99; $p < .001$), and odds of detention were 12 percent higher in Oregon (OR = 1.12; 95% CI: 1.01–1.23; p = .03), also curvilinear (OR = 1.00; 95% CI: .99–1.00; p = .01). Third, concentrated disadvantage was positively associated with odds of detention in Missouri, but not in other states. Specifically, odds of detention were 42 percent higher in counties with one standard deviation higher concentrated disadvantage (OR = 1.42; 95% CI: 1.14–1.77; p = .002). Fourth, income inequality was not associated with odds of detention in any state.

Social Disorganization

There was evidence that detention outcomes were positively associated with crime rates in Missouri, negatively associated with juvenile arrest rates in Missouri while positively associated with juvenile arrest rates in Oregon, and negatively associated with youth population density in Oregon. Ethnic heterogeneity and residential mobility were not associated with detention outcomes in any state, although negative associations between odds of detention and ethnic heterogeneity approached significance in Alabama and Missouri.

Table 8.1 State-level analyses, detention

Fixed effects	*AL*[a]	*MO*[b]	*OR*[c]	*SC*[d]	*TX*[e]	*UT*[f]
	OR (95% CI)	*OR (95% CI)*	*OR (95% CI)*	*OR (95% CI)*	*OR (95% CI)*	*OR (95% CI)*
Intercept	.12*** (.09, .15)	.08*** (.05, .11)	.09*** (.07, .11)	.14*** (.11, .19)	.43 (.36, .51)	.09*** (.07, .11)
***Level-1* variables**						
Black[g]	1.21** (1.07, 1.38)	1.86*** (1.39, 2.49)	1.49*** (1.25, 1.77)	1.31*** (1.15, 1.48)	1.31*** (1.16, 1.49)	1.63*** (1.43, 1.87)
Hispanic[g]	1.12 (.87, 1.46)	1.04 (.71, 1.54)	1.20*** (1.09, 1.33)	1.55*** (1.10, 2.17)	1.20*** (1.10, 1.31)	1.25*** (1.16, 1.33)
Other race/ethnicity[g]	1.23 (.91, 1.66)	1.27 (.83, 1.95)	.97 (.77, 1.24)	1.56* (1.00, 2.43)	1.06 (.88, 1.27)	1.07 (.95, 1.21)
Male	1.60*** (1.33, 1.92)	1.59*** (1.25, 2.02)	1.65*** (1.49, 1.82)	1.48*** (1.28, 1.70)	1.26*** (1.16, 1.36)	1.68*** (1.47, 1.91)
Age	1.11*** (1.08, 1.15)	1.24*** (1.21, 1.28)	1.18*** (1.15, 1.21)	1.16*** (1.11, 1.22)	1.07*** (1.04, 1.10)	1.01 (.98, 1.05)
Violent offense[h]	2.08*** (1.70, 2.53)	1.12 (.87, 1.43)	3.11*** (2.54, 3.82)	1.04 (.85, 1.28)	2.34*** (2.07, 2.64)	2.26*** (2.03, 2.51)
Drug/alcohol offense[h]	1.10 (.80, 1.51)	.72** (.56, .92)	.44 (.37, .52)	1.91*** (1.16, 3.13)	.99 (.86, 1.13)	1.25** (1.09, 1.44)
Weapon offense[h]	2.08*** (1.46, 2.97)	2.66*** (1.70, 4.16)	4.22*** (2.99, 5.96)	.76† (.56, 1.02)	2.44*** (1.96, 3.03)	1.58† (.99, 2.53)
Probation violation[h]	1.99*** (1.38, 2.86)	8.79*** (4.51, 17.13)	26.17** (2.96, 231.29)	1.91* (1.16, 3.13)	4.74*** (3.01, 7.47)	6.22*** (4.74, 8.17)
Status offense[h]	.06*** (.03, .10)	.42*** (.32, .56)	.50*** (.40, .62)	.82 (.58, 1.16)	.21*** (.14, .31)	.52** (.34, .81)
Other offense[h]	.54*** (.43, .68)	.90 (.60, 1.35)	1.14 (.92, 1.42)	.63*** (.51, .78)	.87 (.59, 1.28)	1.62*** (1.39, 1.88)
***Level-2* variables**						
Community threat model						
Percent Black	.98 (.95, 1.01)	.96† (.91, 1.01)	.87 (.48, 1.58)	1.00 (.96, 1.04)	1.05† (.99, 1.11)	.38 (.03, 4.82)
Percent Black (squared)	1.00 (1.00, 1.00)	1.00 (1.00, 1.00)	.99 (.92, 1.07)	1.00 (1.00, 1.00)	1.00 (1.00, 1.00)	1.92 (.56, 6.61)
Percent Hispanic	1.01 (.77, 1.32)	1.22* (1.04, 1.44)	1.12* (1.01, 1.23)	.96 (.80, 1.17)	.99 (.97, 1.01)	1.23 (.83, 1.82)
Percent Hispanic (squared)	1.00 (.98, 1.02)	.99*** (.98, .99)	1.00* (.99, 1.00)	1.00 (.99, 1.02)	1.00 (1.00, 1.00)	.99 (.97, 1.01)
Concentrated disadvantage (CD)[i]	.86 (.47, 1.55)	1.42** (1.14, 1.77)	.96 (.79, 1.18)	.92 (.71, 1.18)	.87 (.69, 1.09)	1.05 (.88, 1.26)
Gini index (0–1)[i]	.88 (.68, 1.14)	1.07 (.84, 1.36)	1.08 (.82, 1.43)	1.09 (.92, 1.29)	1.12 (.98, 1.29)	.99 (.82, 1.19)

Social disorganization model						
Crime rate (per 1,000)	1.00 (.98, 1.02)	1.03*** (1.01, 1.05)	.99 (.96, 1.01)	1.00 (.99, 1.05)	1.00 (.99, 1.01)	.99 (.98, 1.01)
Juvenile crime rate (per 1,000)	1.08 (.88, 1.34)	.92* (.87, .98)	1.08** (1.02, 1.14)	.97 (.91, 1.05)	1.03 (.96, 1.10)	1.03 (.96, 1.10)
Ethnic heterogeneity (0–1)[i]	.81† (.64, 1.03)	.83† (.68, 1.03)	1.13 (.82, 1.56)	.99 (.87, 1.12)	1.00 (.87, 1.16)	.92 (.80, 1.05)
Residential mobility (% moved)	1.04 (.99, 1.10)	1.00 (.95, 1.06)	1.03 (.98, 1.08)	1.02 (.98, 1.06)	1.01 (.99, 1.04)	1.02 (.98, 1.06)
Youth population density (%)	.97 (.87, 1.08)	1.08 (.97, 1.19)	.89* (.80, .98)	1.02 (.96, 1.09)	.98 (.95, 1.02)	.98 (.91, 1.06)
Political economy model						
Median income (×1,000)	1.04*** (1.03, 1.04)	.98† (.95, 1.00)	.99 (.96, 1.02)	.99 (.96, 1.02)	1.02* (1.00, 1.03)	.99 (.98, 1.00)
Conservative voting majority	1.00* (1.00, 1.01)	1.00 (.99, 1.02)	.99* (.98, 1.00)	1.00 (.99, 1.01)	.99* (.99, 1.00)	1.01† (1.00, 1.02)
Population density (per sq/mi) (×100)	.68*** (.65, .70)	1.01 (.98, 1.04)	.92*** (.89, .96)	1.09 (.94, 1.27)	.98 (.95, 1.01)	1.03* (1.00, 1.05)
Random effects						
Random intercept variance component	1.41*** (1.19)	1.03*** (1.01)	.30*** (.55)	.23*** (.47)	.91*** (.95)	.20*** (.44)
Intraclass correlation (ρ)	.30	.24	.08	.07	.22	.06

Note: Estimates for three separate models presented: community threat, social disorganization, and political economy. Coefficients for case-level variables are based on the community threat model.

a N_I = 30,293; N_2 = 65.
b $N_{I =}$ 40,580; N_2 = 111.
c N_I = 31,842; N_2 = 34.
d N_I = 21,314; N_2 = 46.
e N_I = 77,420; N_2 = 189.
f N_I = 33,015; N_2 = 22.
g Reference: White.
h Reference: Property offense.
i Standardized.
† p <.10; * p <.05; ** p <.01; *** p <.001 (two tailed).

First, crime rates were positively associated with odds of detention in Missouri. Specifically, odds of detention were 3 percent higher in counties with 1 percent higher crime rates (OR = 1.03; 95% CI: 1.01–1.05; $p < .001$). Second, juvenile arrest rates were positively associated with odds of detention in Oregon and negatively associated with odds of detention in Missouri. Specifically, in counties with 1 percent higher juvenile arrest rate, odds of detention were 8 percent higher in Oregon (OR = 1.08; 95% CI: 1.02–1.14; $p = .01$) and 8 percent lower in Missouri (OR = .92; 95% CI: .87–.98; $p = .01$). Third, ethnic heterogeneity was not significantly associated with odds of detention in any state, although negative associations approached significance for Alabama and Missouri. Specifically, in counties with one standard deviation higher heterogeneity, odds of detention were 19 percent lower in Alabama (OR = .81; 95% CI: .64–1.03; $p = .08$), and 17 percent lower in Missouri (OR = .83; 95% CI: .68–1.03; $p = .08$). Fourth, residential mobility was not associated with odds of detention in any state. Fifth, youth population density was negatively associated with odds of detention in Oregon. Specifically, odds of detention were 11 percent lower in counties with 1 percent higher youth population (OR = .89; 95% CI: .80–.98; $p = .02$).

Political Economy

For political economy models, there was evidence that detention outcomes were positively associated with median income (i.e. external economy) in Alabama and Texas, positively associated with conservatism (i.e. internal polity) in Alabama while negatively associated with conservatism in Oregon and Texas, and positively associated with urbanism (i.e. internal economy) in Utah while negatively associated with urbanism in Alabama and Oregon.

First, median income was positively associated with odds of detention in Alabama and Texas, while a negative association approached significance in Missouri. Specifically, in counties with $1,000 higher median income, odds of detention were 4 percent higher in Alabama (OR = 1.04; 95% CI: 1.03–1.04; $p < .001$), 2 percent higher in Texas (OR = 1.02; 95% CI: 1.00–1.03; $p = .02$), and 2 percent lower in Missouri (OR = .98; 95% CI: .95–1.00; $p = .06$). Second, conservatism was positively associated with odds of detention in Alabama while negatively associated with odds of detention in Oregon and Texas, and a positive association approached significance in Utah. Specifically, in counties with a 1 percent larger conservative majority, odds of detention were less than 1 percent higher in Alabama (OR = 1.00; 95% CI: 1.00–1.01; $p = .047$), 1 percent higher in Utah (OR = 1.01; 95% CI: 1.00–1.02; $p = .095$), 1 percent lower in Oregon (OR = .99; 95% CI: .98–1.00; $p = .02$), and 1 percent lower in Texas (OR = .99; 95% CI: .99–1.00;

p = .04). Third, urbanism was positively associated with odds of detention in Utah while negatively associated with odds of detention in Alabama and Oregon. Specifically, in counties with an additional 100 persons per square mile, odds of detention were 32 percent lower in Alabama (OR = .68; 95% CI: .65–.70; $p < .001$), 8 percent lower in Oregon (OR = .92; 95% CI: .89–.96; $p < .001$), and 3 percent higher in Utah (OR = 1.03; 95% CI: 1.00–1.05; p = .03).

Petition of Delinquency

Early processing decisions also varied considerably across states (see Appendix A). In 2010, the proportion of referrals that received diversion to informal processing was as follows: 62.3 percent in Missouri (n = 23,371), 44.8 percent in Texas (n = 34,569), 31.4 percent in South Carolina (n = 6,634), 29.7 percent in Oregon (n = 9,253), 29.1 percent in Utah (n = 9,606), 13.6 percent in Alabama (n = 4,047), and 12.2 percent in Connecticut (n = 1,491). In 2010, the proportion of referrals that were formally petitioned, by state, was as follows: 69.2 percent in Utah (n = 22,833), 59.3 percent in Alabama (n = 17,067), 54.9 percent in Connecticut (n = 6,735), 41.3 percent in South Carolina (n = 8,722), 37.6 percent in Texas (n = 28,970), 23.6 percent in Oregon (n = 7,372), and 20.4 percent in Missouri (n = 7,638). Table 8.2 reports the state-level findings for petition.

Community Threat

For community threat models, there was no evidence that percent Hispanic or income inequality was associated with petition outcomes in any state, while there was evidence that percent Black was positively associated with petition in Texas, and evidence that concentrated disadvantage was positively associated with odds of diversion in Missouri.

First, percent Black was significantly associated with odds of petition in Texas and not associated with odds of diversion in any state. Specifically, in counties with a 1 percent larger Black population, odds of petition were 8 percent higher in Texas (OR = 1.08; 95% CI: 1.01–1.15; p = .02). Second, percent Hispanic was not associated with odds of petition or diversion in any state. Third, concentrated disadvantage was positively associated with odds of diversion in Missouri, while a negative association approached significance in Oregon. Specifically, in counties with one standard deviation higher concentrated disadvantage, odds of diversion were 35 percent higher in Missouri (OR = 1.35; 95% CI: 1.10–1.65; p = .004) and 22 percent lower in Oregon (OR = .78; 95% CI: .60–1.01; p = .06). Fourth, income inequality was not associated with odds of petition or diversion in any state.

Table 8.2 State-level analyses, petition of delinquency

	AL[a]	*MO*[b]	*OR*[c]	*SC*[d]	*TX*[e]	*UT*[f]
Diversion[g]						
Fixed effects	OR (95% CI)	OR (95% CI)	OR (95% CI)	OR (95% CI)	OR (95% CI)	OR (95% CI)
Intercept	1.03 (.52, 2.06)	12.96*** (9.05, 18.56)	1.72*** (1.33, 2.22)	2.58*** (1.85, 3.60)	8.83*** (5.57, 14.01)	31.69*** (16.8, 59.8)
Level-1 variables						
Black[h]	.93 (.74, 1.17)	.64*** (.56, .74)	.88† (.75, 1.02)	.76*** (.66, .87)	.75*** (.66, .87)	.43*** (.29, .64)
Hispanic[h]	1.01 (.70, 1.47)	1.27† (.99, 1.63)	1.19*** (1.08, 1.30)	.91 (.69, 1.20)	.90 (.79, 1.04)	1.01 (.81, 1.24)
Other race/ ethnicity[h]	1.40 (.71, 2.77)	.97 (.68, 1.40)	.87* (.76, 1.00)	.97 (.72, 1.31)	1.04 (.83, 1.30)	1.01 (.73, 1.39)
Male	.82** (.71, .94)	.78*** (.71, .86)	.91** (.85, .98)	.67*** (.60, .75)	.66*** (.61, .72)	.79* (.65, .95)
Age	1.03 (.99, 1.07)	.91*** (.87, .96)	1.00 (.98, 1.02)	.91*** (.87, .94)	.87*** (.83, .91)	1.06* (1.01, 1.11)
Violent offense[i]	.55*** (.41, .75)	.54*** (.43, .69)	.63*** (.57, .69)	.64*** (.53, .79)	.39*** (.25, .62)	.51*** (.36, .71)
Drug/alcohol offense[i]	1.73* (1.11, 2.71)	.89 (.48, 1.65)	1.33*** (1.22, 1.44)	1.39*** (1.14, 1.69)	1.33** (1.08, 1.63)	3.24*** (1.83, 5.73)
Weapon offense[i]	.52 (.14, 1.96)	.39*** (.23, .64)	.82 (.57, 1.18)	1.17 (.82, 1.67)	.70 (.43, 1.13)	.33*** (.18, .59)
Probation violation[i]	.15* (.02, .97)	.23*** (.09, .56)	–	.15** (.04, .51)	.61 (.32, 1.14)	–
Status offense[i]	.30** (.13, .66)	.91 (.50, 1.68)	.02*** (.01, .02)	.11*** (.07, .19)	.83 (.24, 2.79)	.28*** (.22, .37)
Other offense[i]	.85 (.57, 1.26)	1.19 (.82, 1.72)	.53*** (.47, .59)	.68** (.53, .87)	.65 (.29, 1.45)	.39*** (.32, .48)
Detention	.63† (.37, 1.05)	1.36 (.73, 2.53)	.48*** (.40, .58)	.13*** (.08, .23)	.39*** (.30, .52)	.22*** (.10, .48)
Level-2 variables						
Community threat model						
Percent Black	1.00 (.93, 1.08)	.99 (.93, 1.05)	1.88 (.65, 5.49)	1.04 (.95, 1.15)	1.00 (.93, 1.07)	.02 (0, 177.8)
Percent Black (squared)	1.00 (1.00, 1.00)	1.00† (1.00, 1.00)	.89† (.77, 1.02)	1.00 (1.00, 1.00)	1.00 (1.00, 1.00)	11.10 (.12, 1039)
Percent Hispanic	.95 (.45, 1.99)	.96 (.78, 1.19)	.94 (.81, 1.10)	1.03 (.70, 1.51)	1.00 (.97, 1.03)	1.35 (.29, 6.38)
Percent Hispanic (squared)	.98 (.93, 1.04)	.99 (.98, 1.01)	1.00 (1.00, 1.01)	1.00 (.98, 1.03)	1.00 (1.00, 1.00)	.98 (.90, 1.06)
Concentrated disadvantage (CD)[j]	1.26 (.33, 4.82)	1.35** (1.10, 1.65)	.78† (.60, 1.01)	.74 (.48, 1.14)	1.36 (.93, 2.00)	.96 (.48, 1.91)
Gini index (0–1)[j]	1.73 (.83, 3.58)	.91 (.75, 1.12)	.90 (.67, 1.21)	.76 (.49, 1.16)	.89 (.73, 1.09)	1.15 (.58, 2.32)

Social disorganization model						
Crime rate (per 1,000)	1.02 (.97, 2.25)	.99 (.98, 1.00)	.95** (.92, .99)	.97** (.95, .99)	1.02* (1.00, 1.03)	1.03 (.95, 1.12)
Juvenile crime rate (per 1,000)	1.20 (.64, 2.25)	1.11** (1.04, 1.19)	1.05 (.95, 1.15)	1.03 (.89, 1.19)	1.02 (.96, 1.09)	.96 (.75, 1.23)
Ethnic heterogeneity (0–1)[j]	1.17 (.67, 2.05)	.65** (.50, .85)	1.12 (.75, 1.67)	1.58** (1.13, 2.19)	.96 (.79, 1.17)	1.23 (.60, 2.51)
Residential mobility (% moved)	.88† (.77, 1.00)	1.01 (.97, 1.06)	1.02 (.94, 1.11)	1.03 (.97, 1.08)	.99 (.96, 1.03)	1.00 (.84, 1.19)
Youth population density (%)	.63* (.42, .95)	1.01 (.91, 1.12)	1.05 (.92, 1.20)	.91 (.79, 1.05)	.96 (.91, 1.02)	1.08 (.85, 1.37)
Political economy model						
Median income (×1,000)	.93 (.84, 1.03)	.99 (.97, 1.01)	1.07** (1.02, 1.11)	1.01 (.93, 1.09)	.99 (.97, 1.02)	1.02 (.96, 1.09)
Conservative voting majority	1.00 (.98, 1.03)	.98* (.97, 1.00)	1.01 (.99, 1.02)	1.00 (.98, 1.02)	1.01 (1.00, 1.02)	.99 (.96, 1.03)
Population density (per sq/mi) (×100)	1.06 (.57, 1.96)	.93*** (.90, .95)	.89* (.81, .98)	1.05 (.76, 1.46)	1.01 (.96, 1.06)	1.06 (.89, 1.26)
Random effects						
Random intercept variance component	3.86*** (1.97)	.90*** (.95)	.43*** (.65)	1.02*** (1.01)	1.23*** (1.11)	1.48*** (1.22)
Intraclass correlation (ρ)	.54	.22	.12	.24	.27	.31
Formal petition[g]						
Fixed effects						
Intercept	23.63*** (13.19, 42.4)	1.07 (.74, 1.55)	.91 (.67, 1.24)	1.05 (.83, 1.34)	2.02 (1.57, 2.60)	40.78*** (22.5, 73.8)
Level-1 variables						
Black[h]	.97 (.86, 1.09)	1.12 (.93, 1.35)	1.46*** (1.26, 1.71)	.95 (.87, 1.04)	1.03 (.95, 1.11)	.65* (.44, .96)
Hispanic[h]	.96 (.79, 1.18)	1.63** (1.16, 2.28)	1.37*** (1.24, 1.52)	1.10 (.84, 1.43)	1.19*** (1.11, 1.27)	1.30* (1.05, 1.60)
Other race/ ethnicity[h]	.88 (.58, 1.32)	.99 (.46, 2.13)	.79*** (.68, .91)	1.12 (.81, 1.53)	.98 (.78, 1.23)	1.27 (.92, 1.76)

(continued)

Table 8.2 Cont.

	AL[a]	*MO*[b]	*OR*[c]	*SC*[d]	*TX*[e]	*UT*[f]
Male	1.21** (1.07, 1.36)	1.14† (.98, 1.34)	1.50*** (1.39, 1.63)	1.31*** (1.17, 1.46)	1.31*** (1.19, 1.44)	1.28** (1.07, 1.54)
Age	1.13*** (1.08, 1.19)	.98 (.91, 1.05)	1.17*** (1.14, 1.19)	1.05† (1.00, 1.10)	.94† (.89, 1.00)	1.24*** (1.18, 1.30)
Violent offense[i]	.60*** (.46, .78)	.55*** (.45, .66)	1.03 (.92, 1.14)	.69*** (.58, .82)	.69*** (.60, .81)	.74† (.53, 1.03)
Drug/alcohol offense[i]	1.48† (.98, 2.25)	.85 (.50, 1.44)	1.38*** (1.26, 1.51)	.86 (.70, 1.05)	1.16 (.96, 1.39)	7.13*** (4.04, 12.58)
Weapon offense[i]	1.45 (.72, 2.92)	.80 (.41, 1.58)	1.88*** (1.36, 2.61)	1.30† (.99, 1.70)	1.30* (1.03, 1.64)	.37*** (.21, .66)
Probation violation[i]	1.99* (1.18, 3.34)	8.18*** (2.80, 23.91)	–	3.87*** (2.58, 5.79)	.64*** (.48, .84)	–
Status offense[i]	.07*** (.04, .14)	1.22 (.60, 2.48)	.02*** (.02, .02)	1.62*** (1.23, 2.12)	.19* (.05, .69)	.24*** (.19, .32)
Other offense[i]	.52*** (.39, .71)	.99 (.58, 1.70)	.72*** (.63, .81)	.76* (.61, .95)	.45** (.27, .75)	.43*** (.35, .53)
Detention	4.32*** (2.96, 6.31)	34.64*** (16.24, 73.9)	10.49*** (9.32, 11.82)	2.50*** (2.06, 3.04)	1.36*** (1.17, 1.58)	25.41*** (12.62, 51.2)
Level-2 variables						
Community threat model						
Percent Black	1.06 (.97, 1.15)	1.04 (.96, 1.12)	.39 (.11, 1.44)	1.02 (.95, 1.08)	1.08* (1.01, 1.15)	.00 (0, 14.4)
Percent Black (squared)	1.00 (1.00, 1.00)	1.00† (1.00, 1.00)	1.07 (.91, 1.27)	1.00 (1.00, 1.00)	1.00† (1.00, 1.00)	22.06 (.33, 1487)
Percent Hispanic	.64 (.33, 1.23)	.96 (.75, 1.23)	.94 (.78, 1.13)	1.01 (.73, 1.39)	1.01 (.98, 1.03)	1.69 (.40, 7.18)
Percent Hispanic (squared)	1.03 (.99, 1.08)	1.00 (.98, 1.01)	1.00 (1.00, 1.01)	1.00 (.98, 1.02)	1.00 (1.00, 1.00)	.97 (.90, 1.04)
Concentrated disadvantage (CD)[j]	.67 (.15, 2.94)	1.13 (.85, 1.50)	.97 (.71, 1.33)	.84 (.51, 1.39)	.90 (.66, 1.23)	1.15 (.61, 2.19)
Gini index (0–1)[j]	1.38 (.71, 2.69)	.88 (.69, 1.12)	.98 (.69, 1.40)	.88 (.65, 1.18)	.96 (.83, 1.10)	1.25 (.65, 2.38)
Social disorganization model						
Crime rate (per 1,000)	.99 (.95, 1.04)	.98† (.96, 1.00)	.92*** (.89, .96)	.99 (.97, 1.01)	1.01* (1.00, 1.02)	1.00 (.93, 1.08)
Juvenile crime rate (per 1,000)	1.01 (.56, 1.82)	1.17*** (1.08, 1.27)	1.08 (.98, 1.19)	.94 (.83, 1.08)	1.01 (.95, 1.06)	1.02 (.81, 1.28)
Ethnic heterogeneity (0–1)[j]	1.53† (.98, 2.37)	.84 (.60, 1.18)	1.21 (.80, 1.85)	1.21 (.96, 1.52)	1.13† (.98, 1.29)	1.41 (.72, 2.73)

Residential mobility (% moved)	.98 (.85, 1.14)	.99 (.94, 1.03)	1.05 (.96, 1.14)	1.01 (.96, 1.07)	1.00 (.97, 1.03)	.96 (.82, 1.13)
Youth population density (%)	.71* (.53, .96)	1.03 (.92, 1.14)	.92 (.81, 1.06)	.90* (.83, .99)	.98 (.94, 1.02)	1.01 (.81, 1.26)
Political economy model						
Median income (×1,000)	.95 (.87, 1.05)	1.01 (.99, 1.04)	1.00 (.95, 1.05)	.99 (.95, 1.03)	1.00 (.99, 1.02)	1.00 (.94, 1.07)
Conservative voting majority	1.00 (.98, 1.02)	.99 (.97, 1.01)	1.01 (1.00, 1.03)	1.00 (.99, 1.02)	1.00 (1.00, 1.01)	.99 (.95, 1.03)
Population density (per sq/mi) (×100)	1.07 (.40, 2.88)	.95*** (.92, .98)	.89* (.80, 1.00)	1.12 (.90, 1.40)	1.01 (.99, 1.03)	1.02 (.86, 1.19)
Random effects						
Random intercept variance component	3.58*** (1.89)	1.30*** (1.14)	.65*** (.81)	.58*** (.76)	.76*** (.87)	1.24*** (.11)
Intraclass correlation (ρ)	.52	.28	.17	.15	.19	.27

Note: Estimates for three separate models presented: community threat, social disorganization, and political economy. Coefficients for case-level variables are based on the community threat model.

a N_1 = 29,703; N_2 = 65.
b N_1 = 37,541; N_2 = 111.
c N_1 = 31,182; N_2 = 34.
d N_1 = 21,129; N_2 = 46.
e N_1 = 77,095; N_2 = 189.
f N_1 = 33,006; N_2 = 22.
g Reference: Dismissal.
h Reference: White.
i Reference: Property offense.
j Standardized.
† p <.10; * p <.05; ** p <.01; *** p <.001 (two tailed).

Social Disorganization

For social disorganization models, there was evidence that petition outcomes were positively associated with crime rates in Texas while negatively associated with crime rates in Oregon, positively associated with juvenile arrest rates in Missouri, and negatively associated with youth population density in Alabama and South Carolina. Ethnic heterogeneity and residential mobility were not associated with petition outcomes in any state, although positive associations between odds of petition and ethnic heterogeneity approached significance in Alabama and Texas. Additionally, there was evidence that diversion outcomes were positively associated with crime rates in Texas while negatively associated with crime rates in Oregon and South Carolina, positively associated with juvenile arrest rates in Missouri, positively associated with ethnic heterogeneity in South Carolina while negatively associated with ethnic heterogeneity in Missouri, and negatively associated with youth population density in Alabama. Residential mobility was not associated with diversion outcomes in any state, although a negative association approached significance in Alabama.

First, crime rates were positively associated with odds of petition in Texas and negatively associated with odds of petition in Oregon, while a negative association approached significance in Missouri. Crime rates were also positively associated with odds of diversion in Texas and negatively associated with odds of diversion in Oregon and South Carolina. Specifically, in counties with 1 percent higher crime rates, odds of petition were 1 percent higher in Texas (OR = 1.01; 95% CI: 1.00–1.02; p = .04), 8 percent lower in Oregon (OR = .92; 95% CI: .89–.96; p <.001), and 2 percent lower in Missouri (OR = .98; 95% CI: .96–1.00; p = .06). In counties with 1 percent higher crime rates, odds of diversion were 2 percent higher in Texas (OR = 1.02; 95% CI: 1.00–1.03; p = .03), 5 percent lower in Oregon (OR = .95; 95% CI: .92–.99; p = .01), and 3 percent lower in South Carolina (OR = .97; 95% CI: .95–.99; p = .01).

Second, juvenile arrest rates were positively associated with odds of petition as well as with odds of diversion in Missouri, while not associated with odds of petition or diversion in other states. Specifically, in Missouri, odds of petition were 17 percent higher (OR = 1.17; 95% CI: 1.08–1.27; p < .001) and odds of diversion were 11 percent higher (OR = 1.11; 95% CI: 1.04–1.19; p = .003) in counties with 1 percent higher juvenile arrest rate. Third, ethnic heterogeneity was positively associated with odds of diversion in South Carolina while negatively associated with odds of diversion in Missouri, and a positive association between ethnic heterogeneity and odds of petition approached significance in Alabama and Texas. Specifically, in counties with one standard deviation higher heterogeneity, odds of diversion were 58 percent higher in South Carolina (OR = 1.58; 95% CI: 1.13–2.19; p = .01) and 35 percent lower in Missouri (OR = .65; 95% CI: .50–.85; p = .002), while odds of petition were 53 percent higher in Alabama (OR = 1.53; 95% CI: .98–2.37; p = .06) and 13 percent higher in Texas (OR = 1.13; 95% CI: .98–1.29; p = .09).

Fourth, residential mobility was not significantly associated with odds of petition or diversion across states, although odds of diversion approached significance in Alabama. Specifically, odds of diversion were 12 percent lower in counties with 1 percent higher mobility (OR = .98; 95% CI: .77–1.00; p = .01). Fifth, youth population density was negatively associated with odds of petition in Alabama and South Carolina, and negatively associated with odds of diversion in Alabama only. Specifically, in counties with a 1 percent larger youth population, odds of petition were 29 percent lower in Alabama (OR = .71; 95% CI: .53–.96; p = .03) and 10 percent lower in South Carolina (OR = .90; 95% CI: .83–.99; p = .03), while odds of diversion were 37 percent lower in Alabama (OR = .63; 95% CI: .42–.95; p = .03).

Political Economy

For political economy models, there was evidence that petition outcomes were negatively associated with urbanism in Missouri and Oregon, but not associated with median income or conservatism in any state. Additionally, there was evidence that diversion outcomes were also negatively associated with urbanism in Missouri and Oregon, negatively associated with conservatism in Missouri, and positively associated with median income in Oregon.

First, median income was positively associated with odds of diversion in Oregon only, and was not positively associated with odds of petition in any state. Specifically, in counties with $1,000 higher median income, odds of diversion were 7 percent higher in Oregon (OR = 1.07; 95% CI: 1.02–1.11; p = .003). Second, conservatism was negatively associated with odds of diversion in Missouri only, and was not positively associated with odds of petition in any state. Specifically, in counties with a 1 percent larger conservative majority, odds of diversion were 2 percent lower in Missouri (OR = .98; 95% CI: .97–1.00; p = .047).

Third, urbanism was negatively associated with odds of petition in Missouri and Oregon, and negatively associated with odds of diversion in Missouri and Oregon as well. Specifically, in counties with an additional 100 persons per square mile, odds of petition were 5 percent lower in Missouri (OR = .95; 95% CI: .92–.98; $p < .001$) and 11 percent lower in Oregon (OR = .89; 95% CI: .92–.98; p = .04), while odds of diversion were 7 percent lower in Missouri (OR = .93; 95% CI: .90–.95; $p < .001$) and 11 percent lower in Oregon (OR = .89; 95% CI: .81–.98; p = .02). Read together, this implies that odds of dismissal at intake were high (relative to diversion or petition) in more urban counties in Missouri and Oregon.

Waiver to Criminal Court

Waiver to criminal court also varied considerably across states (see Appendix A). In 2010, the proportion of waiver-eligible referrals that were transferred to criminal court, by state, was as follows: 3.2 percent in Oregon (n = 173), 2.4 percent in Connecticut (n = 134), 1.6 percent in Alabama (n = 243), 1.4 percent in Missouri (n = 102), .9 percent in Texas (n = 206), .4 percent in South Carolina (n = 32), and .04 percent in Utah (n = 9). Due to the small number of waived cases in South Carolina and Utah, these states were excluded from waiver analyses (along with Connecticut). Table 8.3 reports the state-level findings for waiver to criminal court.

Community Threat

For community threat models, there was evidence that percent Black was negatively associated with waiver to criminal court in Oregon and Texas, percent Hispanic was negatively associated with waiver in Alabama and Missouri, concentrated disadvantage was negatively associated with waiver in Oregon, and income inequality was positively associated with waiver in Oregon while negatively associated with waiver in Alabama.

First, percent Black was negatively associated with odds of waiver in Oregon, with a negative association approaching significance in Texas. Specifically, in counties with a 1 percent larger Black population, odds of waiver were 73 percent lower in Oregon (OR = .27; 95% CI: .08–.89; p = .03), and the relationship appears curvilinear (OR = 1.19; 95% CI: 1.04–1.38; p = .02). Also, odds of waiver were 7 percent lower in Texas in counties with a 1 percent larger Black population (OR = .93; 95% CI: .86–1.01; p = .09), also curvilinear (OR = 1.00; 95% CI: 1.00–1.01; p = .03). Second, percent Hispanic was negatively associated with odds of waiver in Alabama and Missouri. Specifically, in counties with a 1 percent larger Hispanic population, odds of waiver were 40 percent lower in Alabama (OR = .60; 95% CI: .42–.85; p = .005) and curvilinear (OR = 1.03; 95% CI: 1.01–1.05; p = .02), as well as 38 percent lower in Missouri (OR = .62; 95% CI: .46–.84; p = .002), also curvilinear (OR = 1.04; 95% CI: 1.02–1.06; p < .001).

Third, concentrated disadvantage was negatively associated with odds of waiver in Oregon. Specifically, odds of waiver were 32 percent lower in counties with one standard deviation higher concentrated disadvantage (OR = .68; 95% CI: .48–.95; p = .03). Fourth, income inequality was positively associated with odds of waiver in Oregon while negatively associated

Table 8.3 State-level analyses, waiver to criminal court

	AL[a]	*MO*[b]	*OR*[c]	*TX*[d]
Fixed effects	OR (95% CI)	OR (95% CI)	OR (95% CI)	OR (95% CI)
Intercept	.03 (.02, .04)	.00*** (.00, .00)	.00*** (.00, .01)	.00*** (.00, .00)
***Level-1* variables**				
Black[e]	.86† (.73, 1.01)	3.46** (1.58, 7.57)	1.30† (.96, 1.77)	1.97*** (1.48, 2.62)
Hispanic[e]	1.40* (1.05, 1.88)	.55 (.06, 4.80)	.98 (.68, 1.40)	1.79*** (1.35, 2.37)
Other race/ethnicity[e]	.83 (.45, 1.53)	–	1.07 (.63, 1.80)	1.13 (.29, 4.51)
Male	1.13 (.96, 1.33)	5.11*** (2.36, 11.07)	2.10*** (1.41, 3.15)	4.15*** (2.82, 6.11)
Age	1.37*** (1.25, 1.50)	4.99*** (4.35, 5.73)	1.63*** (1.36, 1.95)	3.85*** (3.30, 4.50)
Violent offense[f]	.79 (.59, 1.07)	4.60*** (3.37, 6.29)	14.53*** (8.38, 25.19)	8.71*** (6.24, 12.16)
Drug/alcohol offense[f]	.99 (.77, 1.25)	.60 (.27, 1.34)	.58† (.33, 1.01)	.98 (.36, 2.66)
Weapon offense[f]	1.79 (.83, 3.85)	2.08 (.67, 6.44)	–	2.20† (.98, 4.94)
Probation violation[f]	.61*** (.46, .80)	–	–	.09*** (.04, .18)
Status offense[f]	1.04 (.78, 1.38)	.58 (.21, 1.60)	2.41 (.71, 8.15)	–
Other offense[f]	1.57*** (1.26, 1.97)	.12*** (.08, .18)	8.16*** (3.48, 19.17)	.92 (.48, 1.76)
Detention	.71*** (.60, .83)	4.29*** (2.23, 8.25)	2.06* (1.16, 3.67)	2.46*** (1.79, 3.39)
***Level-2* variables**				
Community threat model				
Percent Black	1.02 (.98, 1.05)	1.04 (.93, 1.15)	.27* (.08, .89)	.93† (.86, 1.01)
Percent Black (squared)	1.00* (1.00, 1.00)	1.00 (1.00, 1.00)	1.19* (1.04, 1.38)	1.00* (1.00, 1.01)
Percent Hispanic	.60** (.42, .85)	.62** (.46, .84)	1.02 (.87, 1.21)	.97 (.94, 1.01)
Percent Hispanic (squared)	1.03* (1.01, 1.05)	1.04*** (1.02, 1.06)	1.00 (1.00, 1.01)	1.00 (1.00, 1.00)
Concentrated disadvantage (CD)[g]	1.72 (.89, 3.31)	1.07 (.73, 1.56)	.68* (.48, .95)	1.01 (.58, 1.78)
Gini index (0–1)[g]	.69** (.52, .90)	.98 (.71, 1.34)	1.97** (1.25, 3.11)	1.30† (.97, 1.72)
Social disorganization model				
Crime rate (per 1,000)	.98* (.96, 1.00)	1.01 (.99, 1.03)	1.03 (.96, 1.10)	1.04*** (1.02, 1.06)
Juvenile crime rate (per 1,000)	.91 (.59, 1.41)	.99 (.90, 1.08)	1.05 (.97, 1.14)	.75*** (.68, .83)

(continued)

Table 8.3 Cont.

	AL[a]	MO[b]	OR[c]	TX[d]
Ethnic heterogeneity (0–1)$_g$	1.24 (.94, 1.63)	.90 (.57, 1.40)	1.63 (.74, 3.60)	1.14 (.92, 1.41)
Residential mobility (% moved)	.91 (.82, 1.02)	1.01 (.96, 1.07)	.91 (.80, 1.03)	.98 (.91, 1.05)
Youth population density (%)	.94 (.77, 1.14)	1.11 (.95, 1.29)	.77 (.54, 1.09)	1.07 (.98, 1.17)
Political economy model				
Median income (×1,000)	1.02 (.98, 1.07)	.98 (.96, 1.01)	.93* (.87, .99)	.97** (.95, .99)
Conservative voting majority	.99 (.98, 1.01)	1.00 (.98, 1.02)	.97* (.95, 1.00)	1.01* (1.00, 1.02)
Population density (per sq/mi) (×100)	.42*** (.34, .52)	.99 (.96, 1.02)	1.00 (.92, 1.09)	1.02 (.98, 1.05)
Random effects				
Random intercept variance component	2.43*** (1.56)	.87 (.93)	1.39*** (1.18)	1.15*** (1.07)
Intraclass correlation (ρ)	.43	.21	.30	.26

Note: Estimates for three separate models presented: community threat, social disorganization, and political economy. Coefficients for case-level variables are based on the community threat model.

a N_1 = 15,356; N_2 = 65.
b N_1 = 7,195; N_2 = 105.
c N_1 = 5,483; N_2 = 34.
d N_1 = 24,351; N_2 = 186.
e Reference: White.
f Reference: Property offense.
g Standardized.
† p <.10; * p <.05; ** p <.01; *** p <.001 (two tailed).

with odds of waiver in Alabama. Also, a positive association approached significance in Texas. Specifically, in counties with one standard deviation higher income inequality, odds of waiver were 97 percent higher in Oregon (OR = 1.97; 95% CI: 1.25–3.11; p = .005), 30 percent higher in Texas (OR = 1.30; 95% CI: .97–1.72; p = .08), and 31 percent lower in Alabama (OR = .69; 95% CI: .52–.90; p = .01).

Social Disorganization

For social disorganization models, there was evidence that waiver to criminal court was positively associated with crime rates in Texas while negatively associated with crime rates in Alabama, and negatively associated with juvenile arrest rates in Texas. Ethnic heterogeneity, residential mobility, and youth population density were not associated with waiver in any state.

First, crime rates were positively associated with odds of waiver in Texas and negatively associated with odds of waiver in Alabama. Specifically, in counties with 1 percent higher crime rates, odds of waiver were 4 percent higher in Texas (OR = 1.04; 95% CI: 1.02–1.06; p < .001) while 2 percent lower in Alabama (OR = .98; 95% CI: .96–1.00; p = .03). Second, juvenile arrest rates were negatively associated with odds of waiver in Texas. Specifically, in counties with 1 percent higher juvenile arrest rates, odds of waiver were 25 percent lower (OR = .75; 95% CI: .68–.83; p < .001).

Political Economy

For political economy models, there was evidence that waiver to criminal court was negatively associated with median income in Oregon and Texas, positively associated with conservatism in Texas while negatively associated with conservatism in Oregon, and negatively associated with urbanism in Alabama.

First, median income was negatively associated with odds of waiver in Oregon and Texas. Specifically, in counties with $1,000 higher median income, odds of waiver were 7 percent lower in Oregon (OR = .93; 95% CI: .87–.99; p = .02) and 3 percent lower in Texas (OR = .97; 95% CI: .95–.99; p = .002). Second, conservatism was positively associated with odds of waiver in Texas and negatively associated with odds of waiver in Oregon. Specifically, in counties with 1 percent greater conservativism, odds of waiver were 1 percent higher in Texas (OR = 1.01; 95% CI: 1.00–1.02; p = .049) while 3 percent lower in Oregon (OR = .97; 95% CI: .95–1.00; p = .02). Third, urbanism was negatively associated with odds of waiver in Alabama. Specifically, in counties with an additional 100 persons per square mile, odds of waiver were 58 percent lower (OR = .42; 95% CI: .34–.52; p < .001).

Table 8.4 State-level analyses, adjudication of delinquency

	AL[a]	*MO*[b]	*OR*[c]	*SC*[d]	*TX*[e]	*UT*[f]
Fixed effects	OR (95% CI)	OR (95% CI)	OR (95% CI)	OR (95% CI)	OR (95% CI)	OR (95% CI)
Intercept	.84 (.65, 1.08)	12.21*** (8.66, 17.22)	17.53*** (11.68, 26.3)	11.14*** (7.70, 16.11)	2.10*** (1.57, 2.81)	3.94*** (3.10, 4.99)
***Level-1* variables**						
Black[g]	1.12* (1.03, 1.23)	.69** (.53, .91)	.84 (.48, 1.46)	.93 (.78, 1.12)	1.40*** (1.26, 1.56)	.85* (.75, .97)
Hispanic[g]	.90 (.71, 1.13)	.72 (.43, 1.19)	.98 (.64, 1.49)	.97 (.55, 1.70)	1.41*** (1.23, 1.62)	1.06 (.99, 1.13)
Other race/ethnicity[g]	.86 (.48, 1.57)	.69 (.21, 2.28)	.81 (.60, 1.08)	.93 (.56, 1.55)	1.29 (.92, 1.82)	.98 (.88, 1.09)
Male	1.58*** (1.42, 1.75)	.98 (.87, 1.12)	.86† (.73, 1.00)	1.00 (.88, 1.14)	1.46*** (1.29, 1.64)	1.00 (.94, 1.06)
Age	1.06*** (1.03, 1.08)	.96† (.92, 1.01)	1.00 (.92, 1.08)	.98 (.91, 1.05)	1.11*** (1.08, 1.15)	.96** (.94, .99)
Violent offense[h]	.66*** (.58, .74)	.88 (.67, 1.16)	2.49*** (1.75, 3.52)	.89 (.67, 1.19)	.81*** (.71, .92)	1.27*** (1.13, 1.43)
Drug/alcohol offense[h]	.75** (.63, .91)	1.10 (.80, 1.50)	.74 (.45, 1.23)	1.13 (.73, 1.75)	.83 (.65, 1.06)	1.18 (.92, 1.50)
Weapon offense[h]	1.11 (.69, 1.79)	.91 (.59, 1.42)	3.31** (1.57, 6.97)	2.30** (1.23, 4.32)	.60*** (.44, .82)	1.18 (.93, 1.51)
Probation violation[h]	.84 (.57, 1.24)	.71† (.49, 1.02)	–	1.15 (.57, 2.32)	1.35 (.78, 2.35)	.74† (.54, 1.03)
Status offense[h]	.17*** (.13, .24)	1.14 (.74, 1.74)	.02*** (.01, .04)	1.07 (.80, 1.43)	.77 (.49, 1.22)	.96 (.73, 1.26)
Other offense[h]	.51*** (.40, .66)	.96 (.76, 1.22)	.59** (.43, .82)	.93 (.77, 1.14)	.83** (.74, .94)	.68* (.49, .95)
Detention	2.43*** (1.96, 3.01)	1.18 (.94, 1.48)	1.60* (1.07, 2.41)	1.70*** (1.23, 2.36)	2.00*** (1.65, 2.43)	2.19*** (1.69, 2.85)
***Level-2* variables**						
Community threat model						
Percent Black	1.00 (.97, 1.04)	1.00 (.94, 1.06)	.33* (.11, .95)	.94* (.87, 1.00)	.89* (.82, .98)	.55 (.02, 14.86)
Percent Black (squared)	1.00 (1.00, 1.00)	1.00 (1.00, 1.00)	1.16* (1.02, 1.32)	1.00 (1.00, 1.00)	1.00† (1.00, 1.01)	1.32 (.27, 6.42)
Percent Hispanic	.86 (.63, 1.17)	1.01 (.83, 1.23)	.93 (.82, 1.05)	.75† (.56, 1.01)	1.03† (1.00, 1.07)	.94 (.54, 1.65)
Percent Hispanic (squared)	1.00 (.98, 1.03)	1.00 (.98, 1.01)	1.00 (1.00, 1.01)	1.02 (1.00, 1.04)	1.00* (1.00, 1.00)	1.00 (.97, 1.03)
Concentrated disadvantage (CD)[i]	.98 (.56, 1.71)	.84 (.67, 1.05)	1.19 (.94, 1.50)	1.04 (.64, 1.70)	1.60* (1.05, 2.46)	1.01 (.82, 1.25)
Gini index (0–1)[i]	1.15 (.90, 1.46)	.84 (.58, 1.20)	.91 (.64, 1.30)	.95 (.65, 1.39)	.82* (.67, 1.00)	1.11 (.89, 1.39)
Social disorganization model						
Crime rate (per 1,000)	1.00 (.99, 1.02)	1.00 (.98, 1.01)	.99 (.96, 1.02)	1.00 (.98, 1.02)	.99† (.97, 1.00)	.98* (.95, 1.00)

Juvenile crime rate (per 1,000)	.74* (.58, .96)	1.14*** (1.05, 1.23)	1.06 (.97, 1.16)	.90† (.80, 1.00)	1.05 (.97, 1.13)	1.00 (.93, 1.07)
Ethnic heterogeneity (0–1)[i]	1.23 (.94, 1.59)	.75† (.65, 1.01)	.79 (.52, 1.20)	.71 (.56, .89)	1.06 (.84, 1.34)	1.04 (.83, 1.30)
Residential mobility (% moved)	1.02 (.97, 1.08)	1.00 (.95, 1.04)	.98 (.89, 1.08)	1.12** (1.03, 1.21)	.99 (.94, 1.05)	.98 (.94, 1.02)
Youth population density (%)	.87 (.73, 1.03)	.96 (.87, 1.06)	.94 (.81, 1.09)	1.09** (.94, 1.26)	1.02 (.96, 1.09)	.93** (.88, .97)
Political economy model						
Median income (×1,000)	.98 (.94, 1.02)	1.01 (.99, 1.04)	.94*** (.90, .97)	.97 (.91, 1.03)	.98† (.96, 1.00)	.99 (.97, 1.01)
Conservative voting majority	1.01 (.99, 1.02)	1.00 (.98, 1.02)	1.00 (.98, 1.02)	1.02* (1.00, 1.03)	1.01*** (1.01, 102)	.99† (.98, 1.00)
Population density (per sq/mi) (×100)	.96 (.75, 1.24)	.97* (.94, 1.00)	1.01 (.94, 1.09)	1.29* (1.02, 1.63)	1.02 (.98, 1.06)	.97 (.92, 1.02)
Random effects						
Random intercept variance component	1.72*** (1.31)	.99*** (1.00)	1.03*** (1.01)	1.17*** (1.08)	1.72*** (1.31)	.19*** (.44)
Intraclass correlation (ρ)	.34	.23	.24	.26	.34	.06

Note: Estimates for three separate models presented: community threat, social disorganization, and political economy. Coefficients for case-level variables are based on the community threat model.

a N_1 = 17,327; N_2 = 65.
b N_1 = 7,534; N_2 = 105.
c N_1 = 7,197; N_2 = 34.
d N_1 = 8,377; N_2 = 46.
e N_1 = 23,870; N_2 = 185.
f N_1 = 22,824; N_2 = 22.
g Reference: White.
h Reference: Property offense.
i Standardized.
† p <.10; * p <.05; ** p <.01; *** p <.001 (two tailed).

Adjudication of Delinquency

Adjudication of delinquency also varied considerably across states (see Appendix A). In 2010, the proportion of petitioned cases that were adjudicated delinquent, by state, was as follows: 93.6 percent in South Carolina (n = 7,840), 90.7 percent in Oregon (n = 6,527), 85.9 percent in Missouri (n = 6,471), 76.1 percent in Utah (n = 17,363), 74.9 percent in Texas (n = 17,867), 45.7 percent in Connecticut (n = 3,017), and 44.8 percent in Alabama (n = 7,831). Table 8.4 reports the state-level findings for adjudication.

Community Threat

For community threat models, there was some evidence that percent Black was negatively associated with adjudication outcomes in Oregon, South Carolina, and Texas. Additionally, in Texas, there was evidence that concentrated disadvantage was positively associated with adjudication outcomes, as well as evidence of a negative association between income inequality and adjudication.

First, percent Black was not positively associated with odds of adjudication in any state, although it was negatively associated with odds of adjudication in Oregon, South Carolina, and Texas. Specifically, in counties with a 1 percent larger Black population, odds of adjudication were 67 percent lower in Oregon (OR = .33; 95% CI: .11–.95; p = .04), 6 percent lower in South Carolina (OR = .94; 95% CI: .87–1.00; p = .049), and 11 percent lower in Texas (OR = .89; 95% CI: .82–.98; p = .01). Findings also suggested that the relationship was curvilinear in Oregon (OR = 1.16; 95% CI: 1.02–1.32; p = .03) and Texas (OR = 1.00; 95% CI: 1.00–1.01; p = .06). Second, percent Hispanic was not significantly associated with odds of adjudication in any state, although it approached significance in South Carolina and Texas. Specifically, in counties with a 1 percent larger Hispanic population, odds of adjudication were 25 percent lower in South Carolina (OR = .75; 95% CI: .56–1.01; p = .05) and 3 percent higher in Texas (OR = 1.03; 95% CI: 1.00–1.07; p = .08), and also curvilinear in Texas (OR = 1.00; 95% CI: 1.00–1.00; p = .03).

Third, concentrated disadvantage was positively associated with odds of adjudication in Texas, but not in other states. Specifically, in Texas, odds of adjudication were 60 percent higher in counties with one standard deviation higher concentrated disadvantage (OR = 1.60; 95% CI: 1.05–2.46; p = .03). Fourth, income inequality was negatively associated with odds of adjudication in Texas. Specifically, odds of adjudication were 18 percent lower in counties with one standard deviation higher income inequality (OR = .82; 95% CI: .67–1.00; p = .049).

Table 8.5 State-level analyses, judicial disposition

	AL[a]	*MO*[b]	*OR*[c]	*SC*[d]	*TX*[e]	*UT*[f]
Judicial release[g]						
Fixed effects	OR (95% CI)	OR (95% CI)	OR (95% CI)	OR (95% CI)	OR (95% CI)	OR (95% CI)
Intercept	.07*** (.04, .11)	.01*** (.01, .02)	.44*** (.34, .58)	.03*** (.01, .08)	.02*** (.02, .03)	.03*** (.02, .04)
Level-1 variables						
Black[h]	.82 (.62, 1.09)	1.15 (.97, 1.35)	1.16 (.89, 1.51)	.76** (.62, .92)	1.13 (.79, 1.62)	1.65* (1.08, 2.53)
Hispanic[h]	2.23† (.95, 5.23)	–	.84† (.71, 1.00)	1.19 (.81, 1.74)	.95 (.70, 1.29)	.99 (.81, 1.21)
Other race/ethnicity[h]	.80 (.15, 4.15)	–	1.24† (.99, 1.56)	.72 (.22, 2.32)	.82 (.16, 4.27)	.94 (.69, 1.27)
Male	.97 (.77, 1.21)	.73** (.60, .89)	.84* (.73, .96)	.97 (.78, 1.22)	1.24** (1.06, 1.45)	1.05 (.86, 1.27)
Age	1.08* (1.01, 1.14)	1.06† (.99, 1.15)	1.00 (.96, 1.05)	.79*** (.74, .85)	1.49*** (1.30, 1.69)	1.04 (.98, 1.10)
Violent offense[i]	1.32* (1.05, 1.66)	1.34 (.62, 2.92)	1.00 (.85, 1.18)	1.07 (.78, 1.15)	1.21 (.91, 1.60)	1.69** (1.20, 2.38)
Drug/alcohol offense[i]	1.04 (.81, 1.35)	1.64* (1.03, 2.60)	.94 (.81, 1.10)	.67 (.37, 1.19)	.85 (.64, 1.14)	.97 (.72, 1.30)
Weapon offense[i]	.42*** (.33, .55)	.28*** (.21, .38)	1.14 (.76, 1.71)	1.67 (.81, 3.43)	.85 (.41, 1.75)	2.96*** (1.62, 5.42)
Probation violation[i]	.67 (.41, 1.11)	2.88*** (2.06, 4.04)	–	.53 (.25, 1.15)	.22* (.07, .74)	2.66*** (2.03, 3.49)
Status offense[i]	1.17 (.64, 2.16)	2.82** (1.33, 5.96)	–	32.47*** (10.81, 97.5)	–	.73 (.44, 1.22)
Other offense[i]	1.35 (.83, 2.18)	3.05*** (2.53, 3.68)	.92 (.74, 1.15)	1.17 (.52, 2.67)	1.05 (.85, 1.29)	1.98*** (1.54, 2.54)
Detention	.59** (.43, .82)	.38*** (.25, .59)	.59*** (.51, .68)	.23*** (.12, .44)	1.01 (.78, 1.31)	1.82*** (1.53, 2.18)
Level-2 variables						
Community threat model						
Percent Black	1.05 (.98, 1.13)	.98 (.78, 1.22)	1.74 (.65, 4.67)	.94 (.86, 1.04)	1.04 (.92, 1.17)	.14 (.00, 11.35)
Percent Black (squared)	1.00 (1.00, 1.00)	1.00 (1.00, 1.01)	.94 (.83, 1.07)	1.00 (1.00, 1.00)	1.00 (1.00, 1.00)	2.48 (.28, 21.94)
Percent Hispanic	.70 (.39, 1.27)	1.68 (.74, 3.82)	1.03 (.90, 1.19)	1.15 (.74, 1.77)	1.00 (.95, 1.06)	1.83 (.84, 3.98)
Percent Hispanic (squared)	1.03 (.99, 1.07)	.96 (.89, 1.04)	1.00 (1.00, 1.00)	.99 (.96, 1.01)	1.00 (1.00, 1.00)	.97 (.93, 1.01)
Concentrated disadvantage (CD)[j]	1.39 (.49, 3.92)	.75 (.37, 1.52)	1.06 (.83, 1.35)	2.07 (.72, 5.94)	.61 (.32, 1.14)	1.33† (.95, 1.88)
Gini index (0–1)[j]	.65† (.41, 1.03)	1.02 (.53, 1.94)	1.08 (.82, 1.43)	.54* (.33, .86)	1.26 (.93, 1.71)	.91 (.65, 1.28)

(continued)

Table 8.5 Cont.

	AL[a]	MO[b]	OR[c]	SC[d]	TX[e]	UT[f]
Social disorganization model						
Crime rate (per 1,000)	1.01 (.97, 1.05)	.98 (.95, 1.02)	1.03* (1.01, 1.06)	.98 (.95, 1.01)	1.00 (.98, 1.03)	1.00 (.96, 1.05)
Juvenile crime rate (per 1,000)	1.06 (.70, 1.60)	1.08 (.94, 1.24)	.98 (.93, 1.03)	1.11 (.90, 1.36)	1.04 (.93, 1.16)	1.05 (.92, 1.20)
Ethnic heterogeneity (0–1)[i]	1.32 (.85, 2.06)	1.74 (.78, 3.89)	1.08 (.75, 1.54)	.76 (.53, 1.09)	1.17 (.83, 1.63)	.91 (.62, 1.33)
Residential mobility (% moved)	.86** (.78, .94)	.89 (.77, 1.03)	.98 (.94, 1.02)	.89 (.77, 1.03)	.97 (.90, 1.04)	1.00 (.91, 1.09)
Youth population density (%)	.87 (.62, 1.23)	.90 (.68, 1.19)	.97 (.87, 1.08)	1.19 (.95, 1.48)	.98 (.89, 1.06)	1.00 (.62, 1.33)
Political economy model						
Median income (×1,000)	.96 (.79, 2.15)	1.02 (.96, 1.09)	.99 (.96, 1.01)	.99 (.91, 1.09)	1.03* (1.00, 1.06)	1.00 (.97, 1.03)
Conservative voting majority	1.00 (.98, 1.02)	.99 (.95, 1.03)	.99* (.98, 1.00)	1.01 (.98, 1.04)	.99 (.98, 1.01)	1.00 (.98, 1.02)
Population density (per sq/mi) (×100)	1.30 (.79, 2.15)	1.02 (.93, 1.11)	1.02 (.98, 1.06)	.73 (.48, 1.11)	.95† (.89, 1.01)	.97 (.89, 1.05)
Random effects						
Random intercept variance component	2.43*** (1.56)	3.35*** (1.83)	.34*** (.58)	1.30*** (1.14)	1.51*** (1.23)	.28*** (.53)
Intraclass correlation (ρ)	.43	.51	.09	.28	.32	.08
Placement[g]						
Fixed effects						
Intercept	.04*** (.02, .06)	.20*** (.15, .26)	.07*** (.05, .10)	.08*** (.06, .11)	.01*** (.01, .01)	.04*** (.03, .06)
Case-level variables						
Black[h]	.96 (.74, 1.23)	1.06 (.87, 1.28)	1.16 (.82, 1.65)	1.16 (.93, 1.45)	1.32** (1.07, 1.63)	1.87*** (1.47, 2.37)

Hispanic[h]	.95 (.45, 2.00)	–	.91 (.71, 1.16)	1.50 (.70, 3.25)	1.21 (.94, 1.55)	1.31*** (1.17, 1.46)
Other race/ethnicity[h]	1.33 (.25, 6.99)	–	1.22 (.86, 1.74)	.93 (.56, 1.55)	.95 (.40, 2.25)	1.01 (.84, 1.21)
Male	1.02 (.70, 1.50)	1.20 (.90, 1.60)	1.09 (.87, 1.37)	1.94*** (1.62, 2.32)	2.71*** (2.02, 3.64)	1.26*** (1.13, 1.41)
Age	.98 (.85, 1.12)	.92* (.86, .98)	1.18*** (1.10, 1.26)	1.64*** (1.50, 1.80)	1.72*** (1.53, 1.94)	1.36*** (1.31, 1.41)
Violent offense[i]	1.32* (1.01, 1.73)	1.38** (1.12, 1.70)	1.45*** (1.17, 1.79)	1.07 (.84, 1.36)	1.93*** (1.59, 2.33)	1.82*** (1.50, 2.22)
Drug/alcohol offense[i]	.85 (.52, 1.39)	.91 (.62, 1.33)	.22*** (.15, .32)	.74* (.55, 1.00)	.44*** (.30, .64)	.93 (.79, 1.10)
Weapon offense[i]	.82 (.58, 1.15)	.69† (.46, 1.03)	.98 (.60, 1.62)	.84 (.51, 1.40)	.75 (.46, 1.21)	1.89** (1.23, 2.91)
Probation violation[i]	2.99*** (2.11, 4.24)	4.88*** (2.22, 10.72)	–	2.74*** (1.22, 3.56)	4.54*** (3.22, 6.39)	4.92*** (4.27, 5.67)
Status offense[i]	.66 (.28, 1.52)	3.91*** (2.27, 6.76)	–	1.18 (.79, 1.75)	–	.39*** (.26, .59)
Other offense[i]	1.07 (.76, 1.52)	2.15*** (1.61, 2.86)	.99 (.73, 1.36)	2.89*** (1.92, 4.34)	.69* (.49, .97)	1.71*** (1.48, 1.98)
Detention	1.46*** (1.17, 1.83)	3.03*** (2.14, 4.30)	2.74*** (2.25, 3.34)	1.36† (1.00, 1.85)	3.17*** (2.60, 3.86)	4.23*** (3.84, 4.67)
Level-2 variables						
Community threat model						
Percent Black	1.00 (.95, 1.05)	.96 (.90, 1.02)	1.98 (.75, 5.20)	1.00 (.95, 1.04)	.96 (.89, 1.03)	.61 (.02, 17.79)
Percent Black (squared)	1.00 (1.00, 1.00)	1.00† (1.00, 1.00)	.93 (.82, 1.05)	1.00 (1.00, 1.00)	1.00 (1.00, 1.00)	1.08 (.21, 5.58)
Percent Hispanic	.97 (.57, 1.63)	1.17 (.94, 1.44)	1.05 (.90, 1.23)	.80† (.62, 1.02)	1.02 (.99, 1.05)	.89 (.51, 1.56)
Percent Hispanic (squared)	1.00 (.96, 1.04)	.99 (.97, 1.01)	1.00 (.99, 1.00)	1.01† (1.00, 1.03)	1.00* (1.00, 1.00)	1.01 (.98, 1.04)
Concentrated disadvantage (CD)[j]	1.26 (.48, 3.27)	.88 (.69, 1.13)	1.06 (.83, 1.34)	1.00 (.68, 1.48)	1.76** (1.20, 2.59)	.80† (.63, 1.03)
Gini index (0–1)[j]	1.29 (.74, 2.24)	.87 (.71, 1.07)	1.07 (.80, 1.44)	.83 (.64, 1.07)	.79** (.66, .94)	.93 (.74, 1.18)
Social disorganization model						
Crime rate (per 1,000)	1.01 (.98, 1.05)	1.00 (.99, 1.01)	1.02† (1.00, 1.05)	1.01 (.99, 1.02)	1.00 (.98, 1.01)	1.01 (.98, 1.04)
Juvenile crime rate (per 1,000)	1.25 (.89, 1.76)	.95* (.90, 1.00)	.96 (.88, 1.06)	.91† (.83, 1.01)	.93† (.86, 1.01)	.99 (.91, 1.08)
Ethnic heterogeneity (0–1)[j]	1.08 (.76, 1.53)	1.06 (.85, 1.33)	1.26 (.90, 1.78)	.95 (.79, 1.13)	1.09 (.92, 1.29)	.88 (.69, 1.11)
Residential mobility (% moved)	.89* (.80, 1.00)	.97† (.94, 1.00)	.99 (.92, 1.07)	1.00 (.96, 1.05)	1.01 (.97, 1.06)	.98 (.92, 1.04)
Youth population density (%)	1.02 (.81, 1.28)	1.03 (.95, 1.12)	.98 (.85, 1.12)	1.07 (.99, 1.15)	1.02 (.96, 1.08)	1.05 (.97, 1.14)

(*continued*)

Table 8.5 Cont.

	AL[a]	*MO*[b]	*OR*[c]	*SC*[d]	*TX*[e]	*UT*[f]
Political economy model						
Median income (×1,000)	.98 (.91, 1.07)	1.01 (.99, 1.03)	1.01 (.97, 1.05)	1.00 (.96, 1.04)	.98* (.97, 1.00)	1.03* (1.01, 1.05)
Conservative voting majority	.99† (.97, 1.00)	.99 (.98, 1.01)	1.00 (.99, 1.01)	1.00 (.99, 1.01)	1.01** (1.00, 1.02)	1.00 (.99, 1.01)
Population density (per sq/mi) (×100)	.94 (.51, 1.73)	.99 (.97, 1.01)	1.06* (1.01, 1.12)	1.04 (.87, 1.25)	.99 (.96, 1.02)	.97 (.92, 1.02)
Random effects						
Random intercept variance component	1.95*** (1.40)	.53*** (.73)	.26*** (.51)	.29*** (.54)	.51*** (.72)	.16*** (.40)
Intraclass correlation (ρ)	.37	.14	.07	.08	.13	.05

Note: Estimates for three separate models presented: community threat, social disorganization, and political economy. Coefficients for case-level variables are based on the community threat model.

a $N_1 = 7{,}648$; $N_2 = 65$.
b $N_1 = 6{,}471$; $N_2 = 105$.
c $N_1 = 6{,}089$; $N_2 = 34$.
d $N_1 = 7{,}809$; $N_2 = 46$.
e $N_1 = 17{,}867$; $N_2 = 182$.
f $N_1 = 17{,}058$; $N_2 = 22$.
g Reference: Community supervision.
h Reference: White.
I Reference: Property offense.
j Standardized.
† $p < .10$; * $p < .05$; ** $p < .01$; *** $p < .001$ (two tailed).

Social Disorganization

For social disorganization models, there was evidence that adjudication outcomes were negatively associated with crime rates in Utah, positively associated with juvenile arrest rates in Missouri while negatively associated with juvenile arrest rates in Alabama, positively associated with residential mobility in South Carolina, and positively associated with youth population density in South Carolina while negatively associated with youth population density in Utah. Ethnic heterogeneity was not associated with adjudication in any state, although negative associations between adjudication and ethnic heterogeneity approached significance in Missouri.

First, crime rates were not positively associated with odds of adjudication in any state, but crime rates were negatively associated with odds of adjudication in Utah and a negative association approached significance in Texas. Specifically, in counties with 1 percent higher crime rates, odds of adjudication were 2 percent lower in Utah (OR = .98; 95% CI: .95–1.00; $p = .04$) and 1 percent lower in Texas (OR = .99; 95% CI: .97–1.00; $p = .095$). Second, juvenile arrest rates were positively associated with odds of adjudication in Missouri and negatively associated with odds of adjudication in Alabama, while approaching a negative association in South Carolina. Specifically, in counties with 1 percent higher juvenile arrest rates, odds of adjudication were 14 percent higher in Missouri (OR = 1.14; 95% CI: 1.05–1.23; $p < .001$), while odds of adjudication were 26 percent lower in Alabama (OR = .74; 95% CI: .58–.96; $p = .02$) and 10 percent lower in South Carolina (OR = .90; 95% CI: .80–1.00; $p = .05$).

Third, ethnic heterogeneity was not significantly associated with odds of adjudication in any state, although a negative association approached significance in Missouri. Specifically, in counties with one standard deviation higher heterogeneity, odds of adjudication were 25 percent lower (OR = .75; 95% CI: .65–1.01; $p = .06$). Fourth, residential mobility was positively associated with odds of adjudication in South Carolina only. Specifically, odds of adjudication were 12 percent higher in counties with 1 percent higher residential mobility (OR = 1.12; 95% CI: 1.03–1.21; $p = .009$). Fifth, youth population density was positively associated with odds of adjudication in South Carolina while negatively associated with odds of adjudication in Utah. Specifically, in counties with a 1 percent larger youth population, odds of adjudication were 9 percent higher in South Carolina (OR = 1.09; 95% CI: .94–1.26; $p = .005$) while 7 percent lower in Utah (OR = .93; 95% CI: .88–.97; $p = .004$).

Political Economy

For political economy models, there was evidence that adjudication outcomes were negatively associated with median income in Oregon, positively associated with conservatism in South Carolina and Texas, and positively associated with urbanism in South Carolina while negatively associated with urbanism in Missouri.

First, median income was negatively associated with odds of adjudication in Oregon and a negative association approached significance in Texas. Specifically, in counties with \$1,000 higher median income, odds of adjudication were 6 percent lower in Oregon (OR = .94; 95% CI: .90–.97; $p < .001$) and 2 percent lower in Texas (OR = .98; 95% CI: .96–1.00; $p = .07$). Second, conservatism was positively associated with odds of adjudication in South Carolina and Texas, while a negative association approached significance in Utah. Specifically, in counties with 1 percent higher conservatism, odds of adjudication were 2 percent higher in South Carolina (OR = 1.02; 95% CI: 1.00–1.03; $p = .04$), 1 percent higher in Utah (OR = 1.01; 95% CI: 1.01–1.02; $p < .001$), and 1 percent lower in Utah (OR = .99; 95% CI: .98–1.00; $p = .08$). Third, urbanism was positively associated with odds of adjudication in South Carolina and negatively associated with odds of adjudication in Missouri. Specifically, in counties with an additional 100 persons per square mile, odds of adjudication were 29 percent higher in South Carolina (OR = 1.29; 95% CI: 1.02–1.63; $p = .04$) while 3 percent lower in Missouri (OR = .97; 95% CI: .94–1.00; $p = .03$).

Judicial Disposition

Judicial dispositions also varied considerably across states (see Appendix A). In 2010, the proportion of delinquent cases that received residential placement, by state, was as follows: 35.8 percent in Missouri (n = 2,319), 20.8 percent in South Carolina (n = 1,621), 14.8 percent in Utah (n = 2,523), 12.2 percent in Connecticut (n = 367), 9.4 percent in Oregon (n = 575), 7.2 percent in Alabama (n = 549), and 6.3 percent in Texas (n = 1,120). The proportion of delinquent cases that received judicial release, by state, was as follows: 26.4 percent in Oregon (n = 1,608), 15 percent in Connecticut (n = 452), 9.7 percent in South Carolina (n = 760), 9.1 percent in Alabama (n = 698), 6.9 percent in Missouri (n = 444), 4 percent in Texas (n = 710), and 3.4 percent in Utah (n = 575). Table 8.5 reports the state-level findings for judicial disposition.

Community Threat

For community threat models, there was no evidence of any association between percent Black and judicial dispositions, while a negative association between judicial placement and percent Hispanic approached significance in South Carolina. There was also evidence that placement was positively associated with concentrated disadvantage in Texas, while in Utah, two associations approached significance: concentrated disadvantage was negatively associated with placement while positively associated with judicial release. There was also evidence that income inequality was negatively associated with placement in Texas, as well as negatively associated with judicial release in South Carolina.

First, percent Black was not significantly associated with odds of placement or odds of release in any state. Second, percent Hispanic was not associated with odds of placement in any state, although a negative association did approach significance for South Carolina. Specifically, odds of placement were 20 percent lower in counties with a 1 percent larger Hispanic population (OR = .80; 95% CI: .62–1.02; p = .07), with some evidence of a curvilinear relationship (OR = 1.01; 95% CI: 1.00–1.03; p = .097).

Third, concentrated disadvantage was positively associated with odds of placement in Texas, while in Utah, a negative association with odds of placement and a positive association with odds of judicial release approached significance. Specifically, in counties with one standard deviation higher concentrated disadvantage, odds of placement were 76 percent higher in Texas (OR = 1.76; 95% CI: 1.20–2.59; p = .004) while 20 percent lower in Utah (OR = .80; 95% CI: .63–1.03; p = .07). Additionally, odds of judicial release were 33 percent higher in counties with greater disadvantage in Utah (OR = 1.33; 95% CI: .95–1.88; p = .09).

Fourth, income inequality was negatively associated with odds of placement in Texas and negatively associated with odds of judicial release in South Carolina (with a negative association with odds of release approaching significance in Alabama). Specifically, odds of placement were 21 percent lower in counties with one standard deviation higher income inequality (OR = .79; 95% CI: .66–.94; p = .009). Income inequality was also negatively associated with judicial release in South Carolina, where odds of release were 46 percent lower in counties with higher income inequality (OR = .54; 95% CI: .33–.86; p = .01), and in Alabama, where odds of release were 35 percent lower in counties with higher inequality (OR = .65; 95% CI: .41–1.03; p = .07).

Social Disorganization

For social disorganization models, there was evidence that placement was negatively associated with juvenile arrest rates in Missouri and negatively associated with residential mobility in Alabama. Approaching significance were positive associations between placement and crime rates in Oregon and negative associations between placement and juvenile arrests in South

Carolina and Texas, as well as a negative association between placement and residential mobility in Missouri. Ethnic heterogeneity and youth population were not associated with odds of placement in any state. Additionally, there was evidence that judicial release was positively associated with crime rates in Oregon and negatively associated with residential mobility in Alabama. Ethnic heterogeneity, juvenile arrest rates, and youth population were not associated with judicial release in any state.

First, crime rates were positively associated with placement as well as judicial release in Oregon. Specifically, in counties with 1 percent higher crime rates, odds of placement were 2 percent higher (OR = 1.02; 95% CI: 1.00–1.05; p = .08) and odds of judicial release were 3 percent higher (OR = 1.03; 95% CI: 1.01–1.06; p = .01) compared to community supervision. Second, juvenile arrest rates were negatively associated with odds of placement in Missouri, South Carolina, and Texas, while not associated with odds of judicial release in any state. Specifically, in counties with 1 percent higher juvenile arrest rates, odds of placement were 5 percent lower in Missouri (OR = .95; 95% CI: .90–1.00; p = .04), 9 percent lower in South Carolina (OR = .91; 95% CI: .83–1.01; p = .06), and 7 percent lower in Texas (OR = .93; 95% CI: .86–1.01; p = .08).

Third, ethnic heterogeneity was not associated with odds of placement or release in any state. Fourth, residential mobility was negatively associated with odds of placement in Alabama and Missouri, while residential mobility was negatively associated with odds of judicial release in Alabama only. Specifically, in counties with 1 percent higher mobility, odds of placement were 11 percent lower in Alabama (OR = .89; 95% CI: .80–1.00; p = .049) and 3 percent lower in Missouri (OR = .97; 95% CI: .94–1.00; p = .07). Similarly, in counties with 1 percent higher mobility, odds of release were 14 percent lower in Alabama (OR = .86; 95% CI: .78–.94; p = .002). Fifth, youth population density was not associated with odds of placement or judicial release in any state.

Political Economy

For political economy models, there was evidence that median income was negatively associated with judicial placement while positively associated with judicial release in Texas, as well as positively associated with judicial release in Utah. There was also evidence that conservatism was positively associated with placement in Texas (with a negative association with placement approaching significance in Alabama) and negatively associated with judicial release in Oregon. Finally, there was evidence that urbanism was positively associated with placement in Oregon, with a negative association with judicial release approaching significance in Texas.

First, median income was negatively associated with odds of placement and positively associated with odds of judicial release in Texas, and positively associated with odds of placement in Utah. Specifically, in counties with \$1,000 higher median income, odds of placement were 2 percent lower in Texas (OR = .98; 95% CI: .97–1.00; p = .01) while 3 percent higher in Utah (OR = 1.03; 95% CI: 1.01–1.05; p = .02). Additionally, odds of judicial release were 3 percent higher in counties with \$1,000 higher median income in Texas (OR = 1.03; 95% CI: 1.00–1.06; p = .049). Second, conservatism was positively associated with odds of placement in Texas and Alabama (approaching significance), and negatively associated with odds of judicial release in Oregon. Specifically, in counties with 1 percent higher conservatism, odds of placement were 1 percent higher in Texas (OR = 1.01; 95% CI: 1.00–1.02; p = .008) while 1 percent lower in Alabama (OR = .99; 95% CI: .97–1.00; p = .096). Additionally, higher conservatism was associated with 1 percent lower odds of judicial release in Oregon (OR = .99; 95% CI: .98–1.00; p = .02). Third, urbanism was positively associated with odds of placement in Oregon, and a negative association with judicial release approached significance in Texas. Specifically, in counties with an additional 100 persons per square mile, odds of placement were 6 percent higher in Oregon (OR = 1.06; 95% CI: 1.01–1.12; p = .02) and odds of judicial release were 5 percent lower in Texas (OR = .95; 95% CI: .89–1.01; p = .07).

Summary of Findings

Findings indicated that juvenile court outcomes varied significantly across counties within states. Variance component models indicated that the proportion of variation in juvenile court outcomes that was attributable to county-level differences was approximately 3–27 percent for detention (highest in Alabama and lowest in Utah), 14–52 percent for petition (highest in Alabama and lowest in South Carolina), 11–56 percent for diversion (highest in Alabama and lowest in Oregon), 18–47 percent for waiver (highest in Alabama and lowest in Missouri), 6–35 percent for adjudication (highest in Texas and lowest in Utah), 3–37 percent for judicial placement (highest in Alabama and lowest in Utah), and 6–46 percent for judicial release (highest in Missouri and lowest in Utah).

To explore whether variation in juvenile processing and sanctions could be explained by contextual influences on the juvenile court, this chapter examined whether community threat, social disorganization, and political economy were associated with odds of detention, petition and diversion, waiver, adjudication, and placement and release, at the level of individual states. The findings indicated some support for the contextual hypotheses, mixed across different outcomes as well as states.

First, several contextual factors were significantly associated with detention outcomes in different states. Among community threats, percent Hispanic (i.e. ethnic threat) was positively associated with odds of detention in Missouri and Oregon while concentrated disadvantage (i.e. economic threat) was positively associated with odds of detention in Missouri. (Percent Black [i.e. racial threat] and income inequality [i.e. inequality threat] were not associated with detention in any state.) Among social disorganization factors, crime rates were positively associated with odds of detention in Missouri, juvenile arrests were positively associated with odds of detention in Oregon while negatively associated with odds of detention in Missouri, and youth population density was negatively associated with odds of detention in Oregon. (Ethnic heterogeneity and residential mobility were not associated with detention outcomes in any state.) Among political economy factors, median income (i.e. external economy) was positively associated with odds of detention in Alabama and Texas, conservatism (i.e. internal polity) was positively associated with odds of detention in Alabama while negatively associated with odds of detention in Oregon and Texas, and urbanism (i.e. internal economy) was positively associated with odds of detention in Utah while negatively associated with odds of detention in Alabama and Oregon.

Second, several contextual factors were significantly associated with petition and diversion outcomes in different states. Among community threats, percent Black was only positively associated with odds of petition (but not diversion) in Texas. (Percent Hispanic, concentrated disadvantage, and income inequality were not associated with odds of petition or diversion.) Among social disorganization factors, crime rates were positively associated with odds of petition as well as odds of diversion in Texas while negatively associated with odds of petition as well as odds of diversion in Oregon and negatively associated with odds of diversion in South Carolina. Juvenile arrest rates were positively associated with odds of petition as well as odds of diversion in Missouri only. Ethnic heterogeneity was positively associated with odds of diversion in South Carolina while negatively associated with odds of diversion in Missouri. Youth population density was negatively associated with odds of petition as well as odds of diversion in Alabama while negatively associated with odds of petition in South Carolina. (Residential mobility was not associated with petition or diversion outcomes, while ethnic heterogeneity was not associated with petition outcomes, in any state.) Among political economy factors, median income was positively associated with odds of diversion in Oregon, conservatism was negatively associated with odds of diversion in Missouri, and urbanism was negatively associated with odds of petition as well as odds of diversion in Missouri and Oregon. This would appear to indicate that odds of dismissal at intake were higher in more urban counties in those last two states. (Median income and conservatism were not associated with odds of petition in any state, however.)

Third, several contextual factors were significantly associated with waiver outcomes in different states. Among community threats, percent Black was negatively associated with odds of waiver in Oregon and Texas, percent Hispanic was negatively associated with odds of waiver to criminal court in Alabama and Missouri, concentrated disadvantage was negatively associated with odds of waiver in Oregon, and income inequality was positively associated with odds of waiver in Oregon while negatively associated with odds of waiver in Alabama. Among social disorganization factors, crime rates were positively associated with odds of waiver in Texas while negatively associated with odds of waiver in Alabama, and juvenile arrest rates were negatively associated with odds of waiver in Texas. (Ethnic heterogeneity, residential mobility, and youth population density were not associated with odds of waiver in any state.) Among political economy factors, median income was negatively associated with odds of waiver in Oregon and Texas, conservatism was positively associated with odds of waiver in Texas while negatively associated with odds of waiver in Oregon, and urbanism was negatively associated with odds of waiver in Alabama.

Fourth, several contextual factors were significantly associated with adjudication outcomes in different states. Among community threats, percent Black was negatively associated with odds of adjudication in Oregon, South Carolina, and Texas, concentrated disadvantage was positively associated with odds of adjudication in Texas, and income inequality was negatively associated with odds of adjudication in Texas. (Percent Hispanic was not associated with adjudication outcomes in any state.) Among social disorganization factors, crime rates were negatively associated with odds of adjudication in Utah, juvenile arrest rates were positively associated with odds of adjudication in Missouri while negatively associated with odds of adjudication in Alabama, residential mobility was positively associated with odds of adjudication in South Carolina, and youth population density was positively associated with odds of adjudication in South Carolina while negatively associated with odds of adjudication in Utah. (Ethnic heterogeneity was not associated with adjudication in any state.) Among political economy factors, median income was negatively associated with odds of adjudication in Oregon, conservatism was positively associated with odds of adjudication in South Carolina and Texas, and urbanism was positively associated with odds of adjudication in South Carolina while negatively associated with odds of adjudication in Missouri.

Fifth, several contextual factors were significantly associated with judicial dispositions in different states. Among community threats, concentrated disadvantage was positively associated with odds of placement in Texas, while income inequality was negatively associated with odds of placement in Texas and negatively associated with odds of judicial release in South Carolina. (Percent Black and percent Hispanic were not associated with odds of placement or release in any state.) Among social disorganization factors, crime rates were positively associated with odds of judicial release in Oregon, juvenile arrest rates were negatively associated with odds of placement in Missouri, and residential mobility was negatively associated with odds of placement as well as odds of release in Alabama. (Crime rates were not associated with odds of placement in any state, juvenile arrest rates were not associated with odds of release in any state, and ethnic heterogeneity and youth population density were not associated with odds of placement or release in any state). Among political economy factors, median income was positively associated with odds of judicial release in Texas and Utah and negatively associated with odds of placement in Texas. Conservatism was negatively associated with odds of release in Oregon, but not associated with odds of placement in any state. Urbanism was positively associated with odds of placement in Oregon, but not associated with odds of release in any state.

Chapter 9

Does Context Matter? Discussing the Findings

The present study was motivated by the fact that juvenile justice processing and punishment vary across communities and systems; yet our understanding of how and why this occurs is quite limited. To that end, the study investigated whether community and court characteristics directly influenced the likelihood that a juvenile offender would experience certain outcomes from intake processing to final disposition. Specifically, the study hypothesized that juvenile court outcomes would be more punitive (i.e. exclusionary) and less treatment-oriented (i.e. inclusionary) in the presence of certain contextual factors. These factors were grouped into three theoretical perspectives: *community threat*, *social disorganization*, and *political economy of the juvenile court*. As expected, juvenile court outcomes *did* vary significantly across courts and systems. In 2010, 12–25 percent of the variation in juvenile court outcomes was attributable to county-level differences and 11–28 percent was attributable to state-level differences. In 2000, 11–24 percent of the variation in these outcomes was attributable to county-level differences and 11–63 percent was attributable to state-level differences. As such, a relatively substantial amount of variation in juvenile punishment was attributable to context.

The study findings indicated limited support for the research hypotheses, however. That is, contextual factors did not appear to *explain* the variation in juvenile court processing across communities and systems. Below, I summarize the findings from Chapters 6–8 (in less technical terms than what appeared in those chapters).

Summary of Findings

Multistate Findings, 2010

Table 9.1 presents the findings from the multistate dataset for the year 2010 (see Chapter 6). The table displays 20 research hypotheses—8 community threat hypotheses, 8 social disorganization hypotheses, and 4 political economy hypotheses—for each of the 7 juvenile court outcomes. This means that a total of 140 research hypotheses were tested (i.e. 7 × 20). The

Table 9.1 Summary of contextual findings, year 2010

Research Hypothesis	*Detention*	*Petition*		*Waiver*	*Adjudication*	*Judicial disposition*	
		Diversion	*Petition*			*Release*	*Placement*
Community Threat							
Racial threat (static)	ns	ns	ns	ns	ns	ns	ns
Racial threat (dynamic)	ns	ns	ns	ns	ns	ns	ns
Ethnic threat (static)	ns	ns	ns	ns	ns	ns	ns
Ethnic threat (dynamic)	ns	ns	ns	ns	ns	ns	ns
Economic threat (static)	ns	ns	ns	ns	ns	ns	ns
Economic threat (dynamic)	ns	ns	ns	ns	-	ns	ns
Inequality threat (static)	ns	ns	ns	+	ns	ns	ns
Inequality threat (dynamic)	ns	ns	ns	-	ns	ns	ns
Social Disorganization							
Crime rate (static)	ns	ns	ns	ns	ns	ns	ns
Crime rate (dynamic)	ns	ns	ns	ns	ns	ns	ns
Juvenile arrest rate (static)	ns	ns	ns	ns	ns	ns	-
Juvenile arrest rate (dynamic)	ns	ns	ns	ns	ns	ns	ns
Ethnic heterogeneity	ns	ns	ns	ns	ns	+	ns
Residential mobility	ns	ns	ns	-	ns	-	-
Youth density (static)	ns	ns	ns	-	ns	ns	ns
Youth density (dynamic)	ns	ns	ns	ns	ns	ns	ns
Political economy							
External polity (election)	ns	+	ns	ns	ns	ns	ns
External economy (wealth)	ns	ns	ns	-	ns	ns	ns
Internal polity (conservative)	ns	ns	ns	ns	+	-	ns
Internal economy (urban)	ns	ns	ns	ns	ns	ns	ns

Note: + = positive association ($p < .05$); - = negative association ($p < .05$); ns = no significant association.

table illustrates whether the test revealed a positive association, a negative association, or no association (at $p < .05$).

Of these 140 tests, only 13 associations were statistically significant. By chance, we would expect approximately 7 significant associations, so this indicates that some of these associations are likely real and not merely statistical artifacts. That said, there are few patterns in the findings. The only contextual factors significantly associated with multiple outcomes were conservatism (i.e. internal polity) and residential mobility (i.e. social disorganization).[1]

First, conservative voting majority was positively associated with odds of adjudication of delinquency and negatively associated with odds of judicial release—supporting internal polity hypotheses $\mathbf{H}_{3D}$ and $\mathbf{H}_{3E}$. Second, residential mobility was negatively associated with odds of waiver, odds of release, and odds of placement. The negative association between this indicator of social disorganization and odds of release is supportive of $\mathbf{H}_{2E}$, that judicial release will be less likely than community supervision in counties with greater residential mobility. The negative associations between residential mobility and odds of adjudication and placement, however, are not supportive of the research hypotheses. The only other significant associations that are supportive of research hypotheses are the positive association between static inequality threat and odds of waiver ($\mathbf{H}_{1C}$) and the negative association between ethnic heterogeneity and odds of judicial release ($\mathbf{H}_{2E}$). The research hypotheses are not supported by the associations between dynamic economic threat and adjudication, dynamic inequality threat and waiver, juvenile arrests and placement, static youth density and waiver, ethnic heterogeneity and judicial release, external polity (i.e. judicial elections) and diversion, or external economy (i.e. median wealth) and waiver. In other words, these associations were all in an unexpected direction.

Moreover, no contextual measure was associated with *every* juvenile court outcome. Thus, no operationalization of community threat, social disorganization, or political economy predicted variation across all juvenile justice outcomes, as might be predicted by the strongest versions of those theories. For example, if juvenile court actors are truly influenced by perceptions of social disorganization, contributing to a more punitive formal social control response, we might reasonably expect that this would operate at *every* level of the juvenile court. That is, we might expect those same contextual realities to influence probation officers, prosecutors, and judges, rather than influencing some juvenile court actors and not others.

Alternatively, given the loosely coupled nature of the juvenile justice system, it might be that some outcomes are influenced by context while others are not. In the present findings, odds of waiver were associated with five contextual variables, odds of judicial release were associated with three contextual variables, and odds of adjudication and placement were each associated with two contextual variables. Odds of diversion were only associated with one contextual factor, while odds of detention and petition were associated with none. This is interesting, since it appears to indicate more contextual influences on *formal* processing stages. It is not clear what might explain this trend. If anything, we would expect more contextual influences on *informal* processing where there is less discretion (i.e. a loosely coupled environment). Might there be more overall variation across counties at these formal stages of processing, contrary to expectations? It would appear not. Variation in outcomes attributable to county-level differences for waiver, adjudication, judicial release, and judicial placement was 24 percent, 23 percent, 25 percent, and 12 percent, respectively. Variation in outcomes attributable to county-level differences for detention, diversion, and petition was 16 percent, 21 percent, and 24 percent, respectively. Again, there are no clear patterns for which stages of processing were more strongly associated with contextual factors.

In total, then, fewer than half of the significant associations (i.e. 5 of 13) *supported* the research hypotheses. Of these five, one supported a community threat hypothesis (out of 40 tests), one supported a social disorganization hypothesis (out of 40 tests), and three supported political economy hypotheses (out of 28 tests). While there was limited support for the research hypotheses, this was especially true for community threat and social disorganization.[2] This is interesting given that the majority of research attention has been paid to community threats—most notably minority threat (see, e.g., Feldmeyer & Cochran, 2018)—as opposed to organizational factors associated with court processing. The main takeaway from the above is that while major juvenile court outcomes vary significantly across states and across counties within states, this variation is not explained by community threat, social disorganization, or political economy.

Multistate Findings, 2000

Table 9.2 presents the findings from the multistate dataset for the year 2000 (see Chapter 7). The table displays 12 research hypotheses—4 community threat hypotheses, 4 social disorganization hypotheses, and 4 political economy hypotheses—for each of the 7 juvenile court outcomes. This means that there were a total of 84 tests of the research hypotheses (i.e. 7 × 12). The table illustrates whether the test revealed a positive association, a negative association, or no association (at $p < .05$).

Of these 84 tests, only 12 proved statistically significant. By chance, we would expect approximately four significant associations, so this indicates that some of these associations are likely real and not merely statistical

Table 9.2 Summary of contextual findings, year 2000

Research Hypothesi	*Detention*	*Petition*		*Waiver*	*Adjudication*	*Judicial Disposition*	
		Diversion	*Petition*			*Release*	*Placement*
Community Threat							
Racial threat (static)	ns	-	ns	ns	ns	ns	ns
Ethnic threat (static)	ns	ns	ns	ns	ns	ns	ns
Economic threat (static)	ns	ns	ns	ns	+	ns	ns
Inequality threat (static)	ns	ns	ns	ns	ns	ns	ns
Social Disorganization							
Crime rate (static)	ns	ns	ns	ns	-	ns	+
Juvenile arrest rate (static)	ns	ns	ns	+	ns	ns	-
Ethnic heterogeneity	ns	ns	ns	ns	ns	ns	ns
Youth density (static)	ns	ns	ns	-	ns	ns	+
Political economy							
External polity (election)	ns	ns	ns	ns	ns	ns	ns
External economy (wealth)	ns	-	ns	ns	ns	ns	ns
Internal polity (conservative)	ns	+	+	ns	+	ns	ns
Internal economy (urban)	ns	ns	ns	ns	ns	ns	ns

Note: + = positive association ($p < .05$); - = negative association ($p < .05$); ns = no significant association.

artifacts. That said, as with the 2010 findings, there are few patterns in these results.

The contextual factor associated with the most outcomes was conservatism (i.e. internal polity). Specifically, conservative voting majority was positively associated with odds of petition and odds of adjudication of delinquency, supporting hypotheses $\mathbf{H_{3B}}$ and $\mathbf{H_{3D}}$ that punitive outcomes would be more likely in more conservative juvenile courts. However, odds of diversion (versus release) were also positively associated with conservatism, contrary to $\mathbf{H_{3B}}$. In effect, these results indicate that *dismissal* was especially unlikely in more conservative counties—an interesting result that possibly indicates that conservative juvenile courts are more sensitive to the perception that they are letting delinquents off without any repercussions for their offenses.

Additionally, three other contextual factors were associated with multiple outcomes: crime rates, juvenile arrest rates, and youth population density. Notably, these are all indicators of social disorganization. First, crime rates were negatively associated with odds of adjudication of delinquency—contrary to $\mathbf{H_{2D}}$—and positively associated with odds of placement—in support of $\mathbf{H_{2E}}$. Second, juvenile arrest rates were positively associated with odds of waiver—in support of $\mathbf{H_{2C}}$—and negatively associated with odds of placement—contrary to $\mathbf{H_{2E}}$. Third, youth population density was negatively associated with odds of waiver—in contrast to $\mathbf{H_{2C}}$ —and positively associated with odds of placement—in support of $\mathbf{H_{2E}}$. In sum, we see a relationship between social disorganization and three outcomes—waiver, adjudication, and placement. For each outcome, interestingly, one association supported while another contradicted the research hypotheses. The only other significant associations that are supportive of research hypotheses are the negative association between static racial threat and diversion ($\mathbf{H_{1B}}$) and the positive association between static economic threat and adjudication ($\mathbf{H_{1D}}$). The negative association between odds of diversion and external economy (i.e. median wealth), however, does not support $\mathbf{H_{3B}}$.

In total, then, approximately half of the significant associations (i.e. 7 of 12) supported the research hypotheses—slightly more support than the research hypotheses received in 2010. (Specifically, 5 out of 140 possible associations supported research hypotheses in 2010—3.6 percent—compared to 7 out of 84 possible associations supporting research hypotheses in 2000—8.3 percent.) Of these 7 associations, 2 supported community threat hypotheses (out of 28 tests), 3 supported social disorganization hypotheses (out of 28 tests), and 2 supported political economy hypotheses (out of 28 tests). Looking at different stages of juvenile processing: diversion, adjudication of delinquency, and secure placement were each associated with three contextual variables, while waiver was associated with two contextual factors and petition was associated with one contextual factor. One similarity with the 2010 findings is that *preadjudication detention was not associated with any contextual factors*. Like 2010, the main takeaway from the above is that while major juvenile court outcomes vary significantly across states and across counties within states, this variation is not explained by community threat, social disorganization, or political economy.

Still, it is worth comparing the findings from 2000 and 2010. Only three associations were observed in both datasets. First, waiver to criminal court was negatively associated with youth population density in 2000 as well as 2010. Second, residential placement was negatively associated with juvenile arrest rates in 2000 as well as 2010. Third, adjudication of delinquency was positively associated with conservative voting majority in 2000 as well as 2010. Of these, only the association between internal polity and adjudication supports the research hypotheses ($\mathbf{H}_{3D}$).[3] That is, there is some support for the notion that juvenile court judges were more likely to find petitioned offenders delinquent, as opposed to dismissing or diverting them, in more conservative counties. Yet findings did not support the notion that detention, waiver, or secure placement was more likely in more conservative counties. (Formal petitions were more likely in more conservative counties in 2000 but not in 2010.) It may be, as Feld (1993) has argued, that the conservative "get tough" movement in juvenile justice was associated with more formal processing (i.e. petition and adjudication) but not necessarily more severe *punishment* (i.e. placement). That is, one sense of "punitive" is *severity of sanction*—such as more juvenile offenders being placed in residential facilities—but another sense of "punitive" is the criminalization of conduct or the inflexibility of doctrines of criminal liability—such as more petitioned juveniles being formally processed and adjudicated delinquent (Whitman, 2003). Even in terms of formal processing rather than punishment, however, the overall contextual patterns are quite weak.

State-Level Findings, 2010

Table 9.3 presents the state-level findings for the year 2010 (see Chapter 8). The table displays 12 research hypotheses—4 community threat hypotheses, 5 social disorganization hypotheses, and 3 political economy hypotheses—for each of the 6 states (Connecticut was excluded). In each cell of the table, notations for the juvenile court outcomes—detention (DT), diversion (DV), petition (PT), waiver (WV), adjudication (AD), judicial release (JR), and judicial placement (JP)—are included if there was a significant association (at $p < .05$), along with an indication of a positive (+) or negative (–) association. This reflects a total of 480 tests of the state-specific research hypotheses.[4]

Table 9.3 Summary of state-level contextual findings

Research Hypothesis	*AL*	*MO*	*OR*	*SC*	*TX*	*UT*
Community Threats						
Racial threat (static)			WV(-),AD(-)	AD(-)	PT(+),AD(-)	
Ethnic threat (static)	WV(-)	DT(+),WV(-)	DT(+)			
Economic threat (static)		DT(+), DV(+)	WV(-)		AD(+), JP(+)	
Inequality threat (static)	WV(-)		WV(+)	JR(-)	AD(-), JP(-)	
Social Disorganization						
Crime rate (static)	WV(-)	DT(+), DV(+)	DV(-), PT(-), JR(+)	DV(-)	DV(+), PT(+),WV(+)	AD(-)
Juvenile arrest rate (static)	AD(-)	DT(-), DV(+), PT(+), AD(+), JP(-)	DT(+)			
Ethnic heterogeneity		DV(-)		DV(+)		
Residential mobility	JR(-), JP(-)			AD(+)		
Youth density (static)	DV(-), PT(-)		DT(-)	PT(-),AD(+)		AD(-)
Political economy						
External economy (wealth)	DT(+)		WV(-),AD(-)		DT(+),WV(-), JR(+), JP(-)	JP(+)
Internal polity (conservative)	DT(+)		DT(-),WV(-), JR(-)	AD(+)	WV(+),AD(+), JP(+)	
Internal economy (urban)	DT(-),WV(-)	PT(-),AD(-)	DT(-), PT(-), JP(+)	AD(+)		DT(+)

Note: DT = detention; DV = diversion; PT = petition; WV = waiver; AD = adjudication; JR = judicial release; JP = placement. Significant association ($p < .05$) indicated with outcome abbreviation and positive (+) or negative (-) association. Empty cells indicate no significant associations.

Of these 480 tested associations, 73 were significant, or approximately 15 percent. By chance, we would expect approximately 24 significant associations, so this indicates that some of these associations are likely real and not merely statistical artifacts.

First, for community threat hypotheses, findings indicated support for each hypothesis in *some* states and for *some* outcomes. For the racial threat hypothesis, which was not supported for any outcome in the multistate analysis, percent Black was positively associated with odds of petition in Texas—in support of the hypothesis. Contrary to the hypothesis, however, percent Black was negatively associated with odds of waiver in Oregon and negatively associated with odds of adjudication in Oregon, South Carolina, and Texas. For the ethnic threat hypothesis, which was not supported for any outcome in the multistate analysis, percent Hispanic was positively associated with odds of detention in Missouri and Oregon—in support of the hypothesis—and negatively associated with odds of waiver in Alabama and Missouri—contrary to the hypothesis.

For the economic threat hypothesis, which was not supported for any outcome in the multistate analysis, concentrated disadvantage was positively associated with odds of detention in Missouri, and positively associated with odds of adjudication and placement in Texas—in support of the hypothesis. Contrary to the hypothesis, however, concentrated disadvantage was positively associated with odds of diversion in Missouri and negatively associated with odds of waiver in Oregon. For the inequality threat hypothesis, which was supported for waiver in the multistate analysis, income inequality was positively associated with odds of waiver in Oregon and negatively associated with odds of judicial release in South Carolina—in support of the hypothesis. Contrary to the hypothesis, however, income inequality was negatively associated with odds of waiver in Alabama and negatively associated with odds of adjudication and placement in Texas.

Second, for social disorganization hypotheses, findings indicated support for each hypothesis in *some* states and for *some* outcomes. Crime rates were not associated with any outcome in the multistate analysis, but crime rates were positively associated with odds of detention in Missouri, negatively associated with odds of diversion in Oregon and South Carolina, and positively associated with odds of petition and odds of waiver in Texas—all in support of the hypothesis. Contrary to the hypothesis, crime rates were also negatively associated with odds of waiver in Alabama, positively associated with odds of diversion in Missouri and Texas, negatively associated with odds of petition in Oregon, negatively associated with odds of adjudication in Utah, and positively associated with odds of judicial release in Oregon. In the multistate analysis, juvenile crime was (only) negatively associated with judicial placement. Across states, in support of the hypothesis, juvenile arrest rates were positively associated with odds of detention in Oregon and positively associated with odds of petition and adjudication in Missouri. Contrary to the hypothesis, however, juvenile arrest rates were negatively associated with odds of detention in Missouri, positively associated with odds of diversion in Missouri, negatively associated with odds of adjudication in Alabama, and negatively associated with odds of placement in Missouri.

In the multistate analysis, ethnic heterogeneity was (only) positively associated with judicial release at disposition. Across states, however, ethnic heterogeneity was not associated with judicial release. Instead, heterogeneity was negatively associated with odds of diversion in Missouri—in support of the hypothesis—and positively associated with odds of diversion in South Carolina—contrary to the hypothesis. In the multistate analysis, residential mobility was negatively associated with odds of waiver, judicial release, and judicial placement. Across states, in support of the hypothesis, residential mobility was positively associated with odds of adjudication in South Carolina and negatively associated with odds of judicial release in Alabama. Contrary to the hypothesis, residential mobility was also negatively associated with odds of judicial placement in Alabama. In the multistate analysis, youth population density was negatively associated with odds of waiver. Across states, in support of the hypothesis, youth population density was negatively associated with odds of diversion in Alabama and positively associated with odds of adjudication in South Carolina. Contrary to the hypothesis, youth population density was negatively associated with odds of detention in Oregon, negatively associated with odds of petition in Alabama and South Carolina, and negatively associated with odds of adjudication in Utah.

Third, for political economy hypotheses, findings indicated support for each hypothesis in *some* states and for *some* outcomes. For external economy, which received support (only) for waiver in the multistate analyses, median income was negatively associated with odds of waiver in Oregon and Texas, negatively associated with odds of adjudication in Oregon, positively associated with odds of judicial release in Texas, and negatively associated with odds of placement in Texas—all in support of the hypothesis. Contrary to the hypothesis, median income was positively associated with odds of detention in Alabama and Texas.

For internal polity, which received support (only) for adjudication in the multistate analyses, conservatism was positively associated with odds of detention in Alabama, positively associated with odds of waiver in Texas, positively associated with odds of adjudication in South Carolina and Texas, negatively associated with judicial release in Oregon, and positively associated with odds of placement in Texas—all in support of the hypothesis. Contrary to the internal polity hypothesis, conservatism was negatively associated with odds of detention as well as odds of waiver in Oregon. For internal economy, which was not associated with any outcomes in the multistate analyses, urbanism was positively associated with odds of detention in Utah, positively associated with odds of adjudication in South Carolina, and positively associated with odds of placement in Oregon. Contrary to the internal economy hypothesis, urbanism was negatively associated with odds of detention in Alabama and Oregon, negatively associated with odds of petition in Missouri and Oregon, negatively associated with odds of waiver in Alabama, and negatively associated with odds of adjudication in Missouri.

In total, then, approximately half of the significant associations (i.e. 35 of 73) supported the research hypotheses for state-level analyses. Of these 35 associations, 8 supported community threat hypotheses (out of 160 tests, or 5 percent), 12 supported social disorganization hypotheses (out of 200 tests, or 6 percent), and 14 supported political economy hypotheses (out of 120 tests, or 11.7 percent). As with the multistate analyses, the overall support is quite limited and there are no clear patterns in the findings. Also similar to the multistate findings, support is weaker for community threats and social disorganization than political economy. The most support for contextual hypotheses was found in Texas, where 11 out of 84 tested associations were in support of the research hypotheses (i.e. 13.1 percent), while the least support involved Utah, where there was only one association in support of the research hypotheses (i.e. 1.4 percent). This may simply reflect statistical power, as these happen to be the states with the largest and smallest level-2 sample sizes ($N = 189$ and $N = 22$, respectively). That said, political economy factors alone were associated with several juvenile justice outcomes in Texas in directions supportive of the hypotheses. It is thus possible that political economy factors influenced juvenile court processing in Texas more than other states.

One notable observation is that while 3.6 percent of hypotheses received support in the multistate analysis for 2010 (i.e. 5 out of 140), 7.3 percent of hypotheses received support in the state-level analyses (i.e. 35 out of 480). This might indicate heterogeneity in contextual influences across states, such that different contextual influences "cancel out" across states, producing less overall support in the multistate analysis. It may be that county-level differences in community threat, social disorganization, and political economy matter more *within* states, and that contextual patterns are harder to detect across states due to state-level differences in how context influences juvenile court processing.

State Variation in Juvenile Justice Outcomes

Despite the limited support for the influence of macro-social context on juvenile court processing, one major takeaway of the study findings is that juvenile court outcomes did vary significantly across *state* juvenile justice systems. In some cases, this may just reflect differences in how state juvenile justice systems operate. Indeed, states differed considerably in terms of what percentage of cases received each juvenile court outcome (see Appendix A).

While these descriptive differences are of great interest, they do not capture whether the differences in case processing across states are statistically significant after controlling for case-level differences. As such, I conducted supplemental analyses with *states as predictors of juvenile court outcomes*. To do so, I employed two-level multilevel models including case-level control variables *only*. (County-level measures were excluded due to collinearity issues.) The focus of the analysis was on whether states differed significantly in the probability that a case referral would receive each juvenile court outcome after controlling for case-level factors (such as offense type, age, and race/ethnicity). Following multilevel regression analyses, I estimated predicted probabilities for each outcome across states, then tested whether these probabilities were significantly different across states (i.e. marginal effects). Table 9.4 displays the findings.

Table 9.4 Outcome probabilities across states

	Outcome	*Predicted probability*	*Contrast*
	Detention		
a	Alabama	.1311	e, *f*, g
b	Connecticut	.1235	*f*
c	Missouri	.1248	*d*, e, *f*, g
d	Oregon	.1655	*c*, *f*
e	South Carolina	.1698	*a*, *c*, *f*
f	Texas	.3902	*a*, *b*, *c*, *d*, e, g
g	Utah	.1969	*a*, *c*, *d*, *f*
	Dismissal (Intake)		
a	Alabama	.1263	*b*, *d*, e, *f*, g
b	Connecticut	.3344	*a*, *c*, *f*, g
c	Missouri	.1091	*d*, e, *f*, g
d	Oregon	.3439	*a*, *c*, e, *f*, g
e	South Carolina	.2724	*a*, *c*, *d*, *f*, g
f	Texas	.1839	*a*, *b*, *c*, *d*, e, g
g	Utah	.0254	*a*, *b*, *c*, *d*, e, *f*
	Diversion		
a	Alabama	.0809	*c*, *d*, e, *f*, g
b	Connecticut	.1395	*c*, *d*, e, *f*, g
c	Missouri	.5831	*a*, *b*, *d*, e, g
d	Oregon	.3325	*a*, *b*, *c*, *f*
e	South Carolina	.3124	*a*, *b*, *c*, *f*
f	Texas	.5584	*a*, *b*, *d*, e, g
g	Utah	.3280	*a*, *b*, *c*, *f*
	Petition		
a	Alabama	.7929	*b*, *c*, *d*, e, *f*, g
b	Connecticut	.5261	*a*, *c*, *d*, *f*, g
c	Missouri	.3079	*a*, *b*, e, *f*, g

Table 9.4 Cont.

	Outcome	*Predicted probability*	*Contrast*
d	Oregon	.3236	*a, b,* e, *f, g*
e	South Carolina	.4151	*a, c, f, g*
f	Texas	.2577	*a, b, c, d,* e, *g*
g	Utah	.6466	*a, b, c, d,* e, *f*
	Waiver to criminal court		
a	Alabama	.0209	e, *f, g*
b	Connecticut	.0295	*g*
c	Missouri	.0154	e, *g*
d	Oregon	.0259	e, *f, g*
e	South Carolina	.0060	*a, c, d, g*
f	Texas	.0105	*a, b, d, g*
g	Utah	.0005	*a, b, c, d,* e, *f*
	Adjudication of delinquency		
a	Alabama	.4920	*c, d,* e, *f, g*
b	Connecticut	.4591	*c, d,* e, *f, g*
c	Missouri	.9293	*a, b, f, g*
d	Oregon	.8980	*a, b, f, g*
e	South Carolina	.9232	*a, b, f, g*
f	Texas	.7989	*a, b, c, d,* e
g	Utah	.7731	*a, b, c, d,* e
	Judicial release		
a	Alabama	.0761	*b, c, d, f*
b	Connecticut	.1921	*a, c, f, g*
c	Missouri	.0092	*a, b, d,* e, *f, g*
d	Oregon	.2761	*a, c,* e, *f, g*
e	South Carolina	.0844	*c, d, f*
f	Texas	.0474	*a, b, c, d,* e
g	Utah	.0513	*b, c, d,* e
	Community supervision		
a	Alabama	.8565	*b, c, d,* e, *g*
b	Connecticut	.6584	*a, f, g*
c	Missouri	.5624	*a,* e, *f, g*
d	Oregon	.6048	*a,* e, *f, g*
e	South Carolina	.6953	*a, c, d, f, g*
f	Texas	.8829	*b, c, d,* e, *g*
g	Utah	.7872	*a, b, c, d,* e, *f*
	Secure placement		
a	Alabama	.0674	*b, c, d,* e, *g*
b	Connecticut	.1495	*a, c,* e, *f*
c	Missouri	.4284	*a, b, d,* e, *f, g*
d	Oregon	.1191	*a, c,* e, *f*
e	South Carolina	.2203	*a, b, c, d, f, g*
f	Texas	.0699	*b, c, d,* e, *g*
g	Utah	.1615	*a, c,* e, *f*

Note: The "contrasts" column reports which probabilities are significantly different across states (i.e. marginal effects) at $p < .05$.

First, the probability of preadjudication detention among referrals to juvenile court ranged from 12.4 percent in Connecticut to 39 percent in Texas. Tests of differences (see "Contrasts") indicated that referrals were significantly more likely to receive detention in Texas than in any other state. Next most likely was in Utah, where the probability of detention was 19.7 percent, significantly greater than in Alabama (13.1 percent), Missouri (12.5 percent), or Oregon (16.6 percent). In South Carolina, the probability was 17 percent, significantly greater than in Alabama or Missouri. Although it was the lowest among states, Connecticut's probability of detention did not differ significantly from most other states (indicating a wide confidence interval, or less precise estimate). There was thus one group of states with low probability of detention (Alabama, Connecticut, and Missouri), a second group of states with slightly higher probability of detention (Oregon, South Carolina, and Utah), and Texas standing out as the extreme outlier with a high probability of detention.

Second, the probability of dismissal at intake among referrals to juvenile court ranged from 2.5 percent in Utah to 34.4 percent in Oregon. Tests of differences indicated that referrals were significantly less likely to be dismissed in Utah than any other state—making it the outlier here. Dismissal was most likely in Connecticut and Oregon (no significant difference), followed by South Carolina, then Texas, then Alabama and Missouri (no significant difference), then Utah. Correspondingly, the probability of informal diversion ranged from 8.1 percent in Alabama to 58.3 percent in Missouri. Diversion was most likely in Texas and Missouri (no significant difference), followed by Oregon, South Carolina, and Utah (no significant difference), and least likely in Alabama and Connecticut (no significant difference). For formal petition, probabilities ranged from 25.8 percent in Texas to 79.3 percent in Alabama. Formal petition was most likely in Alabama, followed by Utah, Connecticut, and South Carolina (no significant difference), then Missouri and Oregon (no significant difference), and was least likely in Texas. Looking at these intake processing outcomes together, there are states where most referrals were formally petitioned—Alabama and Utah—states where more than half of the cases were diverted to informal processing and formal petition was less common—Missouri and Texas—and states where rates of dismissal at intake were quite high—Connecticut, Oregon, and South Carolina. This would appear to indicate different approaches to intake screening among states, since similar cases may be dismissed in one state (e.g. Oregon), diverted in another (e.g. Missouri), and petitioned in yet another (e.g. Alabama).

Third, the probability of judicial waiver to criminal court ranged from .05 percent in Utah to 3 percent in Connecticut. Tests of differences indicated that referrals were significantly less likely to be waived to criminal court in

Utah than any other state. Beyond Utah as the extreme outlier (since almost no cases were judicially waived there), states could be grouped into those where waiver was more likely, about 1.5–3 percent probability (Alabama, Connecticut, Missouri, and Oregon), and states with lower waiver probability, about .5–1 percent (South Carolina and Texas). Since other forms of waiver are not included in this analysis (i.e. prosecutorial direct-file and statutory exclusion), however, these comparisons should be interpreted with caution.[5] Fourth, the probability of adjudication of delinquency ranged from 45.9 percent in Connecticut to 92.9 percent in Missouri. Tests of differences indicated that odds of adjudication were highest in Missouri, Oregon, and South Carolina (no significant difference), followed by Texas and Utah (no significant difference), and were lowest in Alabama and Connecticut (no significant difference).

Finally, for judicial disposition, the probability of judicial release ranged from .9 percent in Missouri to 27.6 percent in Oregon. Tests of differences indicated that Missouri was the extreme outlier, with significantly lower probability of release than any other state. Judicial release was most likely in Connecticut and Oregon (no significant difference), followed by Alabama and South Carolina (no significant difference), then Texas and Utah (no significant difference), then Missouri. For community supervision, probabilities ranged from 56.2 percent in Missouri to 88.3 percent in Texas. Community supervision was most likely in Alabama and Texas, followed by Utah, then Connecticut and South Carolina (no significant difference), then Missouri and Oregon (no significant difference). Correspondingly, the probability of residential placement ranged from 6.7 percent in Alabama to 42.8 percent in Missouri. Missouri here stands out as the outlier, with significantly higher probability of secure placement than any other state. This is followed by South Carolina, then Connecticut, Oregon, and Utah (no significant difference), and least likely in Alabama and Texas (no significant difference).

Looking at these judicial disposition outcomes together, it appears that there are states in which most delinquent cases are sentenced to community supervision (Alabama, Texas, and Utah), states where a substantial proportion of delinquent cases are committed to residential placement (South Carolina and Missouri), and states where rates of judicial release following adjudication of delinquency are quite high (Connecticut and Oregon). Interestingly, states with high placement rates also tend to have high adjudication rates—suggestive of more "punitive" systems—but these states also tend to have lower formal petition rates. This may indicate that less serious cases are simply not petitioned in some states; as a result, petitioned cases are more likely to be adjudicated delinquent and then committed to secure placement because they represent a more serious group of offenders.

State Profiles

What emerges from the above is that each state has its own model of juvenile justice processing. If we roughly group states into "low," "medium," and "high" for each stage of processing, we can summarize each state as follows.[6]

Compared to others, Alabama's juvenile justice system was relatively low on preadjudication detention, high on formal petition while low on diversion and dismissal (at intake), high on waiver to criminal court, low on adjudication of delinquency, and high on community supervision while low on secure placement (and medium on judicial release). Alabama appeared to treat adjudication quite differently from other states, allowing most cases to be petitioned but then diverting or dismissing them at the adjudicatory stage. This is neither more nor less punitive than other states which might perform the same function earlier, at intake processing by the probation officer. It is simply a different processing model.

Connecticut's juvenile justice system was low on preadjudication detention, high on dismissal at intake, high on waiver to criminal court, low on adjudication of delinquency, and high on judicial release while medium on community supervision and secure placement. Connecticut did not process most of its cases formally, but rather dismissed them at intake or later at adjudication. (Only about one quarter of all referrals were ultimately adjudicated delinquent.) Even among those cases that were adjudicated delinquent, there was a high rate of judicial release. This might indicate that community alternatives to formal sanctions were widespread in Connecticut, which was the wealthiest of the states profiled here. It may also reveal that a philosophy of "non-intervention" had taken hold in Connecticut.

Missouri's juvenile justice system was low on preadjudication detention, high on diversion, high on waiver to criminal court, high on adjudication of delinquency, and high on secure placement while medium on community supervision and extremely low on judicial release. This suggests that the Missouri juvenile justice system performed efficient screening at the petition stage, sending only the most serious delinquents into formal processing and diverting most non-serious cases. This resulted in a high diversion rate as well as high adjudication and placement rates, likely for a smaller sample of more serious offenders (as noted above). It would appear to be a model that is quite consistent with the original, interventionist and diversionary vision of the juvenile court.

Oregon's juvenile justice system was medium on preadjudication detention, low on formal petition while medium on diversion and high on dismissal, high on waiver to criminal court, high on adjudication of delinquency, and high on judicial release while low on community supervision and medium on secure placement. These findings suggest that only the most serious cases were formally petitioned in Oregon, most of which were then also adjudicated delinquent. Judges also diverted a larger share of these delinquent youth at the disposition stage—which might have occurred earlier in other states, such as at petition or adjudication. As with Connecticut, the high dismissal probability at intake might suggest that there were community alternatives that were not officially counted as diversion. While Connecticut and Oregon are geographically quite distinct, they are both coastal states far outside the South—and represent the two most politically progressive states (i.e. Democrat) in the analysis.

South Carolina's juvenile justice system was medium on preadjudication detention, high on dismissal at intake while medium on diversion and petition, medium on waiver to criminal court, high on adjudication of delinquency, and high on secure placement while medium on community supervision and judicial release. This fits into the pattern of lower probability of petition coupled with higher probability of adjudication and detention (e.g., Missouri)—suggesting screening of more serious cases at intake. Overall, it may be fair to characterize South Carolina as a relatively "punitive" juvenile justice system.

Texas' juvenile justice system was extremely high on preadjudication detention, low on formal petition while high on diversion and medium on dismissal, medium on waiver to criminal court, medium on adjudication of delinquency, and high on community supervision while low on judicial release and secure placement. Texas stood out as a real outlier in terms of detaining juvenile referrals during intake processing, yet was *not* more punitive in terms of other outcomes. In fact, most cases were diverted rather than formally processed, and adjudication and placement rates were low even among the lower numbers of (possibly more serious) petitioned youth. In fact, Texas was one of the more *lenient* systems of juvenile justice except for preadjudication detention—where it was the most punitive. Mears (2017) suggests that in one large county in Texas, the juvenile probation officer was motivated by rehabilitation while the prosecutor "emphasized due process above all else" (p. 102). Such role conflict may produce difficult-to-interpret results, with some aspects of the system appearing lenient while others appear punitive.

Finally, Utah's juvenile justice system was high on preadjudication detention, high on formal petition while medium on diversion and extremely low on dismissal, low on waiver to criminal court, medium on adjudication of delinquency, and high on community supervision while medium on secure placement and low on judicial release. Utah dismissed almost no cases, waived almost no cases, and discharged almost no cases at judicial disposition. Instead, most cases were handled formally, within the juvenile justice system, with some filtering at adjudication and judicial release. The judge, then, appears to have substantial discretion in this system. Placement rates were neither especially low nor high compared to other states, and community supervision was the typical outcome for a juvenile offender that was adjudicated delinquent. In some sense, this looks like an especially "interventionist" juvenile justice system in terms of processing outcomes, exercising a large amount of formal social control but not in an excessively punitive manner.

The above illustrates that the manner in which juvenile offenders are processed can differ dramatically across juvenile justice systems. In some states, preadjudication detention is common while in others it is rare. Certain states more aggressively utilize diversion at the adjudicatory stage, while others divert cases at intake (by the probation officer) and apply more formal processing to petitioned cases. Some states send a larger share of juvenile delinquents to secure placement, but this often seems to be a function of having a more select group of juvenile offenders who are adjudicated delinquent in the first place (i.e. a selection effect). This results in quite different rates of petition, adjudication, and placement across states—but in ways that complicate whether some states are more "punitive" than others.

In terms of each state's statutory purpose clause, a few observations are worthwhile. First, five states employed "balanced and restorative justice" rhetoric, but there are many differences among these states in terms of processing. Each state system has selected a "balance" of goals that result in stark differences in processing outcomes. Interestingly, only one state in this study employed "due process" language—Texas—and it is the outlier in terms of preadjudication detention. However, it was *not* the most punitive state in any other dimension. It would appear that the "due process" orientation of the Texas juvenile justice system resulted in formal treatment for immediate referrals (i.e. detention), but did not result in more formal or punitive outcomes in later processing. Additionally, only one state employed the traditional "parens patriae" language—Missouri. Interestingly, Missouri served as an outlier at intake, sending most referrals to informal processing (i.e. diversion). This appears consistent with its more traditional orientation. It may be that statutory purpose clauses are most revealing for states that have *not* adopted the majority "balanced and restorative justice" language, but instead retain their own unique purposes, corresponding to the original mission of the juvenile court (i.e. parens patriae) or to the formal criminalization of the court (i.e. due process).

Study Limitations

Several limitations confronted the present study. First, the study utilized a large, multijurisdictional sample in order to possess sufficient statistical power to test myriad contextual factors that were predicted to influence juvenile justice processing. However, such a sample may pose the concern that different state systems are simply not comparable.[7] For example, Myers and Talarico (1987) argue, "We consider it appropriate, if not essential, to focus on the sentencing process within a single state" (p. 16). The same argument could be made in favor of studying only one *court* at a time, as even differences within state juvenile justice systems may complicate interpretation of findings. There are tradeoffs here between precision and generalizability. Research on a single jurisdiction may be better positioned to interpret its findings—but less well positioned to make conclusions about juvenile justice more generally. On the one hand, limiting focus to individual jurisdictions means never moving beyond 51 different, possibly conflicting, conclusions about the relationship between juvenile justice and community context. On the other hand, multijurisdictional research runs the risk of being overbroad, ignoring important differences among the trees in the quest to understand the forest. As such, these research strategies should complement each other in trying to discover patterns in juvenile justice processing. Indeed, the ideal research strategy would include different levels of analysis, from court-specific qualitative inquiry to quantitative analyses of "big data" that combine multiple jurisdictions. The present research takes the latter "macro" approach, but this is not necessarily superior to less generalizable, more in-depth research such as qualitative work.

Another limitation is that while this study aimed at a comprehensive exploration of the influence of macro-social context on juvenile court processing, the analytical models did not include every relevant case or county-level variable. At the case-level, this is particularly apparent. In addition to unmeasured characteristics such as developmental maturity, substance abuse, family situation, attitudinal factors (e.g. remorse), victim characteristics, and strength of evidence—variables that are rarely included in criminal justice system research (Baumer, 2013)—the present study also did not include a measure of prior record. This is because three states (Missouri, Oregon, and Texas) did not provide this information. As such, approximately 60 percent of referrals—and, more importantly, 70 percent of counties—were missing an indicator of prior record. Dropping these observations was not desirable given that one of the chief strengths of the dataset was the large number of level-2 units. This provided sufficient statistical power for multilevel analysis to examine many contextual (i.e. level-2) variables (see Johnson, 2010).

The possibility of omitted variable bias at the county level (i.e., level 2) was largely mitigated by the comprehensive catalogue of contextual variables included in the present study. A related issue, however, is whether context is properly measured by variables created at the county-level, or whether certain levels of analysis are omitted. As Wenger (2019) observes, "there is no a priori reason to believe that complex theoretical constructs, like disadvantage, inequality, residential stability, and so on operate at only one geographic level" (p. 7). Quantitative research is limited, of course, by what can be measured in quantifiable terms (see, e.g., Mears, 1998; Michell, 1997; Schedler, 2012). It is quite possible that the most important contributors to juvenile court outcomes, including the influence of context, cannot be measured with county-level Census data. For example, social disorganization was developed as a neighborhood-level theory, so higher levels of aggregation, such as the county, may not be appropriate (see Pratt & Cullen, 2005). Similarly, the best way to test organizational theory would ideally involve court-level data collection, probably including in-depth, qualitative interviews with court personnel. For political economy of the juvenile court, the measures in the present study were proxies that allowed for quantitative measurement of a concept that may be more elusive. For example, internal polity (i.e. judicial conservatism) was measured using the proxy of conservative voting majority in the county, which may not align with judicial ideology. That is, judges may be more or less conservative than the surrounding community. Judges within a particular court may also differ in their ideological orientations from one another, and only a direct survey of individual judges would capture such differences in judicial philosophy. Similarly, external economy (i.e. community wealth and resources) was measured by county median income, but many nuances of community resource allocation are not included in this measure. Internal economy (i.e. bureaucratization) was measured by urbanism, but may also be more accurately captured by direct observation—perhaps some urban courts are highly bureaucratized, while others are not. In each case, the present study used general county-level proxy measures that sacrifice precision for the ability to measure *something* that plausibly approximates the construct of interest.

The above measurement issues, notably omitted variable bias and construct validity, plague most research of criminal and juvenile justice processing (Baumer, 2013).[8] A related point is that observational research may be inherently limited in studying court decision-making. As Ulmer (2012) observes,

> [A]lmost all the theoretical frameworks applied to sentencing, such as focal concerns, uncertainty avoidance/causal attribution, rational choice, and racial threat ideas directly or indirectly rest on depictions of individual social psychological processes. *None of these processes can be directly observed with sentencing or even earlier case processing outcome data.*
>
> (pp. 33–34, emphasis in original)

In other words, even the most robust quantitative and qualitative research—in terms of data, methods, and analysis—cannot "directly tell us what was going on in courtroom workgroup members' heads, or the content of their interactions with each other" (Ulmer, 2012, p. 34). The possibility of unmeasured—or *unmeasurable*—variables serves as an important global limitation to observational social science research, encouraging caution and humility in formulating conclusions based on such imperfect evidence.

Interpretation of Findings

Why does the influence of contextual factors on juvenile punishment appear so limited? The variation in juvenile court outcomes across counties and states was substantial, but does not appear attributable to sociopolitical or organizational context, at least as measured in the present study. Here, I close the chapter with four possible interpretations of the findings.

First, the most obvious interpretation is that community threat, social disorganization, and political economy do not influence the operations of the juvenile justice system and the imposition of juvenile sanctions. In terms of the dominant sociopolitical theoretical framework, community threat received little support. This is consistent with prior research, where community threat hypotheses have received mixed support (Feldmeyer & Cochran, 2018). Since the threat perspective is rooted in conflict theory, as described in Chapter 3, one possible implication is that conflict theory simply does not capture how justice systems operate. This is not a novel suggestion. Almost three decades ago, Hagan (1989) argued that "conflict theories do not provide sufficient attention to the structural relationships that emerge from a joining of organizational and political forces in the direction of criminal justice operations" (p. 117). More recently, King and Light (2019) confessed: "We have tested and found support for the group threat perspective in our own research but have become skeptical of the theory's relevance for explaining criminal punishment, including racial sentencing disparities" (p. 404). The present findings corroborate these conclusions, casting doubt on the validity of the community threat perspective in the juvenile justice context. Importantly, however, rival contextual theoretical frameworks—social disorganization and the political economy of the juvenile court—also received limited support. At a minimum, then, the conflict perspective is not *uniquely* poor at predicting variation in juvenile court outcomes. Instead, it appears that county-level factors simply were not related to variation in juvenile court outcomes across different courts and systems.

This brings us to a second interpretation of the findings. As noted in the limitations above, it may be that the county is the wrong unit of analysis and aggregates too much, such that the contextual measures used in the present study were too broad to account for the variation of interest. Specifically, these contextual measures did not assess variation *within* courts. Britt (2000) observes that contextual hypotheses about criminal justice decision-making assume "that judges within the same court jurisdiction will respond in the same way to broader contextual issues such as racial and ethnic composition," and yet, "it is difficult to see how judges would perceive social and economic conditions similarly and then punish offenders in the same way" (pp. 729–730). That is, focusing on the demographics of the surrounding community may not capture the relevant court context, and judges may not even be aware of many community characteristics of interest to researchers. For example, Ulmer and Johnson (2004) found limited support for community threats but found strong evidence that organizational court characteristics—size, trial rate, and guideline departure rate—were significantly related to sentencing guideline departures (see also Johnson, 2005, 2006; Ulmer & Johnson, 2017). While the present study included measures of political economy, these too were based on community measures (i.e. county-level data) rather than court-specific measures. Moreover, the focus on community context may fail to capture factors that distinguish courts, or that distinguish judges, prosecutors, and probation officers within courts (see Kim, Spohn, & Hedberg, 2015). It is thus possible that *court*-level measures may be more appropriate than *county*-level measures. Future research must seek better measures of these court-level influences, mainly through primary data collection that aims to capture the richness of courtroom workgroups (see Ulmer, 1997, 2012, 2019).

One challenge to this interpretation, however, is that county-level variation *was* identified. Thus, it may be that the county is *not* the wrong level of analysis—after all, substantial variation across counties was observed. While "meso"-level research that explores variation *within* juvenile courts would add much to our knowledge, we also know that there is "macro"-level variation across courts and the counties in which they are embedded. While the present findings showed little support for community threat, social disorganization, or political economy, it was the last of these that received the most support. This might indicate that more intellectual resources should be directed toward organizational characteristics of the juvenile court, its political economy as well as its internal culture, to explain variation in juvenile punishment across counties. As Arazan, Bales, and Blomberg (2019) recently observed,

> [N]oticeably absent from the previous literature is discussion of accurately modeling courtroom organization theories that clearly discuss the court being embedded within the community and reflective of community norms and values. Technically, as courts are embedded within their local communities, a better structure for these multilevel analyses

> would be at least a three-level structure that accounted for the embedded structure of offender within courts within communities.
>
> (p. 42)

As such, it may be that more "macro"-level research is needed, but that it should focus on underexamined organizational variables instead of the more commonly examined demographic variables related to community threats and social disorganization. While the present research included several contextual variables measuring different aspects of political economy, such as judicial elections and county politics, it may be that there are other organizational factors that require further examination such as caseload pressure or court culture.

While this second interpretation is perhaps the most optimistic one—variation in juvenile justice processing *can* be explained by contextual factors that we have not yet measured adequately—a more pessimistic interpretation of the findings is that variation in juvenile court outcomes is *irreducibly complex*. After all, prior research has not identified *any* contextual variables that are consistently associated with juvenile court outcomes. This may simply mean that there are no contextual factors that are associated with juvenile court outcomes across different communities and systems. Instead, certain contextual factors may influence some courts, at some times and places, but not others. The complex social world may not admit of clean regularities, a challenge for social scientists who desire to explain it (see Hayek 1955, 1967). Barker (2006), for example, is critical of overly "simple" goal-oriented contextual theories that do not take into account the complexities of organizational decision-making:

> Punishment as a public policy does not neatly reflect the public will nor the will to power. Nor does it embody the needs of capital or easily respond to the electoral calculations of politicians or the power schemes of elites. Instead, public policies are messy, they often fail, and they can bring about just as many unintended as intended consequences.
>
> (p. 34)[9]

There are more than 3,000 counties in the United States, each with its own particular court system (or multiple court systems) and culture. One interpretation of mixed support for community threat in prior research is that such threats influence the decision-making in some small fraction of these courts (Zane, 2018). What would we make of this? One the one hand, it would disconfirm conflict theory as a general theory of court processing; on the other hand, conflict theory could still explain how *some* courts operate. The same observation could be made for all possible contextual influences.

This would frustrate macro-level investigations, since no factors would appear to explain outcomes across different contexts. Interestingly, this is consistent with the argument that single jurisdictions should be studied because court processes across states may be simply incomparable (Myers & Talarico, 1987). Unfortunately, it would leave us with the inability to make generalizable claims about juvenile punishment in the United States. As noted above, it would mean never moving beyond 51—or even 3,000—different, possibly conflicting, conclusions about the contextual influences on the juvenile justice system. The state-level analyses in Chapter 8 suggested slightly more support for the contextual hypotheses than did the multistate analyses, but support was still quite limited (i.e. 7.3 percent support versus 3.6 percent support). Thus, in the present study, it does not appear that *any* of the contextual hypotheses were valid in *any* jurisdictions.

A fourth and final interpretation of the findings is that *state-level* differences are more important than court-level differences within states, and court-level variation is best understood through the lens of each unique state juvenile justice system. It may be that most contextual variation in juvenile court outcomes is merely a product of statewide differences in how juvenile justice systems operate. While the present study examined contextual influences within each state—and found limited support for the influence of community characteristics—it is possible that state-level differences in context and culture produce most of the variation in juvenile court outcomes. Adding to the observation of Arazan et al. (2019) above, it may be that what is really needed is a *four*-level analytical model: individual cases nested within juvenile court organizations nested within communities nested within state juvenile justice systems. To my knowledge, such a research design has not yet been attempted in juvenile justice research, but this would allow for a better understanding of where most contextual variation is taking place. In the concluding chapter, I will take up this topic of state-level variation in more depth.

Notes

1 Additionally, several contextual variables approached significance for multiple outcomes: change in concentrated disadvantage, income inequality, juvenile arrest rate, ethnic heterogeneity, and youth population density. Interestingly, these are all indicators of social disorganization and economic threat—suggesting that the economic characteristics of the surrounding community may be more important than racial and ethnic demographics or the political economy of the court.

2 In each case, we would expect associations by chance to occur approximately twice, so chance could explain the observed support. For political economy, however, the support is slightly greater than expected by chance.

3 The other two findings involve indicators of social disorganization, and show that juvenile court processing was *less* punitive in counties with higher social disorganization—contrary to hypotheses.

4 Only four state-level analyses were conducted for waiver to criminal court.
5 In several states (Connecticut, Missouri, Texas), juvenile cases could only be waived by the judge, so the data should have included all waivers to criminal court. In several states, however, cases could also be automatically waived by statutory exclusion (Alabama, Oregon, South Carolina, and Utah). In those states, it might be that many or most juvenile offenders transferred to the criminal justice system were not included in the data. None of the included states allowed for prosecutorial waiver (i.e. concurrent jurisdiction) as of 2010, however (Griffin, Addie, Adams, & Firestine, 2011). Additionally, three states (Connecticut, South Carolina, and Texas) had an upper age of jurisdiction lower than 17, meaning that the criminal justice system had original jurisdiction for some older juveniles in those states.
6 Obviously, this is a relative metric. As Kutataledze (2009) points out, this is in fact the only sense in which we can assess levels of state punitiveness, as there are no absolute metrics for whether a system is "punitive" or "lenient":

> [Comparative analysis] is the most effective method of conducting state punitiveness research, as a jurisdiction (e.g., Russia) can be perceived as minimally punitive when compared to one jurisdiction (e.g., Iran) and highly punitive when compared to another (e.g., Germany). It is impossible to argue that one state is highly punitive unless it is compared with another state.
>
> (p. 246)

7 A large sample size also poses increased risk of Type I error—that standard errors will be so small that all variables will reach *statistical* significance despite a lack of *analytical* significance. In other words, some large samples are "too big to fail" (Lin, Lucas, & Shmueli, 2013, p. 906). In the present study, however, the multilevel approach largely mitigates this concern because the relevant sample size is at level-2 rather than level-1 for the purpose of calculating standard errors (see Johnson, 2010).
8 For example, an earlier study of the social context of criminal sentencing concludes: "Every scientific enterprise suffers from some methodological shortcomings, and ours is no exception. Of central importance were the unavailability of potentially critical variables and the questionable validity of others" (Myers & Talarico, 1987, p. 176). In the decades since this observation was made, most research still suffers from the same basic issues.
9 Similarly, in the context of the criminal justice system, Campbell (2018) observes,

> What we now call mass incarceration is not the product of any preconceived master plan, and there is no definitive set of legal, policy, and institutional structures responsible for mass imprisonment's rise and persistence. In fact, state histories help illuminate how lawmakers were often responding to cycles of self-created crises in haphazard ways that exacerbated the very problems they were allegedly attempting to solve.
>
> (p. 223)

Punishment practices arise from complex organizational pressures that evolve over time, not in response to any overarching "goal" that can easily explain the patterns we observe—what Sowell (1996) calls the animistic fallacy.

References

Arazan, C. L., Bales, W. D., & Blomberg, T. G. (2019). Courtroom context and sentencing. *American Journal of Criminal Justice, 44*(1), 23–44.

Barker, V. (2006). The politics of punishing: Building a state governance theory of American imprisonment variation. *Punishment & Society, 8*(1), 5–32.

Baumer, E. P. (2013). Reassessing and redirecting research on race and sentencing. *Justice Quarterly, 30*(2), 231–261.

Britt, C. L. (2000). Social context and racial disparities in punishment decisions. *Justice Quarterly, 17*(4), 707–732.

Campbell, M. (2018). Varieties of mass incarceration: What we learn from state histories. *Annual Review of Criminology, 1*, 219–234.

Feld, B. C. (1993). Criminalizing the American juvenile court. *Crime & Justice, 17*, 197–280.

Feldmeyer, B., & Cochran, J. C. (2018). Racial threat and social control: A review and conceptual framework for advancing racial threat theory. In J. D. Unnever, S. L. Gabbidon, & C. Chouhy. (Eds.), *Building a black criminology: Race, theory, and crime* (pp. 283–316). New York, NY: Routledge.

Griffin, P., Addie, S., Adams, B., & Firestine, K. (2011). *Trying juveniles as adults: an analysis of state transfer laws and reporting.* Washington, D.C.: Office of Juvenile Justice and Delinquency Prevention.

Hagan, J. (1989). Why is there so little criminal justice theory? Neglected macro-and micro-level links between organization and power. *Journal of Research in Crime and Delinquency, 26*(2), 116–135.

Hayek, F. A. (1955). Degrees of explanation. *The British Journal for the Philosophy of Science, 6*(23), 209–225.

Hayek, F. A. (1967). The theory of complex phenomena. In F. A. Hayek (Ed.), *Studies in philosophy, politics, and economics* (pp. 22–42). London, UK: Routledge.

Johnson, B. D. (2005). Contextual disparities in guidelines departures: Courtroom social contexts, guidelines compliance, and extralegal disparities in criminal sentencing. *Criminology, 43*(3), 761–796.

Johnson, B. D. (2006). The multilevel context of criminal sentencing: Integrating judge- and county-level influences. *Criminology, 44*(2), 259–298.

Johnson, B. D. (2010). Multilevel analysis in the study of crime and justice. In A. R. Piquero & D. Weisburd (Eds.), *Handbook of quantitative criminology* (pp. 615–648). New York, NY: Springer.

Kim, B., Spohn, C., & Hedberg, E. C. (2015). Federal sentencing as a complex collaborative process: Judges, prosecutors, judge-prosecutor dyads, and disparity in sentencing. *Criminology, 53*(4), 597–623.

King, R. D., & Light, M. T. (2019). Have racial and ethnic disparities in sentencing declined? *Crime & Justice, 48*(1), 365–437.

Kutateladze, B. (2009). *Is America really so punitive? Exploring a continuum of U.S. state criminal justice policies.* El Paso, TX: LFB Scholarly Publishing.

Lin, M., Lucas Jr, H. C., & Shmueli, G. (2013). Too big to fail: Large samples and the p-value problem. *Information Systems Research, 24*(4), 906–917.

Mears, D. P. (1998). The sociology of sentencing: Reconceptualizing decisionmaking processes and outcomes. *Law & Society Review, 32*(3), 667–724.

Mears, D. P. (2017). *Out-of-control criminal justice: The systems improvement solution for more safety, justice, accountability, and efficiency*. Cambridge, UK: Cambridge University Press.
Michell, J. (1997). Quantitative science and the definition of measurement in psychology. *British Journal of Psychology, 88*(3), 355–383.
Myers, M. A., & Talarico, S. M. (1987). *The social contexts of criminal sentencing*. New York, NY: Springer-Verlag.
Pratt, T. C., & Cullen, F. T. (2005). Assessing macro-level predictors and theories of crime: A meta-analysis. *Crime & justice, 32*, 373–450.
Schedler, A. (2012). Judgment and measurement in political science. *Perspectives on Politics, 10*(1), 21–36.
Sowell, T. (1996). *Knowledge and decisions*. New York, NY: Basic Books.
Wenger, M. R. (2019). Omitted level bias in multilevel research: an empirical test distinguishing block group, tract, and city effects of disadvantage on crime. *Justice Quarterly*. https://doi.org/10.1080/07418825.2019.1649449.
Whitman, J. Q. (2003). *Harsh justice: Criminal punishment and the widening divide between America and Europe*. New York, NY: Oxford University Press.
Ulmer, J. T. (1997). *Social worlds of sentencing: Court communities under sentencing guidelines*. Albany, NY: State University of New York.
Ulmer, J. T. (2012). Recent developments and new directions in sentencing research. *Justice Quarterly, 29*(1), 1–40.
Ulmer, J. T. (2019). Criminal courts as inhabited institutions: Making sense of difference and similarity in sentencing. *Crime & Justice, 48*, 483–522.
Ulmer, J. T., & Johnson, B. (2004). Sentencing in context: A multilevel analysis. *Criminology, 42*(1), 137–178.
Ulmer, J. T., & Johnson, B. D. (2017). Organizational conformity and punishment: Federal court communities and judge-initiated guidelines departures. *Journal of Criminal Law and Criminology, 107*(2), 253–292.
Zane, S. N. (2018). Exploring the minority threat hypothesis for juveniles in criminal court: Static versus dynamic threat and diffuse versus targeted effects. *Youth Violence and Juvenile Justice, 16*(4), 418–441.

Chapter 10

Implications for Research and Policy

Given the observation that juvenile court outcomes varied significantly across communities and systems, it is surprising that the contextual factors under examination—ranging from indicators of community threat to social disorganization to political economy—were largely unrelated to juvenile punishment. Generally, a discussion of punishment in the United States tends to take an aggregate, national focus. But this can be quite misleading. As Barker (2009) argues, "American states punish differently from one another and do so in ways that have not been fully documented or explained" (p. 170).[1] The same could certainly be said for juvenile justice. In fact, it might be that the most important contextual perspective would focus on state *systems* rather than community characteristics. In short, more comparative research is needed on juvenile justice systems in the United States. Below I sketch four implications that follow from this, three for future research and one for policy reform.

Implications for Research

Description and Classification

First, research could attempt to catalogue how punitive each juvenile justice system is relative to others. This would be largely a matter of description and classification, rather than explanation, but even this represents a challenging project. Faced with complexity and variation in juvenile confinement across jurisdictions, Krisberg, Litsky, and Schwartz (1984) asked, "Can we accurately measure the benefits or harms experienced by youth confined in different penal settings?" (p. 179).

Comparing states in terms of levels of punitiveness tends to focus on incarceration rates because they can be measured in a straightforward manner. For example, in one classic work on the scale of imprisonment in the criminal justice system, Zimring and Hawkins (1991) observed that in 1980, the imprisonment rate was *ten times higher* in North Carolina than in New Hampshire. More recently, Campbell (2018) observed that incarceration rates in 2015 ranged from 300 (per 100,000 residents) in states such as Maine, Minnesota, Rhode Island, and Vermont, to around 900 in states such as Alabama, Louisiana, Mississippi, and Oklahoma. While the difference among states is less dramatic than in 1980, this still represents a threefold difference in incarceration rates. This provides plausible evidence that state systems vary substantially in how they respond to crime, assuming that different levels of crime cannot fully explain these differences in incarceration.

As others have documented, state juvenile justice systems also vary considerably in their rates of detention and commitment. Krisberg et al. (1984) documented that in 1979, detention admission rates ranged from 256 (per 100,000 juveniles) in South Carolina to 5,685 in Nevada—a more than 20-fold difference. By 2017, the most recent year for which data is available, incarceration rates were much lower overall but still varied considerably, from 3 (per 100,000) in South Dakota and 7 in Michigan to 163 in Wyoming. The average commitment rate in 2017 (34 per 100,000 juvenile residents) has actually been cut in half since 2010, where the rate ranged from 12 in Michigan to 202 in Oregon and 181 in Wyoming (Sickmund, Sladky, Kang, & Puzzanchera, 2019). There are similarities over time in rates of commitment across states, but region does not fully explain the differences. As Zimring and Hawkins (1991) concluded with respect to incarceration rates in 1980, "neither geography nor demographics provide a complete explanation for the diversity" of punishment practices across states (p. 148).[2]

Moreover, as noted in the introduction, commitment rates are not the only aspect of punishment to be measured. Frost (2008), for example, distinguishes between the *propensity to punish* and the *intensity of punishment*. The author classified states across three measures of punitiveness—imprisonment rate, propensity to imprison, and average prison length—which were themselves only weakly-to-moderately correlated. While most states were "average" along one or more dimensions, two states stood out. Only Minnesota was "under" punitive across all three dimensions, while only Oklahoma was "over" punitive across all three dimensions. Frost (2008) concluded that whether a state is "punitive" depends in large part on definition and measurement.

In his macro-level comparative study of punitiveness in the criminal justice system, Kutateladze (2009) employed 44 different measures of punitiveness across various dimensions of the system, and then compared all 51 states (including D.C.). One of these dimensions, juvenile justice, was evaluated according to age of jurisdiction, scope of juvenile transfer laws, number of juveniles in adult prisons, juvenile incarceration rate (i.e. residential placement), juveniles serving LWOP sentences, and overcrowding in juvenile detention and residential facilities. The author found that, overall, Southern juvenile justice systems were the most punitive and Western and

Northeastern juvenile justice systems were the least punitive (with Midwest states rated as "moderately punitive"). But regional patterns were relatively weak, as the ranking of states in terms of punitiveness varied across the different measures, and few states were either the most or the least punitive across all dimensions. For the states included in the present study, South Carolina was ranked as the most punitive (also most punitive overall), followed by Alabama (fourth punitive overall), Connecticut (19th overall), Texas (20th overall), Missouri (29th overall), Utah (40th overall), and Oregon (46th overall). These states thus run the spectrum from "extremely punitive" (i.e. Alabama and South Carolina) to "minimally punitive" (i.e. Oregon).[3]

The present findings complicate this picture, however, as we saw that different states used different kinds of processes that might be labeled as more or less punitive.[4] Certain states were more punitive in terms of preadjudication detention (Texas and Utah), some were more punitive in terms of formal petition instead of diversion (Alabama and Utah), some were more punitive in terms of judicial waiver to criminal court (Alabama, Connecticut, and Oregon), some were more punitive in terms of high rates of adjudication of delinquency among petitioned cases (Missouri, Oregon, and South Carolina), and some were more punitive in terms of high rates of secure placement among delinquent cases (Missouri and South Carolina). In some cases, low and high levels of punitiveness were combined in interesting ways, such as high preadjudication detention rates coupled with low formal petition and placement rates in Texas, high rates of formal petition coupled with low adjudication and placement rates in Alabama, and low rates of formal petition and high diversion rates coupled with high adjudication and placement rates in Missouri. Consistent with Kutateladze (2009), South Carolina did appear to be more punitive across most of these dimensions. This kind of detailed classification study is quite valuable for taking the "bird's eye view" and encouraging critical thinking about different aspects of punitiveness across juvenile justice systems, beyond just comparing commitment rates.

Quantitative Explanation

Comparative research can also attempt to test state-level hypotheses about juvenile court outcomes, seeking to explain punitive differences in state juvenile justice systems. For example, a number of studies have sought to explain variation in incarceration rates across state criminal justice systems in terms of state-level variables such as crime rates, political ideology, racial composition, and other factors (Campbell, Vogel, & Williams, 2015; Greenberg & West, 2001; Jacobs & Carmichael, 2001; Smith, 2004; Spelman, 2009). The findings of this research do not produce many clear conclusions, however. One exception might be political conservatism, which has been associated with higher imprisonment rates in several studies (Beckett & Western, 2001; Greenberg & West, 2001; Jacobs & Carmichael, 2001; Jacobs & Helms, 1996). Even here, however, others have found that the relationship depends on whether "conservatism" is measured in terms of those in political power or the general public (see, e.g., Carmichael, 2011; Carmichael & Burgos, 2012).[5]

In the context of juvenile justice, few studies have attempted to explain state variation in juvenile punishment. Mears (2006) stands out as the clearest example of such research, and was motivated by the observation that "variation in the use of juvenile incarceration remains and yet has gone largely unstudied" (p. 483).[6] This study looked at four possible explanations for state-level differences: (1) symbolic threats; (2) increased crime; (3) criminal justice policies; and (4) punitive regional culture. Mears (2006) found no support for symbolic threat and found that the South was *not* more punitive once other factors were controlled for in the analysis. Instead, the findings supported a relationship between crime and juvenile incarceration—as well as support for juvenile punishment policies corresponding to criminal justice policy (measured as adult incarceration rates).

Perhaps more quantitative research on state-level variation is needed, moving beyond standard demographic variables that are typically used in the literature. In observing the substantial and unexplained variation in state correctional populations, Mears (2017) writes:

> What explains the variation in these rates? Differences in crime may account for some of it, but not most of it. The bulk of variation likely stems from variation in the effectiveness of state and local efforts in reducing crime and recidivism and in philosophical views about appropriate approaches to and amounts of retribution and justice.
>
> (p. 87)

For example, little attention is paid to how states allocate resources on their criminal justice systems, as well as within their justice systems. Mears (2017) points out that in 2012, states ranged from spending less than 5 percent of their state budget on criminal justice and corrections (e.g. Maine) to spending close to 10 percent of their budget (e.g. Nevada). In terms of per capita spending on criminal justice and corrections, states ranged from around $400 per capita in Maine and South Carolina to near or above $1,000 per capita in California and New York. Within each system, moreover, these resources were allocated differently. Spending on police ranged from 35 percent in Kentucky to 56 percent in Illinois, spending on courts ranged from 14 percent in South Carolina to 28 percent in Connecticut, and spending on corrections ranged from 23 percent in Hawaii to 41 percent in Arkansas. Mears (2017) writes:

> States thus devote dramatically different amounts of their budgets to crime and justice efforts. They do so over and above differences in population or crime rates. And they allocate their funds to police, court, and corrections functions differently. The end result is what amount to 50 state experiments ... in addressing crime and justice.
>
> (p. 93)

These state experiments provide an opportunity to test more variables that may explain differences in juvenile justice processing across states. Some hypotheses, like differences in state law and policy, could be most easily tested. Other differences, such as how decision-making is shared among intake officers, prosecutors, and judges in the juvenile court, might also be studied with more primary data collection. Still other differences, such as court cultures or general philosophies animating the juvenile court, may prove more elusive for quantitative analysis. Nelken (2010) points out that comparative research is difficult due to the number of possible differences among systems (i.e. variables) combined with the small number of systems that can be meaningfully compared (e.g. different countries or US states). This leads to under-powered analyses as well as theories of punishment that "explain too much" and risk becoming tautological.[7] While this is especially pronounced for comparisons of criminal justice systems in different countries, including cross-national comparisons of different juvenile justice systems (see Tonry & Chambers, 2012), there are challenges even with state comparisons within the United States. Quantitative analysis comparing states is also limited by the number of macro-level variables that can be examined. This brings us to our next research implication.

Qualitative Explanation

There is also a need for in-depth qualitative research comparing different state justice systems. In large part, this is to move beyond "macro"- social variables and focus more on organizational variables that are not easily measured with existing, widely available data. Garland (2013) argues that due to a "sociological bias" that focuses on distal, structural causes—what which he calls "deep" or "background" causes—research has tended to exclude examination of more proximate, institutional causes:

> My suggestion is that we should shift our attention—for the time being—away from the broad range of social forces that exert pressure

> for penal change and instead concentrate more narrowly on the institutional processes that directly produce specific penal outcomes.
>
> (p. 482)

Similarly, three decades ago Zimring and Hawkins (1991) wrote that "unexplained variations in patterns among the states should be regarded as an invitation to do policy research at the individual state" (p. 154). In particular, they concluded that there is "substantial value in comparative studies that focus on a small number of political jurisdictions over time in an effort to illuminate the evolution and impact of penal policy" (p. 218).

In his presidential address for the American Society of Criminology, Garland (2013) made a similar plea, calling for more "small-*n* comparative studies that are in-depth, qualitative and quantitative analyses, focused on penal state processes—a form of analysis that is still surprisingly rare" (p. 489). Quantitative analyses that compare states, discussed above, are limited by the number of macro-level variables that can be examined, which tend to be static and aggregate rather than the "processes, event sequences, and the choice-point contingencies that shape institutional outcomes" (Garland, 2013, p. 491). Many state-level differences will thus elude aggregate measures, and only in-depth comparative historical research will be able to provide greater understanding of how these differences may contribute to criminal justice policies and outcomes.[8] This is not to say that quantitative research on state variation is not useful for detecting patterns, such as regional differences in punishment practices, but it may be limited in its ability to explain fully the organizational and institutional influences on justice system processing:

> Large-*n* correlation studies … provide us with important information about co-variation or the clustering of factors and, in the most sophisticated studies, about interaction effects. … Their findings usefully point us to recurring associations and patterns, but we need more in-depth studies to identify the various ways in which different institutional structures connect to different action orientations and the penal outcomes that result.
>
> (Garland, 2013, p. 491)

With state criminal justice systems operating like "fifty-one different countries" (Zimring & Hawkins, 1991, p. 137), the opportunities for greater understanding through comparative qualitative research are substantial. A body of qualitative research focused on how individual state systems operate has emerged in recent years, often focusing on political culture as well as particular "state histories" (see generally, Campbell, 2018). While much of this work investigates individual courts or systems, some is comparative.

For example, Barker (2009) developed a theory of penal regimes in terms of democratic governance along two dimensions: level of centralization of political structures and level of civic engagement in collective action. According to this theory, states could be grouped into four categories along these two dimensions: decentralization and high civic engagement produces "deliberative democracy"; decentralization and low civic engagement produces "polarized populism"; centralization and high civic engagement produces "corporatism"; and centralization and low civic engagement produces "elite pragmatism." Barker (2009) predicted lower imprisonment rates in participatory democracy states, average imprisonment rates in pragmatic states, higher imprisonment rates in populist states, and highest imprisonment in patronage states. To evaluate these predictions, the author performed a case study of three states with different types of democratic processes. First, polarized populism in California translated into a retributive penal regime with high imprisonment rates. Second, deliberative democracy in Washington translated into a parsimonious penal regime focused on de-escalation and community reintegration—hence low imprisonment rates. And third, elite pragmatism in New York translated into a managerial penal regime with medium imprisonment rates and a more "targeted" and cost-efficient approach that "sorted violent and drug offenders into prison and diverted most others away" (p. 175). This kind of qualitative inquiry into political culture, an application of political sociology, would be useful for understanding variation in juvenile justice processing. It may be that aggregate measures are simply not sufficient. Notably, no such work has been done in the context of the juvenile justice system.

Implications for Policy

Finally, in terms of possible policy implications, the variation in juvenile court processing across contexts—including both variation across state systems and variation across courts within states—might suggest that taking a national approach to juvenile justice reform is misplaced. Garland (2013) points out that in the United States, "Control of penal power is primarily local, not national. It emerges from the bottom up, not from the top down" (p. 509). Similarly, in the context of mass incarceration, Lynch (2011) observes,

> [T]he problem of American mass incarceration might be explored more fruitfully as a ground-up process, rather than as a top-down process. … [S]hifting the starting point from the macro to the micro offers a more contextualized, interactive, and grounded understanding of how massive penal change occurred in the United States over such a relatively brief period. (p. 682)

Lynch (2019) argues for "re-inhabiting criminal sentencing research," mainly through primary data collection that aims to capture the richness of courtroom workgroups in a more "bottom-up approach" that examines how discretion operates in a dynamic context with social, legal, and political influences (p. 20).[9] In a similar vein, Ulmer (2019) argues:

> Typical empirical efforts analyze sentencing and, less often, other case processing outcomes, sometimes with a focus on between-court variation and contextual influences on outcomes. ... We need more qualitative and multimethod research that can flesh out the inhabited institutions we study—courts.
>
> (p. 509)

A possible policy implication that follows from these observations is that reform must also happen at the local level because bottom-up reform is more likely to respond to the complexity of the juvenile justice system than top-down policy changes. Others have pointed out that historical differences among state cultures, and the path dependencies they generate, make it unlikely that we should *expect* uniform punishment across states:

> Tensions between the nation's states and regions predates the formation of the United States, and the US Constitution was designed to unify states with sometimes-stark socioeconomic and structural differences. ... Deep-seated cultural differences have persisted within America's political cultures in various forms and remain an important factor in shaping state punishment.
>
> (Campbell, 2018, p. 222)

While there are national movements to reform the juvenile justice system, it may be that a "one size fits all" approach that does not appreciate cultural and organizational differences across systems is likely to lead to frustration and policy failure. Going forward, it may be useful to take more seriously that, in a federalist system like the United States, each state is its own laboratory of democracy (see Derthicke, 2008). Each juvenile justice system thus constitutes an experiment in juvenile justice policy that may provide helpful guidance to other systems—but ultimately must be understood on its own terms.

Concluding Thoughts

The fundamental, orienting premise of this study has been that there is no one juvenile justice system in the United States. The research findings bore this out, as state systems differed dramatically in how cases were processed and how juvenile punishment was administered. Despite substantial variation in juvenile justice outcomes across systems, however, the contextual research hypotheses were largely unsupported (within as well as across states). In short, the findings failed to explain *why* juvenile courts vary in their processing outcomes. The main takeaway of the study might simply be the complexity of the juvenile justice system—and the importance of trying to understand the system on its own terms rather than imposing some grand theory of punishment onto the juvenile court.

Sometimes metaphors can lead us astray. For example, Sowell (1996) observes that it is often remarked that a certain society is "punitive, permissive, frivolous, uptight, generous, uncaring, etc." (p. 11). But,

> There is no one named society who decides anything. ... Unless national laws are to vary literally from moment to moment, some decision-making units must make decisions which are binding on other units which either disagree or were not consulted.
>
> (p. 12)

The same could be said of references to the "juvenile justice system." There is no one decision-making unit that determines how to respond to youth crime in the United States, or even in any individual state. A systems approach to studying the juvenile justice system, forcefully advocated by Mears (2017), appears best suited to this challenge since it "requires continues examination of the complexity inherent to criminal justice" (p. 123). Unlike monocausal theories of punishment, a "systems view does not require a single theory that explains virtually every aspect of relevance" (p. 122). As scholars of juvenile justice, and criminal justice more broadly, we must embrace this complexity with an attitude of intellectual humility.[10] We do yet not fully understand why juvenile punishment practices vary so much across systems. We should continue to try to find out.

Notes

1 Elsewhere, Barker (2006) similarly argues that the United States "is not a coherent or singular state but rather made up of mixed democratic practices, a rich political imagination and varying sub-national polities—polities responsible for the creation, enactment and implementation of nearly all criminal justice policy" (p. 6).

2 Zimring and Hawkins (1991) found that Southern states had the highest imprisonment rates while Northeastern states had the lowest rates. Examining regional prison populations going back to 1930, the authors found relative stability over time, with the highest prison rates in the South and lowest rates in the Northeast. Others have found the same general pattern (see, e.g., Frost, 2008). While this might plausibly lend itself to an explanation of political and cultural differences

across regions, there was also substantial variation across state commitment rates *within* regions. Overall, the authors observed, there was more variation in rates of imprisonment across individual American states than across countries in Western Europe. Frost (2008) observed that this remained true in 2005.

3 This rank ordering of states included in the present research was not uniform across dimensions of punitiveness, however. For "age of jurisdiction," the most punitive state (in 2009) was Connecticut and the least punitive was Oregon. For "juvenile transfer laws," the most punitive state was Utah and the least punitive state was Missouri. For "juvenile inmates in adult prisons," the most punitive states were Alabama, Connecticut, and South Carolina, and the least punitive state was Utah. For "juvenile incarceration rate," the most punitive states were Alabama and South Carolina, and the least punitive state was Missouri. For "juveniles serving life without parole," the most punitive state was Missouri and the least punitive states were Oregon, Texas, and Utah. For "overcrowding in juvenile facilities," the most punitive state was Texas and the least punitive state was Utah.

4 Phelps (2017) points out that while Southern states tend to have the highest incarceration rates, *probation* rates are the highest in the Northeast: "The story of state variation in probation complicates many of our established truths about the rise of the carceral state, especially that punishment is most concentrated in Southern states with a history of conservative politics and large minority populations" (p. 66).

5 The overall conclusions from this (small) literature may be summarized with a quote from Zimring and Hawkins (1991), reflecting on the increase in rates of imprisonment from 1960 to 1990:

> [T]here is no simple set of social variables thought to be related to imprisonment that would explain the increase as a consequence of forces external to government criminal justice policy. To those who might be inclined to regard that finding as tantamount to a demonstration that the pattern was the product of variations in government policy, the absence of any plausible specific policy as a major causal agent is both perplexing and frustrating.
>
> (p. 175)

6 An earlier study had attempted to explain changes in the juvenile incarceration rates over time, but only for *public* facilities (McGarrell, 1991).

7 As an example, Nelken (2010) criticizes neo-Marxist theories that attribute higher punishment to more "neo-liberal" societies (with more exclusionary cultures and politics) than corporatist or social-democratic societies (with more inclusionary social policies). He points to a study that reaches this conclusion based on finding a clear pattern among *12 countries*: neoliberal countries had much higher incarceration rates (from 115 in Australia to 701 in the United States) than corporatist countries (from 93 in France to 100 in Italy) and social-democratic countries (70 in Finland and 73 in Sweden). But the analysis was quite under-powered and general in its categories. Ultimately, we are left with a suggestive correlation in need of greater explanation, and many other differences that go unexamined.

8 Lynch (2011) is similarly critical of macro-level research in the context of mass incarceration:

> One problem with this approach is that it assumes these factors mean the same thing over time and in different jurisdictions. It also has meant that some potential causes of mass incarceration are not included because they are not easily reducible to quantitative measures. As a result, to the extent that researchers have tried to develop empirically testable hypotheses about the American incarceration explosion, they have had to make some questionable assumptions about how law, policy making, politics, and social relations happen, including assuming that these processes work the same way across and within different states and regions of the country.
>
> (p. 675)

9 Lynch's (2011) specific recommendations include the following: (1) multilevel modeling to better capture the role of context and place; (2) mixed methods research that draws on interview and survey data to incorporate how decisions are made; (3) using differential statistical techniques, such as decomposition methods, to move beyond merely "controlling" for legal factors in regression; (4) looking at interactions of different court actors to produce decisions, such as judge/prosecutor dyads; (5) examining patterns of policy and outcomes over time; and (6) new, original data collection that includes interviews, surveys, and ethnographic field research to "offer more direct measures of court actors' cognitions and behaviors" (p. 20). This may also be a promising approach in the context of juvenile justice research (see Peck, 2018).

10 Sowell (1996) observes,

> [T]he question in criminal justice is not what decision we should make if we were God, but what decisions we can make effectively, given that we are only human, with all that that implies in terms of limitations of individual knowledge.
>
> (p. 283)

References

Barker, V. (2006). The politics of punishing: Building a state governance theory of American imprisonment variation. *Punishment & Society*, *8*(1), 5–32.

Barker, V. (2009). *The politics of imprisonment: How the democratic process shapes the way American punishes offenders*. New York, NY: Oxford University Press.

Beckett, K., & Western, B. (2001). Governing social marginality: Welfare, incarceration, and the transformation of state policy. *Punishment & Society*, *3*(1), 43–59.

Campbell, M. (2018). Varieties of mass incarceration: What we learn from state histories. *Annual Review of Criminology*, *1*, 219–234.

Campbell, M. C., Vogel, M., & Williams, J. (2015). Historical contingencies and the evolving importance of race, violent crime, and region in explaining mass incarceration in the United States. *Criminology*, *53*(2), 180–203.

Carmichael, J. T. (2011). Punishing juvenile offenders as adults: An analysis of the social and political determinants of juvenile prison admissions across the United States. *Sociological Focus, 44*(2), 102–123.

Carmichael, J. T., & Burgos, G. (2012). Sentencing juvenile offenders to life in prison:The political sociology of juvenile punishment. *American Journal of Criminal Justice, 37*(4), 602–629.

Derthicke, M. (2008). Federalism. In P. H. Schuck & J. Q. Wilson (Eds.), *Understanding America:The anatomy of an exceptional nation* (pp. 121–146). New York: Public Affairs.

Frost, N. (2008). The mismeasure of punishment: Alternative measures of punitiveness and their (substantial) consequences. *Punishment & Society, 10*(3), 277–300.

Garland, D. (2013). Penality and the penal state. *Criminology, 51*(3), 475–517.

Greenberg, D., & West, V. (2001). State prison populations and their growth, 1971–1991. *Criminology, 39*(3), 615–654.

Jacobs, D., & Carmichael, J. T. (2001). The politics of punishment across time and space: a pooled time-series analysis of imprisonment rates. *Social Forces, 80*(1), 61–89.

Jacobs, D., & Helms, R. E. (1996). Toward a political model of incarceration: a time series examination of multiple explanations for prison admission rates. *American Journal of Sociology, 102*(2), 323–357.

Krisberg, B., Litsky, P., & Schwartz, I. (1984). Youth in confinement: Justice by geography. *Journal of Research in Crime and Delinquency, 21*(2), 153–181.

Kutateladze, B. (2009). *Is America really so punitive? Exploring a continuum of U.S. state criminal justice policies.* El Paso, TX: LFB Scholarly Publishing.

Lynch, M. (2011). Mass incarceeration, legal change, and locale: Understanding and remediating Amercian penal overindulgence. *Criminology & Public Policy, 10*(3), 673–698.

Lynch, M. (2019). Focally concerned about focal concerns: A conceptual and methodological critique of sentencing disparities research. *Justice Quarterly, 36*(7), 1148–1175.

McGarrell, E. F. (1991). Differential effects of juvenile justice reform on incarceration rates of the states. *Crime & Delinquency*, 37(2), 262–280.

Mears, D. P. (2006). Exploring state-level variation in juvenile incarceration rates: Symbolic threats and competing explanations. *The Prison Journal, 86*(4), 470–490.

Mears, D. P. (2017). *Out-of-control criminal justice: The systems improvement solution for more safety, justice, accountability, and efficiency.* Cambridge, UK: Cambridge University Press.

Nelken, D. (2010). *Comparative criminal justice: Making sense of difference.* London, UK: Sage.

Peck, J. H. (2018). The importance of evaluation and monitoring within the Disproportionate Minority Contact (DMC) Mandate: Future directions in juvenile justice research. *Race & Justice, 8*(4), 305–329.

Phelps, M. S. (2017). Mass probation: Toward a more robust theory of state variation in punishment. *Punishment & Society, 19*(1), 53–73.

Sickmund, M., Sladky, T.J., Kang, W., and Puzzanchera, C. (2019). Easy Access to the Census of Juveniles in Residential Placement." Retrieved from: www.ojjdp.gov/ojstatbb/ezacjrp/.

Sowell, T. (1996). *Knowledge and decisions*. New York, NY: Basic Books.

Smith, K. (2004). The politics of punishment: Evaluating political explanations of incarceration rates. *Journal of Politics*, *66*(3), 925–938.

Spelman, W. (2009). Crime, cash, and limited options: Explaining the prison boom. *Criminology & Public Policy*, *8*(1), 29–77.

Tonry, M., & Chambers, C. (2012). Juvenile justice cross-nationally considered. In B. C. Feld & D. M. Bishop (eds.), *The Oxford handbook of juvenile crime and juvenile justice* (pp. 871–897). New York, NY: Oxford University Press.

Ulmer, J. T. (2019). Criminal courts as inhabited institutions: Making sense of difference and similarity in sentencing. *Crime & Justice*, *48*, 483–522.

Zimring, F. E., & Hawkins, G. (1991). *The scale of imprisonment*. Chicago, IL: The University of Chicago Press.

Appendices

Appendix A Case-level descriptive statistics, by state (year = 2010)

Variables	*AL*		*CT*		*MO*		*OR*		*SC*		*TX*		*UT*	
	%	*n*	%	*n*	%	*n*	%	*n*	%	*n*	%	*n*	%	*n*
Detention														
Detained	12.99	3,934	12.97	1,591	11.51	4,670	11.07	3,524	18.08	3,853	41.64	32,239	19.59	6,466
Released	87.01	26,529	87.03	10,674	88.49	35,910	88.93	28,314	81.92	17,461	58.36	45,181	80.41	26,549
Total	100.00	30,293	100.00	12,265	100.00	40,580	100.00	31,842	100.00	21,314	100.00	77,420	100.00	33,015
Petition														
Petition filed	59.28	17,607	54.91	6,735	20.35	7,638	23.64	7,372	41.28	8,722	37.58	28,970	69.18	22,833
Diverted	13.62	4,047	12.16	1,491	62.25	23,371	29.67	9,253	31.4	6,634	44.84	34,569	29.1	9,606
Dismissed	27.10	8,049	32.93	4,039	17.40	6,532	46.68	14,557	27.32	5,773	17.58	13,556	1.72	567
Total	100.00	29,890	100.00	12,265	100.00	37,541	100.00	31,182	100.00	21,129	100.00	77,095	100.00	33,006
Waiver														
Transferred	1.58	243	2.41	134	1.42	102	3.16	173	.43	32	.85	206	.04	9
Retained	98.42	15,113	97.59	5,436	98.58	7,093	96.85	5,313	99.57	7,377	99.15	24,145	99.96	20,172
Total	100.00	15,356	100.00	5,570	100.00	7,195	100.00	5,486	100.00	7,409	100.00	24,351	100.00	20,181
Adjudication														
Delinquent	44.75	7,831	45.71	3,017	85.89	6,471	90.69	6,527	93.59	7,840	74.85	17,867	76.08	17,363
Not delinquent	55.25	9,667	54.29	3,584	14.11	1,063	9.31	670	6.41	537	25.15	6,003	23.92	5,461
Total	100.00	15,356	100.00	6,601	100.00	7,534	100.00	7,197	100.00	8,377	100.00	23,870	100.00	22,824
Disposition														
Placement	7.18	549	12.16	367	35.84	2,319	9.44	575	20.76	1,621	6.27	1,120	14.79	2,523
Community supervision	83.70	6,401	72.85	2,198	57.30	3,708	64.15	3,906	69.51	5,429	89.76	16,037	81.84	13,960
Released/ diverted	9.13	698	14.98	452	6.86	444	26.41	1,608	9.73	760	3.97	710	3.37	575
Total	100.00	7,648	100.00	3,017	100.00	6,471	100.00	6,089	100.00	7,810	100.00	17,867	100.00	17,058

Race/ethnicity														
White	51.03	15,458	39.60	4,857	64.18	26,046	65.66	20,907	39.07	8,328	50.05	38,745	60.44	19,954
Black	45.60	13,814	35.57	4,363	33.34	13,531	7.62	2,426	57.04	12,158	23.77	18,403	3.09	1,021
Hispanic	2.61	791	22.54	2,765	1.90	770	19.18	6,108	2.48	529	50.05	38,745	27.68	9,139
Other race/ ethnicity	.76	231	2.28	280	.57	233	7.54	2,401	1.4	299	1.05	813	8.79	2,901
Total	100.00	30,293	100.00	12,265	100.00	40,580	100.00	31,842	100.00	21,314	100.00	77,420	100.00	33,015
Sex														
Male	66.37	20,105	67.64	8,296	65.26	26,481	64.65	20,586	68.43	14,586	71.85	55,623	69.91	23,082
Female	33.63	10,188	32.36	3,969	34.74	14,099	35.35	11,256	31.57	6,728	28.15	21,797	30.09	9,933
Total	100.00	30,293	100.00	12,265	100.00	40,580	100.00	31,842	100.00	21,314	100.00	77,420	100.00	33,015
Age														
7–9	3.49	1,056	.41	51	2.88	1,169	.39	125	.53	112	–	–	.26	85
10	1.42	432	.63	77	1.76	715	.54	173	.54	116	.69	531	.55	183
11	2.16	657	1.87	229	3.08	1,249	1.32	419	2.16	461	1.72	1,329	1.27	419
12	4.47	1,361	5.11	627	6.51	2,642	3.93	1,250	5.98	1,274	4.74	3,671	3.58	1,181
13	7.45	2,266	12.37	1,517	11.01	4,469	8.93	2,845	10.71	2,283	10.27	7,951	8.41	2,775
14	11.57	3,511	20.84	2,556	17.64	7,157	15.55	4,950	17.27	3,680	17.64	13,657	14.07	4,645
15	17.96	5,445	31.72	3,890	23.66	9,600	20.97	6,677	26.56	5,661	26.92	20,844	20.19	6,667
16	23.81	7,204	24.79	3,040	30.43	12,347	24.12	7,679	31.54	6,722	33.35	25,821	23.65	7,808
17	25.41	7,677	2.2	270	2.60	1,057	23.67	7,538	4.4	938	4.57	3,540	23.99	7,919
18–20	2.26	684	.07	8	.43	175	.58	186	.31	67	.10	76	4.04	1,333
Total	100.00	30,293	100.00	12,265	100.00	40,580	100.00	31,842	100.00	21,314	100.00	77,420	100.00	33,015
Offense type														
Violent	11.30	3,424	20.68	2,537	22.34	9,067	13.14	4,184	22.89	4,879	19.65	15,216	6.81	2,249
Property	22.24	6,738	24	2,944	29.01	11,771	29.34	9,343	25.06	5,341	26.99	20,898	31.34	10,347
Drug/alcohol	6.56	1,988	6.55	803	8.22	3,335	25.44	8,102	9.44	2,012	14.59	11,292	17	5,613
Weapon	.79	239	1.96	240	1.21	492	.98	311	2.38	507	1.26	977	1.2	395
Probation violation	5.32	1,613	4.9	601	.54	221	.01	4	6.38	1359	11.83	9,157	11.77	3,886
Status	32.48	9,838	13.78	1,690	23.63	9,589	22.64	7,208	11.88	2,532	11.16	8,640	6.85	2,263
Other	21.30	6,453	28.13	3,450	15.04	6,105	8.45	2,690	21.98	4,684	14.52	11,240	25.02	8,262
Total	100.00	30,293	100.00	12,265	100.00	40,580	100.00	31,842	100.00	21,314	100.00	77,420	100.00	33,015

Appendix B Case-level descriptive statistics, by state (year = 2000)

Variables	*AL*		*CT*		*MO*		*SC*		*TX*		*UT*	
	%	*n*	%	*n*	%	*n*	%	*n*	%	*n*	%	*n*
Detention												
Detained	14.65	5,249	21.87	4,037	9.3	5,725	12.24	3,127	37.68	39,088	19.27	10,888
Released	85.35	30,575	78.13	14,421	90.7	55,856	87.76	22,411	62.32	64,644	80.73	45,620
Total	100.00	35,824	100.00	18,458	100.00	61,581	100.00	25,538	100.00	103,732	100.00	56,508
Petition												
Petition filed	69.49	24,886	63.13	11,652	18.31	10,041	40.86	10,385	38.02	39,303	66.34	22,655
Diverted	9.92	3,554	6.22	1,148	48.16	26,407	24.1	6,124	43.37	44,825	26.90	9,187
Released	20.59	7,374	30.65	5,658	33.53	18,382	35.04	8,904	18.61	19,237	6.76	2,310
Total	100.00	35,814	100.00	18,458	100.00	54,830	100.00	25,413	100.00	103,365	100.00	34,152
Waiver												
Transferred	1.87	396	1.54	126	1.95	188	.22	18	.55	171	.30	57
Retained	98.13	20,763	98.46	8,072	98.05	9,444	99.78	8,134	99.45	31,045	99.70	19,055
Total	100.00	21,159	100.00	8,198	100.00	9,632	100.00	8,152	100.00	31,216	100.00	19,112
Adjudication												
Delinquent	56.37	13,790	55.68	6,418	76.89	7,573	92.57	9,363	76.21	24,266	82.80	18,179
Not delinquent	43.63	10,672	44.32	5,108	23.11	2,276	7.43	751	23.79	7,573	17.20	3,775
Total	100.00	24,462	100.00	11,526	100.00	9,849	100.00	10,114	100.00	31,839	100.00	21,954
Disposition												
Placement	28.61	3,945	16.63	1,067	35.00	2,650	20.14	1,883	10.15	2,462	10.00	1,818
Community supervision	68.56	9,455	75.32	4,834	62.78	4,754	56.66	5,297	89.62	21,748	90.00	16,361
Released/ diverted	2.83	390	8.06	517	2.22	168	23.19	2,168	.24	58	–	–
Total	100.00	13,790	100.00	6,418	100.00	7,572	100.00	9,348	100.00	24,266	100.00	18,179
Race/ethnicity												
White	52.49	18,803	46.68	8,616	70.01	43,110	44.64	11,400	36.58	37,949	75.95	42,919
Black	46.26	16,571	30.62	5,652	27.99	17,235	54.02	13,795	22.38	23,219	1.84	1,037

Hispanic	.74	266	20.26	3,740	0.87	533	–	–	40.03	41,524	14.09	7,962
Other race/ ethnicity	.51	184	2.44	450	1.14	703	1.34	343	1.00	1,040	8.12	4,590
Total	100.00	35,824	100.00	18,458	100.00	61,581	100.00	25,538	100.00	103,732	100.00	56,508
Sex												
Male	70.38	25,214	67.2	12,404	68.63	42,263	68.73	17,552	70.24	72,857	73.55	41,562
Female	29.62	10,610	32.8	6,054	31.37	19,318	31.27	7,986	29.76	30,875	26.45	14,946
Total	100.00	35,824	100.00	18,458	100.00	61,581	100.00	25,538	100.00	103,732	100.00	56,508
Age												
7–9	2.48	890	1.88	346	3.18	1,959	1.78	452	–	–	1.61	912
10	1.49	534	1.9	350	2.44	1,501	1.56	398	.97	1,009	1.28	726
11	2.45	876	4.49	829	3.93	2,419	3.39	867	2.45	2,542	1.91	1,081
12	4.68	1,678	9.19	1,696	7.59	4,675	7.46	1,906	5.76	5,972	3.84	2,172
13	8.45	3,026	17.03	3,143	12.51	7,706	12.49	3,190	12.15	12,608	7.75	4,381
14	13.77	4,934	27.01	4,985	18.83	11,594	19.06	4,868	19.69	20,420	12.57	7,101
15	19.37	6,938	36.19	6,680	23.62	14,548	24.65	6,296	26.14	27,113	18.24	10,310
16	22.06	7,901	2.15	396	25.98	15,997	26.65	6,806	29.19	30,284	23.00	12,995
17	22.82	8,176	.15	28	1.71	1,050	2.85	729	3.60	3,738	23.74	13,412
18–20	2.43	871	.03	5	.22	132	.10	26	.04	46	6.05	3,418
Total	100.00	35,824	100.00	18,458	100.00	61,581	100.00	25,538	100.00	103,732	100.00	56,508
Offense type												
Violent	8.78	3,147	16.88	3,115	18.25	11,240	23.96	6,118	15.86	16,454	14.21	8,029
Property	25.87	9,267	26.87	4,959	32.55	20,045	23.73	6,060	29.51	30,613	26.01	14,695
Drug/alcohol	7.72	2,764	4.68	863	7.16	4,411	7.12	1,819	11.01	11,420	16.22	9,163
Weapon	.96	344	1.01	186	1.08	663	2.25	575	1.30	1,344	1.71	967
Probation violation	10.6	3,796	9.42	1,738	.43	264	5.39	1,376	10.49	10,878	4.05	2,290
Status	24.76	8,870	21.96	4,054	33.08	20,370	16.94	4,326	18.93	19,633	5.26	2,972
Other	21.32	7,636	19.19	3,543	7.56	4,588	20.73	5,264	12.91	13,390	32.55	18,392
Total	100.00	35,824	100.00	18,458	100.00	61,581	100.00	25,538	100.00	103,732	100.00	56,508

Appendix C County-level descriptive statistics, by state (year = 2010)

	AL[a]	*CT*[b]	*MO*[c]	*OR*[d]	*SC*[e]	*TX*[f]	*UT*[g]
	Mean (SD)	*Mean (SD)*	*Mean (SD)*	*Mean (SD)*	*Mean (SD)*	*Mean (SD)*	*Mean (SD)*
Community threat							
Percent Black	28.32 (22.28)	7.67 (5.03)	4.01 (6.94)	1.04 (1.11)	36.86 (16.49)	8.07 (7.12)	.76 (.51)
Percent Hispanic	3.15 (2.93)	9.86 (5.26)	2.40 (2.51)	10.92 (8.31)	4.18 (3.11)	31.74 (23.32)	9.64 (3.64)
Concentrated disadvantage	0 (1.85)	0 (1.93)	0 (1.62)	0 (1.47)	0 (1.81)	0 (1.69)	0 (1.59)
Gini index (0–1	.46 (.03)	.44 (.05)	.42 (.03)	.43 (.02)	.46 (.03)	.45 (.03)	.40 (.03)
Social disorganization							
Crime rate (per 1,000)	30.69 (13.36)	24.74 (5.61)	23.82 (14.08)	26.01 (9.33)	44.17 (12.26)	27.89 (12.37)	23.52 (10.08)
Juvenile arrest rate (per 1,000)	1.50 (1.03)	4.74 (1.41)	4.54 (3.07)	7.46 (3.26)	3.90 (2.14)	4.53 (3.03)	7.77 (3.21)
Ethnic heterogeneity (0–1)	.38 (.12)	.35 (.14)	.15 (.11)	.29 (.12)	.48 (.08)	.45 (.13)	.27 (.09)
Residential mobility (% moved)	13.76 (4.07)	12.83 (2.64)	15.35 (5.17)	17.45 (3.64)	13.00 (3.84)	16.55 (4.41)	16.14 (4.29)
Youth population density (%)	23.51 (1.49)	22.12 (1.35)	23.53 (2.17)	22.04 (3.06)	23.21 (2.06)	25.34 (3.53)	31.85 (3.33)
Political economy							
Median income (×1,000)	36.97 (8.23)	68.94 (8.12)	39.84 (8.10)	44.70 (6.63)	38.53 (8.13)	43.37 (10.00)	52.10 (10.23)
Conservative voting majority	9.13 (30.2)	2.27 (7.52)	-4.03 (16.00)	18.82 (23.54)	-4.46 (21.87)	26.04 (25.16)	61.04 (16.44)
Population density (per sq/mi) (×100)	.92 (1.05)	7.23 (5.47)	1.36 (5.32)	1.17 (3.10)	1.41 (1.33)	1.39 (3.48	1.53 (3.59)

a $N_1 = 30{,}484; N_2 = 65$.
b $N_1 = 12{,}265; N_2 = 8$.
c $N_1 = 40{,}853; N_2 = 111$.
d $N_1 = 31{,}842; N_2 = 34$.
e $N_1 = 21{,}314; N_2 = 46$.
f $N_1 = 77{,}420; N_2 = 189$.
g $N_1 = 33{,}016; N_2 = 22$.

Index

For Product Safety Concerns and Information please contact our EU
representative GPSR@taylorandfrancis.com
Taylor & Francis Verlag GmbH, Kaufingerstraße 24, 80331 München, Germany

www.ingramcontent.com/pod-product-compliance
Ingram Content Group UK Ltd.
Pitfield, Milton Keynes, MK11 3LW, UK
UKHW022353190926
475702UK00015B/2268
* 9 7 8 1 0 3 2 0 3 8 1 5 5 *